Blair Chamberlin was born in Jamaica where his grandfather was a harbourmaster. When the depression hit the island in the thirties the economic situation was dire so his father, a plantation overseer, brought the family to England.

Chamberlin was educated by monks and after pre-sea training college went to sea in 1949. A severe injury in Saigon coincided with the birth of his daughter, so he 'swallowed the anchor.' He subsequently worked in the offshore industry in the UK, Dutch and Norwegian sectors before coming ashore...

Once established ashore he worked in advertising/publicity on both the client company and agency sides. A widower, he lives alone in Norwich.

SWING THE LAMP

Blair Chamberlin

SWING THE LAMP

AUSTIN & MACAULEY

A CIP catalogue record for this title is available from the British Library.

ISBN 978 1 905609 51 2

www.austinmacauley.com

First Published (2009)
Austin & Macauley Publishers Ltd.
25 Canada Square
Canary Wharf
London
E14 5LB

Printed & Bound in Great Britain

DEDICATION

In affectionate memory of my brothers
Eric Russell & Julian Ambrose Chamberlin
and of
A.I.D.(Gus), A.O.M-S (Amos), and R.G.S (Jigger)
who were all seafaring men.
And remembering especially
T.E.H-J (Tottie)
who wasn't.

'Swing the Lamp' a derisory quip, almost certain to be heard from someone in a group of professional seamen who are being expected to accept from one of their number highly imaginative accounts of derring do, of giant sharks encountered, violent storms endured and similar travellers' tall tales.

INTRODUCTION

Bellatrix was a real ship with real people. She was by far the oldest of the twenty-odd ships I served in during my career at sea, and she was certainly the most uncomfortable. There was no running hot water – your steward brought an enamel jug of hot water from the galley 15 minutes before your watch. This was used in a little 'tip-up' basin which had a spring loaded cold water tap and discharged into a bucket in the base of the compendium.

There was no iced water on tap and potable water was always a problem – the quantity we carried could easily become critical and sometimes it became contaminated. Air conditioning was a faintly remembered dream – each cabin had a rackety fan, fixed to the deck head, which frequently burned out its ancient armature windings. She was only comfortable at sea in hot weather when we rigged home-made wind scoops in the portholes to direct a cooling airstream into the accommodation. Many people slept on deck. In port, in the tropics, the cabins were like saunas – portholes and doors had to be locked against sneak thieves. She supported a thriving and competitive throng of cockroaches and steam beetles (mini cockroaches), many of which got to your supper tray before you did if you didn't take adequate precautions.

But she was the happiest ship I ever sailed in – fortunately the character of a ship does not depend solely on creature comforts. She had a 'tight' crew; there was no animosity between departments as can sometimes happen. By and large, misfits didn't last long. Most men were single and stayed in her for long periods. During my tenure the chief engineer – a childless, wartime widower – had reputedly been in her for over eight years through two changes of ownership and three name changes. She had become his permanent home.

To make the narrative flow I have had to monkey with chronology – life at sea does not always produce notable events neatly in a strict time sequence. I have occasionally juxtaposed unrelated events for dramatic purposes or to be ironic.

I have also related events which took place in other ships with other men (sometimes identified) with whom I sailed because the occurrence(s) described are either too traumatic/funny/poignant or otherwise memorable, to be excluded from an anthology such as this. This created a dilemma. Had I followed chronology strictly and attributed events to the personalities and vessels actually involved, I would have had to introduce a plethora of ship names and transient characters who would march briefly through these pages but who would otherwise have been irrelevant. It would have made the narrative treatment impossible to preserve and the story would have degenerated into a collection of anecdotes. (This was the style that I first attempted. It was rather cumbersome. I am grateful to Mr Frank Plowright of Michael Joseph who took the trouble to contact me to offer advice and suggested that I reorganise the material into a narrative form). I have therefore integrated these events/experiences with happenings in *Bellatrix* – but always in context and in character.

So, it is possible that old shipmates will recognise names and events but not the venue. To prevent them from blowing a fuse while taxing their brain (a positive hazard at our age) in struggling to account for why they could not remember having sailed in so memorable ship as *Bellatrix*, I will put their minds at rest. They didn't! Their stories were shangahi-ed.

So my apologies notably to:

Dave B-W. While not an engineer he was as frequent a hostage to fortune as 'Bubbles', our luckless second engineer. 'Outrageous fortune' lay in wait with a veritable arsenal of slings and arrows with which to assail him. He contributes to the character described in Chapter 19. I rescued him on his first day as a first-trip, 16-year-old midshipman when he had been ejected stark naked from the half-deck (where the midshipmen lived) on a raw, late November afternoon in Gladstone Dock, Liverpool. It was a bitter day. In mid-afternoon the frost still glittered on every surface and the clouds hung in tatters down to street level. He was close to tears and desperate when I found him hammering on the half-deck door pleading to be let in.

'You're doing exactly what they want you to do,' I told him and installed him in my cabin on the after end of the boat deck with a blanket and turned up the heat. 'Just sit tight,' I said, 'And watch them start to panic when they can't find you.'

He was constitutionally designed to be a victim – and he never disappointed.

Paul H. We last met in The Boot pub in Wallasey before he swapped the MN for the Canadian Navy. He served at one time and was married in HMCS *Crusader* to Joan P whom he had met when she was a hostess in the British Merchant Navy Officers' Club, in the Hotel Astor in Times Square, New York.

'KKK'. His agility had to be seen to be believed. He could 'brachiate' (using only his arms) up a rope like a monkey. He had no concept of 'cause and effect' and was a dangerously unrestrained practical joker. Looking back, it is easy to conclude that he was a bit deranged; I learned many years later that he had committed suicide by eating salt! This was an eccentric and horribly unpleasant way to make an exit especially when an easier and more comfortable method was readily available – a handful of tablets washed down with a bottle of whisky, then a step over the side to oblivion. I have known one or two to go that way before and since.

Matt P. He could play any stringed instrument. He augmented his earnings by playing guitar and banjo at various venues while we were in port. He had played at 'The Prospect of Whitby' in London and once 'guested' at a well-known jazz club in New York (I think it was Eddie Condon's). He was studying for his master's ticket and while on 'ticket leave' became involved with a music group, turned professional and quit the sea. In the late fifties I saw him on '6.5 Special', a BBC TV programme – a fore runner of 'Top of the Pops'!

Paul P. His claim to fame was the he had been bitten by a shark in the Persian Gulf while serving in tankers – and had an impressive scar to prove it.

Doc W. he had served as a tank commander during the war and the horrific sights he had witnessed and the miracles he had seen performed by surgeons in the field prompted him to take up medicine after he was de-mobbed. He was a brilliant quack and had a fund of the most horrendously gruesome tales and dirty stories and knew every single verse of 'Eskimo Nell'.

Chuffy Y. He had to leave the table on one occasion to go on watch, just as someone had posed the question 'What has more tits than a sow and sings?' When he enquired later what was the answer, nobody would tell him and it became a standing joke amongst us. He became quite obsessive about it! It wasn't till he was going down the gangway when leaving the ship in London at the end of the voyage that someone relented and put him out of his misery. 'Hey Chuffy,' he yelled. 'The answer is 'The Luton Girls' Choir!'.'

They were all rather special and would have fitted seamlessly among the oddballs who crewed *Bellatrix*.

CHAPTER ONE

He wasn't very bright or particularly lovable, but he was a character and when the captain shot him twice, once through the head and once – needlessly – through the chest from behind the left shoulder, it almost sparked off a mutiny. The second shot, sheer vindictiveness, was delivered with evident relish, the snout of the .22 rifle so close to the twitching corpse that the muzzle blast singed his wiry, ginger hair. He had been in *Bellatrix* longer than anyone could remember, longer even than the chief engineer, who seemed part of the engine room fittings. The old man and I had joined her together in Manila, a bare seven weeks before his cruel end came one sultry Sunday morning as we cleared the Sunda Strait between Java and Sumatra en route to South Africa from Tanjong Priok in Indonesia. His name was Dempsey; he had been the ship's dog.

I first saw the captain in the agent's Manila office. He was thick-set and a good head shorter than me. When the agent introduced us, I said 'Good morning, Sir,' and held out my hand. He looked straight through me, ignored my extended hand, turned his back and walked to the window without saying a word. My heart sank. His reaction did not augur well for a pleasant voyage or a happy ship. My subsequent experience of him revealed that he resented anyone who was taller than him; he lost no opportunity to make them defer to his status in as humiliating a manner as possible in even the most trivial matters. He was a Turkish Cypriot and quite handsome in a raddled way, with a fleshy, deeply pock-marked face; he looked tough and craggy, if rather dissolute. I had no inkling of the vile creature that lurked within the tawny, hairy carcass; he delighted in being as offensive as possible to those under his authority who had no means of redress; he quickly established himself as the most hated man I have ever known.

When we joined *Bellatrix* she was lying at the buoys, working into lighters alongside using her own derricks. The starboard gangway had been damaged some time previously when she had been manoeuvring alongside a wharf and snagged the ladder against a bollard. Lighters were clustered round her port side so that gangway was also inaccessible; the only way to board her was by a rope ladder to the after well deck. He had boarded first, walked aft and entered the crew's quarters to see what he could see. I checked the baggage into the cargo net and saw the hoist clear of the launch before climbing the ladder. As my head cleared the bulwark I heard a crisp voice demanding 'Whose bloody gear is this? Get it shifted before someone breaks their bloody neck.' I was astonished to find myself looking at the double of the film actor Dirk Bogarde dressed in American 'suntans' with a second mate's braid up. The likeness was startling. 'Sorry Two-Oh,' I said. 'Some of it's mine, most of it's the old man's.' Before he could reply, the new captain emerged from the crew's accommodation behind him and bellowed 'Do you got a problem, Second Mate?' The second mate spun on his heel. 'Er, no, Sir – just trying to get this gear sorted out. It's blocking the walkway.'

'Well, take it to my quarters.'

'Very good, Sir.'

He summoned a passing seaman and instructed him to carry the captain's baggage forward. As the sailor bent to disentangle the bags and cases from the cargo net, the old man stepped up and pushed him violently away from the pile of baggage and turned on the mate in fury. 'I said **take** it to my quarters. I din' say not'ing 'bout telling someone to do it.'

The second mate flushed deeply through his tan. 'Do you mean me personally, Sir?' he asked in disbelief.

'I'm talking to you, **boy**. I don' talk to nobody else, **boy**. Just do it and you don' get no trouble.' He turned and stumped up the ladder to the main deck.

The second mate stared after him speechless, pale-faced and quivering with suppressed rage. He removed the white, floppy cotton sun hat from his head, mopped his face with it then replaced it. He turned to me choking with anger, scarcely able to articulate his fury. 'What a **prick**! And in front of a seaman too. Where in God's holy name did they trawl up that... that... **specimen**?'

'Dunno... but the agent told me he was lucky to get this command. I guess the company's desperate; he's got a bad name so they say...'

'Promises to be an interesting trip... roll on ----ing death!' He stared at me sombrely for a long moment, then suddenly grinned and stuck out his hand. 'I'm Amos, chief baggage handler to ignorant arseholes. Are there just the two of you? We're expecting a new third mate as well.'

'Just us, so far as I know. Look, if you'll have my gear taken up, I'll give you a hand with his.'

* * * * *

Amos was an extraordinary character. He was the most talented man I have ever known and was wasted at sea. His accomplishments seemed endless and whatever he did was perfectly done, apparently with consummate ease. He was born in China and taken to Australia as a boy when the Sino-Japanese war broke out. For the whole of his conscious life his parents had farmed in Australia and his boyhood was spent, it seemed, galloping round an estate the size of the Isle of Wight on a series of homicidal horses. His physique was that of a 'sundowner'. He was lithe, tough, nimble as a grasshopper and could make a standing jump from the deck to a tabletop with no apparent effort. He could walk for ever on his hands and had an alarming tendency to invert himself without warning when he was drunk – wherever he happened to be – 'because', he said, 'it's not so far to fall.'

He was very funny, although his wit could be unmercifully penetrating; a slanging match with him was something definitely to be avoided. He was the only person I have met who could curse in the biblical sense, calling down a string of hair-raising disasters ('may your balls grow square and fester at the corners') on the head of any who displeased him. The diatribe, always impromptu, was delivered without repetition and with a great deal of whimsy that was guaranteed to have onlookers in stitches. He never lost his temper and while his opponent was soon reduced to calling him rude names and threatening physical violence, Amos was able, somehow, to identify and highlight every weak spot, every failed enterprise, every frustrated hope in the poor chap's life. It was masterly – though sometimes cruel. His facility with words and his whimsicality enlivened discussions about even the most mundane matters; he once described a difficult and frustrating project as 'trying to push butter up a tiger's arse with a hot needle.'

His relationship with the new master, whom he quickly christened 'Animus', never recovered from their disastrous first encounter. Animus had taken a violent dislike to Amos, whom he always called 'boy' and did everything to make his life unbearable. The meanest, pettiest and most spiteful action was not beneath him if it enabled him to goad his victim. Amos was meticulous almost to a fault – a good trait in a navigator, but carried into private life it can seem pernickety and it clearly irritated the careless and anti-social Animus. One of Amos's quirks was to have pencils honed to an almost impossible sharpness. I never knew how he did it. His chartwork was a masterpiece – the writing tiny, beautifully formed and as clear as headlines. Animus would deliberately crush the pencil points into oblivion, one by one. It was hardly the act of a rational man and at first I refused to believe it was deliberate, but Amos actually proved it to me.

The unpleasant aspects of life under the authority of Animus were too numerous to list. They varied from insulting pinpricks to major, frightening disruptions of accepted behaviour. He hated Americans, English and French; he despised the Germans and Italians. The Portuguese and Spanish were 'bloody, bastard half-castes' and the entire spectrum of the coloured races was dismissed as '----ing coolies' or 'dog meat'– except for the women. They apparently were acceptable.

His sheer indifference to professional standards was alarming, an attitude mirrored in his private life and relationships – his language was foul, his personal hygiene was intermittent and seemed to be dictated by whimsy and his habits were deliberately offensive. His only apparent interest in life was women – of any age, race or condition. Looking back it is easy to conclude that he was probably more than a bit mad.

He was also a vicious man. The habit which upset us most was his indiscriminate shooting. He had a .22 rifle and would blast away at anything he cared to. He was a pretty good shot and it was sad enough to see a gull blown from the top of a Samson post or the foremast in a flurry of feathers, but at least death was instantaneous and unexpected. It was infinitely sadder to witness the murder or maiming of dolphins and porpoises in the bizarre and depraved form of clay pigeon shooting that he invented. He would catch them in their random leaps as they cleared the water in their graceful looping passage, effortlessly matching our speed and joyously riding the 'force field' of the bow wave just ahead of the ship. It is unlikely that a .22 bullet would kill one, certainly not quickly – except for a lucky shot. The thought of one of those beautiful animals carrying Animus's bullet in agony, perhaps for years, was distressing in the extreme, but there was nothing we could do about it.

I learned from Animus that swearing in English has curious and undeclared rules of syntax. His cussing was comical. While it is perfectly acceptable, syntactically, to say in English 'bloody fool' or 'silly bugger', it is farcical for some indefinable reason to say 'bloody bugger' and this was one of his favourite portmanteau epithets. The ultimate and ugliest English obscenity is a curious and versatile word. It can be used as a noun, verb or adjective. Animus contrived to use it in all its grammatical versions in the same sentence; the result was hilarious and robbed his obscene monologues of any impact at all.

His crazy campaign against Amos became dangerous when he withheld critical information in the form of 'Notices To Mariners' – a series of Admiralty data sheets listing up-to-date information essential to safe navigation which it is the second mate's duty, as the ship's navigator, to record. It was a difficult enough job to keep abreast and record them all anyway – *Bellatrix* carried more charts than I have ever seen in any other ship – many of them ancient. Charts are expensive, and out-of-date ones can be hazardous; ships usually carry the operational minimum relevant to their particular routes. As most ships run scheduled routes they carry relatively few charts. The whole purpose of Animus's guerilla tactics was to put Amos in the wrong so he could be criticised loudly and in public because various changes had not been recorded on the relevant charts.

Amos saved his own and everyone else's sanity by inventing a series of scurrilous conversations ostensibly between Animus and various international lady celebrities such as Mae West and Queen Juliana of The Netherlands. They were very rude and excruciatingly funny (the confusion between Queen Juliana and Animus over what constituted a 'Dutch Cap' ought to have been recorded for posterity in the annals of humour – he opined that installing a Dutch Cap was likely to hurt your ears and affect your eyesight!) There was a particularly ghoulish exchange between Animus and Ilse Koch, the 'Bitch of Belsen'. In a thick music-hall German accent Ilse told 'Mein Kapitan' how much she admired his hairy carcass and prolific tattoos. She would do anything, yes anything, to see and touch them. He, being the lustful pig that he was, missed the implications in his hot pursuit of her blonde magnificence. While he was otherwise engaged Ilse complained that she couldn't really appreciate the tattoos because of all the hair. Would he mind if she depilated him with a cut-throat razor, 'und nakt schkin to nakt schkin ist zo wunderbar, mein kapitan'. Animus enjoying her acquiescence raised no objection. Ilse got her razor, and Ilse armed with a cut-throat razor was, as the Americans say, 'a whole different ball game', especially with tattoos within reach. This vignette was probably the zenith of Amos's acting career. Various chunks of it became catch phrases on board. For example, if anyone was feeling particularly anti-Animus for some reason, he could say within the captain's hearing 'Und nakt schkin to nakt schkin ist zo wunderbar'; those within earshot knew that it was the equivalent to kicking Animus hard in the crotch. It made everyone feel better.

Amos was a talented mimic and his version of the captain's garbled English when he became excited seemed more real than the original. The most extraordinary thing, however, was that although as physical types they were as different as it was possible to be, Amos managed to convey exactly Animus's craggy, anti-social and almost surrealistic male animalism. In the vicious, undeclared war between them, although Amos was frequently bloodied and punch-drunk, he was the undoubted winner, hands down.

If any man on board had retained somehow, unaccountably, an atom of approbation for Animus, it was dispelled over the Dempsey affair. Dempsey was the ugliest dog in creation. Nobody knew where he had been picked up as he was *Bellatrix*'s oldest resident. He looked as if he had been hastily and inexpertly assembled from randomly selected spare doggy parts and the whole thing covered by a badly fitting, wiry ginger coat. His front legs were shorter than his hinder ones and the feet turned out so badly that he was obliged to shuffle because he couldn't lift them off the deck in a fore and aft motion. Every now and then one of his knees would let him down and he would collapse with a grunt onto his chin. He was afraid of nothing and apparently had been christened Dempsey after the boxer. He was not lovable but his bossy attitude and his rather pompous air of always being engaged on 'rather important business' made him a character. Somebody was always telling the latest Dempsey story.

Soon after I joined *Bellatrix* we carried a pair of prize greyhounds as live freight and they were exercised every morning and evening on the boat deck. They were quite valuable. Dempsey regarded the boat deck as his inviolable territory and as nobody relished a dispute with him he got away with it. He evidently resented the intrusion of the two snooty upstarts and decided to make his feelings on the matter known to one and all. On their second perambulation – the morning after they arrived – he shuffled up behind the precious pair as they trotted regally along behind their handler and sent them leaping cross-eyed into the air with quivering hysterics by prodding them unexpectedly in their private parts with his hard, icy nose. Unfortunately for him, the sailor who was exercising them was as ugly, bossy and indomitable as he was and drove him off with a swift kick in the ribs and a very rude imprecation. Dempsey was deeply offended and for several mornings he would lie in wait and leap out on the exercise party with clashing jaws and his fearsome but phony growl. This simulated attack would send the pampered darlings prancing in panic to the limit of their leads, ensnaring the sailor and creating a small maelstrom of noisy activity on the boat deck. The irritated sailor would restore calm by cuffing the pampered pets and remonstrating with Dempsey by the application of his steel-toe-capped boot.

Dempsey was not stupid. He eventually got the message and devised an alternative strategy. He restricted himself to lurking in unexpected places and when the greyhounds and their handler came in view he would merely have to feint with his nose at their tail ends to induce a fit of the vapours and palpitations in his prey without attracting retributive justice in the form of the seaman's boot. It seemed to satisfy him and he would sit grinning quietly to himself, tongue lolling, while the victims of his terror campaign huddled trembling against the sailor's legs, rolling their eyes to look nervously over their shoulders at their bête noire.

He was an independent cuss and it was impossible to compel him to do anything against his will. Dempsey was very useful, in fact. The boat deck was his undisputed province and he 'protected' it, so that in port there was small chance of any sneak thief setting foot on it – an endemic nuisance in many ports. It made us feel very secure. Long before I joined he had developed the habit of using the space between the lifeboats on the starboard side of the boat deck as his toilet, irrespective of weather. It was quite nerve-racking to witness his virtuoso performance in the teeth of a force ten beating on the starboard side. He was a real old seadog. He would face into the wind, bracing himself expertly against the convulsions of the ship, his ragged ears flapping uncontrollably, a look of blissful concentration on his face until his evacuation was complete. A previous mate had formalised this lavatorial arrangement by laying an oiled canvas sheet on the deck and covering it with sand (we called it 'Dempsey's Dungkirk'), so everybody was happy. If Dempsey had noticed the transition from an ad hoc dumping ground to an officially approved toilet place he gave no sign and the system worked splendidly.

Shortly before my arrival, however, the newly-appointed mate – wielding his new broom – worked valiantly to convert the ship from a reasonable condition to cruise liner standards and a curious contest began. While accepting Dempsey's squatter's rights, he was offended by the Bohemian arrangement and had the carpenter make up a sand tray and install it, replacing the old canvas/sand toilet, (fifteen-love). Dempsey examined the new facility minutely then expressed his contempt for it by aiming just short of the tray, (fifteen-all). The mate countered by dragging the tray further inboard, (thirty-fifteen). Dempsey considered the situation then simply shortened his trajectory, (thirty-all). The mate had the carpenter extend the tray, (forty-thirty). With mathematical precision, Dempsey defiled the deck just outside the tray (deuce). The old man had watched the contest with some amusement. He decided the mate needed coaching and took him in hand. 'For God's sake give in – he won't.' The old toilet arrangement was reinstated (advantage Dempsey) and his matinee performance was conducted with an air of elaborate unconcern – dead centre of the canvas/sand patch, (game, set and match).

He hated ladders but occasionally would stumble along to the back door of the galley where he would sit politely, ears pricked in interest, his nose twitching uncontrollably at the delicious smells. If it seemed that nobody was about he would gingerly test the water by putting his foot inside the galley door, then freezing. If no enraged shout ensued he would creep in to see what he could steal. What he never learned, or perhaps failed to remember, was that there was always somebody about – a galley is manned round the clock. The inevitable result of his illegal incursion was a hefty clonk on the head with a ladle. The first blow always took him by surprise. He would shake his head and blink, hoping he had imagined it. The second blow would nearly drive his head into his shoulders and couldn't be ignored. Grumbling loudly Dempsey would slink outside to sit by the door gazing hopefully at the galley hands or other passers-by with many a tentative wave of his naked, rat-like tail. Eventually even **his** buoyant spirit would succumb and, with hope extinguished, he would shamble off like a quadrupedal Quasimodo, feet splayed, rump in the air, head hanging. He presented an incredibly dismal picture, one it was impossible not to sympathise with.

Although not obvious from this portrait, Amos was a dead-ringer for the film actor Dirk Bogarde and exploited the likeness shamelessly – he was a veritable 'babe-magnet'. We often benefited from the fall-out – girls usually hunt in packs!

The author with Dempsey — the ugliest dog in creation. He was a sort of Airedale, semi-decrepit and irretrievably moth-eaten and looked as if he had been hastily and inexpertly assembled from a random selection of doggy spare parts. His major deformity (his short front legs) is obvious in this sketch.

Dempsey was prone to fleeting paralysis. He rarely left the boat deck except for his occasional forays to the galley; he found it difficult to negotiate ladders because of his deformities. In addition to the sudden collapse of one or other of his dodgy knees, his back legs would sometimes refuse to function. It was usually only momentary and he seemed to suffer no more than the indignity of grovelling around and twitching for a few minutes. It was very distressing to witness but we came to terms with it eventually, long after Dempsey had figuratively shrugged his shoulders and got on with living. If you went to help him during one of these episodes he would roll his eyes at you and break your heart with his pathetic expression. So far as I am aware he was never known to snap. He certainly showed no signs of suffering and exhibited no after-effects at all. We were convinced it was simply a sort of 'short circuit' – a nerve or muscle malfunction – brought on by his deformity, not a 'fit' in the real sense of the word.

Animus had witnessed a couple of these attacks in the past and had made no comment. One Sunday morning Dempsey collapsed at the foot of the boat deck to bridge ladder as Animus was coming up on to the bridge for the noonday sight. Without a word he returned to his quarters, collected his rifle, kicked the dog into the sand patch toilet and shot him twice. The mate witnessed it from the wing of the bridge but it was all over before he realised what was happening, let alone having any opportunity to intervene. Nothing he could have done would have prevented it. When he raised the matter in shock Animus gave him a dusty answer. 'I don' have no ----ing rabious dog on my -----ing ship. His ----ing water is poison.' When the mate contested the allegation Animus would have none of it and threatened him with the sack in the next port of call.

The matter went into the official log as the destruction of a rabid animal and, of course, Animus was acting completely within his powers, if you accepted his diagnosis. We didn't know where Dempsey had come from but I would have thought he had been on board long enough for any incipient rabies to show itself long before his executioner and I had joined *Bellatrix*. But then, who is to say that he had not got ashore somewhere or perhaps had been infected on board by a stray cat? Animus was fireproof. His comment on Dempsey's 'poison water' defeated us. We never decided whether Animus thought the dog's urine was infectious or was making a garbled reference to hydrophobia.

The butchery stunned us all. Shock and horror at the callous killing were palpable and there was an unpleasant, indefinable undercurrent noticeable throughout the ship. I thought it was barely-suppressed hatred; the mate diagnosed it as anxiety, if not fear. 'The man's plainly out of his syphilitic mind', Amos said, 'Who knows what he'll do next?' He contended that the old man was deranged by tertiary syphilis. He certainly lacked discretion in his choice of sexual partners as we had seen in some of the primitive ports we had visited since his arrival, so Amos may not have been a mile off target.

In a show of what the army would probably call 'dumb insolence', we gave Dempsey a seaman's funeral. Everybody was in on it but the chief engineer, who had known him longer than anyone else, and was deeply angered by his death, was the instigator. We didn't realise till later that he had given the matter a great deal of thought – he was a wily old coot and with over 40 years at sea was a match for any 'wise arse' skipper. The carpenter sewed the sad little corpse into a weighted canvas shroud and we asked the mate for a flag to cover it but he refused to sanction the use of any national flag – 'that's going too far', he said; so Dempsey was placed on a hatch board and covered with the Blue Peter – the international flag signal for imminent departure. We couldn't stop the ship without the old man's consent of course, but with most of the ship's officers who were not on watch in attendance we intended to slide him over the side with dignity as far forward as possible so he wouldn't be chopped up by the screw. It was inconceivable that we should just dump him over the wall like a bucket of galley slops.

At three o'clock, as the cortege proceeded forward carrying the improvised bier, we were astonished to hear the steady beat of the engines fade and die away and soon *Bellatrix* lay dead in the water. With the ship stopped the heat was oppressive; no breath of wind scarred the shining sea. The silence was broken appropriately enough by the rhythmic tolling of a loose block striking a derrick boom somewhere as *Bellatrix* rolled heavily in the huge, glossy Indian Ocean swells, which slid under us and rolled away towards the northeastern horizon. At the forehatch by the break of the bow we gathered in full view of the bridge, silently lifted the hatch board to rest the outboard end on the bulwark and after a moments pause, tipped it gently. Dempsey slid from under the Blue Peter and with scarcely a splash embarked on his final voyage. It was quiet, dignified and intensely moving. But as Amos told us later, the real drama was taking place on the bridge.

Dempsey had been killed just before noon and his burial took place at three o'clock. The chief engineer, who had suggested the ritual over pre-lunch tots, had unknown to us devised a scheme. He decided that at three o'clock we would have a lube-oil pump failure and at the appointed hour the second engineer called the bridge to request permission to stop the main engine. Amos was on watch and knowing of the projected rites immediately guessed what was afoot and called Animus to the bridge. The old man had no option but to give permission. The engine was stopped and simultaneously the funeral cortege appeared on the foredeck below him.

Animus threw a fit. He instantly suspected the truth and gobbling with fury, rang the engine room to demand that the engine room log be brought immediately to the bridge. 'I am logging the time of this order', he told the second engineer, 'and I will log the time you arrive on the bridge.'

31

'I can't leave the engine room, Sir, I am responsible for the watch below and we are working on the lube oil pump. I will send the donkeyman.' Within minutes the donkeyman, trailing a line of oily footprints, appeared on the bridge panting like a steam engine. Animus snatched the log and opened it. Amos thought he was going to tear it to pieces and was sure a major eruption was imminent as Animus seemed about to explode in a spray of Turkish Cypriot body parts and fluids. But sadly, before this ultimate calamity occurred, an irate chief engineer appeared and demanded to know why his men were being dragged away from their duties and why the log had been removed from the engine room without reference to him. It was the captain's practice to countersign departmental logs every Monday morning. Why did he need it on Sunday?

The captain spoke commercial English adequate for most purposes but it was not colloquial or fluent, to say the least. When he became excited he was barely coherent. In extremis he reverted partly to his mother tongue and partly to French with a smattering of Arabic, Italian and Greek. This unprecedented event robbed him of his uncertain command of English. He spluttered and blustered in a rich amalgam of Mediterranean languages totally incomprehensible to his audience and finally hurled the log at the chief and bellowed 'Get offa my ----ing bridge.'

We had the chance to examine the evidence later. The first indication of trouble with the lube-oil pump was entered at 1230. Between then and the stoppage at three o'clock there were two other relevant entries charting the deterioration of the pump interspersed with the record of other engine room matters. The chief was fireproof. We had a whip round and presented him with two bottles of his favourite tipple. He accepted the libation with a grave 'Bless you, my children.'

When we complimented him on his impeccable planning, he grinned. 'I'm too old a goose to be cooked on a quick flame,' was all he said.

Just before we arrived in Durban, Animus collapsed with violent stomach pains. He was found rolling in agony on the deck by the tiger (the captain's personal steward is invariably known as 'the old man's tiger'; I have never heard a satisfactory explanation why.) The pain was so severe that he couldn't straighten up long enough to summon help either by the telephone on his desk or through the voice pipe to the bridge which hung near the pillow on his bunk. He was quickly whisked off to hospital. There was no rejoicing, but it felt as if a dense, stifling blanket had been lifted from the ship, allowing us to suck fresh air into tortured lungs. Amos was unrepentant. 'It's probably third stage syph of the ----ing spleen,' he said bitterly. We accused him of sticking pins into Animus's effigy. 'Bloody good idea,' he said, 'wish I'd thought of it.'

Animus never returned to *Bellatrix*. We had endured his reign of unreason for just over ten weeks; it had seemed as many months.

CHAPTER TWO

When I joined *Bellatrix* in Manila she'd had an almost complete crew change of her officers in the previous three months except for the missing third mate, who was to have joined in Manila, and the chief engineer. He had been in her for an age and seemed likely to leave her ultimately in a final plunge, just like poor old Dempsey, if he had any say in the matter.

A couple of months earlier Amos and the mate had arrived in Saigon together to join her and had to wait a few days for her arrival. On their first morning they went together to the British Embassy to register. At that time 'pac-a-macs' – thin, ultra-lightweight plastic raincoats which were carried in a little pocket-sized pouch – were just making their appearance. At first they seemed ideal for tropical use but unfortunately, being impermeable, they had the effect of a sauna and we soon discarded them. In any case I had found them restrictive and preferred to use an enormous angling umbrella. However, Amos had just acquired his new mac and took it with him as at that time it was the height of the rains. After completing their business at the Embassy, they drifted round the beautiful city and wound up at an internationally famous coffee house.

French Indo China was in turmoil in those days. It was just before the disaster of Dien Bien Phu, where the Foreign Legion suffered the most comprehensive defeat in its history. Revolution was in the air and the French were experiencing considerable terrorist activity; cars were frequently raked with gunfire in the suburbs, grenades tossed into cinemas and bombs left in cafes and bars. It seemed there were few places we visited that we didn't hear of, and sometimes experience first-hand, the effects of the struggle of some group or other to throw off the yoke imposed by another. It sharpened the reflexes enormously.

Amos and the mate had just left the café to return to their hotel when he realised that he had left behind the little packet containing his raincoat. The maitre d'hotel intercepted him at the entrance and enquired could he be of assistance. 'Oui, merci', said Amos, 'J'ai perdu mon plastique'. Poor Amos. How easy it is when one has but a partial grasp of a language to use a simple word that has another, awful connotation. 'Plastique' was also a form of (pre-Semtex) high explosive used at that time by terrorists. A brief, frozen silence followed his announcement, then the place erupted as the clientele departed precipitately through doors and windows and over balconies. It surprised Amos somewhat. He thought it rather odd but when nothing else happened he put it down to Gallic eccentricity, retrieved his mac and left. It was not until he was relating the incident to the mate and a couple of jeep loads of foreign legionnaires, sirens howling, whizzed by to pull up dramatically at the café that it all came together. Legionnaires being legionnaires, Amos and the mate ducked into a nearby bar and sat it out.

I came to realise that this episode was typical of the odd experiences visited on *Bellatrix* and her crew. She seemed to have an extraordinary assortment of extraordinary characters to whom extraordinary things happened. This is perhaps partly explained by the fact that she seemed to be used by the owners as a dumping ground for irreverent hard cases and 'nutters' who were professionally competent but who didn't fit in elsewhere, and as a proving ground for recent promotions who had not yet acquired the staid veneer of their newly-exalted status. We had a tremendous turnover in skippers. They hardly ever stayed longer than one or two trips at most, for one reason or another. Animus hadn't lasted three months.

Amos had just joined the company and this was his first trip as second mate. He had taken a tanker officer's course in France and thought he was coming to a tanker. He spoke reasonable French and had a mental 'tic' about the French familiar 'mon brave' and 'mon vieille ' and used them in his speech as 'my brave' and 'my old'. I don't know why. He wasn't a silly or pretentious man at all. It irritated me and in a fit of pique I told him so one day. 'Sorry, my Old,' he said, 'I'll try to remember.'

The new third mate was a huge Scot – six feet six, burly, black-bearded, with deep-set, hooded eyes. On first acquaintance he seemed taciturn and introverted and had a rather menacing presence but I quickly came to realise that he was shy. His seeming reluctance to speak was because he had a stammer of which he was very self-conscious but which disappeared completely when he was relaxed or with familiar and trusted company. Gus caught up with us in Zamboanga, a timber port in Western Mindanao in the Philippines.

It was an odd place. The huge mahogany logs floating in the bay were kept in check by a boom comprised of logs chained together. The ship came alongside the log boom and loaded the logs with her own derricks. The only way to get ashore was to jump precariously from log to log which tipped and rolled under you, or undertake a considerable outrigger canoe journey to circumnavigate the log pound, then make good by a longish walk the distance made in the canoe. Neither Gus nor I were built for outrigger canoes. They are narrow-gutted while we were both broad-beamed; the shortest trip was purgatory for us and terrified the tiny boatmen.

He was supposed to have joined *Bellatrix* in Manila at the same time as Animus and me, but by a series of accidents and miscalculations he missed us. He arrived in a tiny passenger ship just as we passed him outward bound, threading our way through the forest of masts and funnels of the scores of sunken ships that littered the still waters of Manila Bay – a poignant and depressing testimonial to the ferocious skill of both Japanese and American pilots. For the next few weeks he chased us round the thousands of islands of the Philippines in a series of inter-island steamers, sharing the primitive accommodation with a succession of shrouded corpses going home for burial, wedding parties who included him in their prolonged celebrations, and farmyard livestock which attempted to share his bedroll and food. The last stage was by a narrow gauge, wood-burning train which eventually deposited him within striking distance of Zamboanga when at last he was able to stand on the beach and watch us tie up to the log boom.

The log pound was the playground of hordes of impudent children with beautiful, solemn faces and flashing, cheeky smiles. They flitted over the logs like water sprites, touching them so lightly and fleetingly that they scarcely dipped under their passage. By contrast even the fleetest footed amongst us must have looked like drunken hippos. They played a dangerous game with us that we could never win and were in constant fear of losing. As we painfully inched our way ashore over the wet, rolling logs, a gang of them would jump aboard and start it spinning. They would leap to safety while their victim, in fear of life and limb, would try to ride out the madly bucking log or leap to a more stable one where the joke would be repeated. Until Gus, no one had fallen off although frequently it was a close run thing. It was extremely dangerous; the logs were heavy, and once rolling their impetus was lethal. If you fell between them you stood a good chance of being pulped. If they closed over your head without bursting it like a soap bubble you would be assured of drowning. They were low in the water and being so heavy, wet and dripping with slime they were almost impossible to move laterally.

Gus had dumped his dunnage with the local priest and set out over the logs to come aboard. The secret of a reasonably secure footing was to remove your shoes but keep your socks on, this gave some traction on the slimy timber. New at the game, Gus didn't know this and set off across the logs in crepe soled brothel-creepers. His tormentors appeared from nowhere, like mosquitoes scenting warm blood. Despite his intimidating bulk, terrifying aspect and bull-like bellow, they realised instinctively that in their element he was impotent. We heard the uproar and came on deck to watch the fun and saw this gigantic figure stumbling and swaying, trying to make it back to the safety of dry land through the flitting wraiths that were the log children. Suddenly it wasn't funny any more. As he jumped for another log nearer the shore his feet slipped from under him and he fell. The children fled.

His enormous stature saved him from serious injury. Some one as small as Amos would almost certainly have been killed or maimed. Gus fell backward and spanned the gap which had opened up between two logs. One tree trunk was under his knees and the other, fortunately spinning the right way for him, was under his shoulders. He spread his arms and managed to retain sufficient grip to stop himself sliding into the gap. With only his backside in the water and a good purchase on the logs beneath his legs and shoulders he was able to arch his back as they clashed together and so avoid injury. Eventually, with our help and with the frightened children hiding ashore, he made it safely back to the beach. He was quite calm and philosophical about it. When a group of adults came nervously to him to apologise and insisted on taking his clothes to be washed, he grinned at them, bought a crate of Coke and sent it over to the terrified children. I liked him instantly. The near disaster, or perhaps it was the Coca Cola, did what we could never do. We had no more trouble with the homicidal mites that trip, but he had established a precedent; we were obliged to bribe them with a crate of Coke each trip but the benefit was cheap at the price.

With Gus's delayed arrival the new crew was complete and we had a nominal two years to shake down together and work the ship through whatever adventures we might encounter. We had already survived our first trauma – Animus himself. The stroke of fate that had removed him now delivered us into the hands of an even more extraordinary character.

The dreaded log pound in Zamboanga P.I., the scene of Gus's 'downfall' and of our ritual and repeated humiliation.

At six feet-six inches, 18 stone, with craggy features and a penetrating gaze, Gus looked an archetypal hard man who could frighten a squad of paratroopers by smiling at them! His character did not match his appearance; he was rather shy, considerate and contemplative character.

The dreaded log pound was the playground of a swarm of homicidal mites with beautiful solemn faces and flashing smiles.

'Prissy' Prosser was a tall, thin, cadaverous man with a beautiful voice as rich and deep as the base register of a pipe organ, and the bluest, densest five o'clock shadow I have ever seen. We never saw him unshaven but we reckoned he would be able to grow a beard within a week to match any of the luxuriant growths on board.

His great interest in life, other than holystoned decks and immaculate bright work (brass fittings), was incredibly – dress designing! He was well placed to indulge his hobby; he had access to and was often given materials that would have made the trade ashore green with envy. Prissy worked with magnificent silks and brocades, shantung, sharkskin and velvet from China and Japan, cotton and batik designs from Malaya and Indonesia. In Hong Kong he could obtain the finest English tweeds, worsted and woollens at ridiculously low prices. We had copies of Chester Barrie suits made ashore from the finest English materials for about the price of an off-the-peg chainstore tweed jacket at home.

He and Animus could have come from different planets. The contrasts in men and styles could hardly have been greater. Although Prissy was taciturn, his general appearance, manners and hygiene were exceptional – as his nickname suggests. He had sailed as second mate in the Bibby Line before the war and being RNR had been shanghaied by the Navy at the outbreak of hostilities. He spent some time as pilot in HM Submarines then transferred to the Canadian Navy. After the war he married and settled in Canada; he never went home and we assumed the marriage had foundered. There was a son, at least, somewhere. Conversation with him on a sustained level was almost impossible. He was sociable and polite and would respond pleasantly enough, but he never thought it necessary to contribute anything to keep the conversation alive.

We first saw him at the coal wharf in South Africa's East London. The wharf was filthy and depressing. His pristine figure, immaculate in a bronze sharkskin suit which he had made himself, appeared among the coal tips and picked its delicate way aboard. We thought he was rather special then but it was left to poor old Amos to discover exactly how special. On our first trip together we left South Africa bound for Panama and the West Coast. The weather was perfect. One breathless, limpid evening Amos and I and a couple of others had tried to play deck tennis.

After a few sets we called a halt – it was just too uncomfortable and enervating to play on. We were sitting on the hatch abaft the centre-castle accommodation – this had become the social centre of *Bellatrix* in hot weather and was almost an extension of the saloon and the officers' smoke room – when Prissy stuck his head over the rail on the deck above and beckoned Amos.

When he returned to finish his beer, I quizzed him. 'What's up?'

'Nothing. He wants to see me when I've cleaned up, that's all.' It sounded a little ominous. We never knew how a new skipper would show his teeth. It could be that he didn't approve of us drinking on the hatch, or playing deck tennis; perhaps Amos had dropped a clanger. It could be one of a dozen things or nothing at all. I did not see Amos again till the next day.

When I queried the result of his visit to father he shrugged it off, but I detected a slight discordance in his off-hand response. Thereafter he seemed to spend quite a lot of time with the old man one way or another and some malicious tongues began to wag, but he wouldn't come clean and was clearly reluctant to discuss it. This wasn't like Amos at all, although we didn't know each other too well at that time.

The mate was the unwitting cause of Amos's exposure – not to say unfrocking. Spotting something in the water ahead he had called the old man by voice pipe from the wheelhouse but got no response. Gus was in the chartroom writing up some notices[1] for Amos so the mate asked him to go down and find the skipper. Gus stomped down off the bridge, hammered on Father's stateroom door and stepped into the cabin at his instruction. He stopped dead as if he had been hit with a brick. Amos, swathed in silks, was standing majestically in the centre of the cabin; the old man was sitting cowboy fashion on a chair, sketch block in hand, his forehead wrinkled in concentration while making lightning sketches on his clipboard. Poor old Amos went rigid but Prissy didn't bat an eyelid. 'Don't move', he admonished him, then departed to the bridge, leaving Amos to glare red-faced at Gus, silently challenging him to make an injudicious remark or even allow his face to register his jumbled thoughts. Amos told us all about it later. I suppose he thought it best to tell the story before garbled versions of it circulated. I have never seen anyone so impotently furious and embarrassed.

Amos was about five feet six or seven and built like a ballet dancer. He moved lightly and delicately and to be honest had a slightly neat 'feminine' look to him; dimensionally he would have made a splendid model for the skipper's purposes, I suppose. It would have been a foolish man who made the obvious sneer, however. Despite his lithe and 'ladylike' appearance, he was agile and athletic – a bundle of sinew and stringy muscle – and had a very dour, vinegary streak. He was unpushable. Amos, sufficiently enraged, would have been a very awkward man to deal with. At that moment he was as embarrassed, angry and volatile as ever I saw him. His mistake, of course, had been to try to keep the business quiet. Had he made a joke of it to begin with, we would have joshed him about it, then sympathised and ultimately accepted it as part of the skipper's pattern of eccentricity. We didn't know each other very well at that time of course. We were still only faces to each other and hadn't shaken down into personalities and

---

[1] Recording the data from 'Notices To Mariners' on the relevant charts – one of the second mate's duties.

prejudices. Had it happened later he would certainly have confided in one or both of us for his own protection.

We ultimately came to accept Prissy's unusual hobby and even took a pride in some of his creations which he shyly showed us in a 'parade' one evening when we were at anchor, waiting for a berth. Amos was never able to come to terms with his extra-curricular activity, however, and it baffled and infuriated him long after Prissy had left *Bellatrix*. He became so obsessive about it that we dared not even pull his leg over it eventually.

Prissy had grandiose plans to have a genuine fashion parade on board, sell his designs, then have them made up cheaply in bulk in Hong Kong. It seemed a splendidly simple and workable idea, except that we had no conception of how good or bad his creations were. They looked equally as unreal as the fuzzy sketches worn by skeletal pen-and-ink ladies in the Sunday papers. We were all for it. We had visions of svelte, leggy, sun-tanned Californian models swarming all over us, begging to be shown the golden rivet[2]. Prissy's ideas hardened off to the point that he decided to have his fashion show in Long Beach or San Francisco. We were enthusiastic contributors to his fantasy.

'Why not a cruise?' we said. His guests could join as we left Long Beach and he could put on his show en route to 'Frisco. They would be wined and dined and could hardly resist his blandishments. But it all came to nought for one reason or another but I think he was just reluctant to expose himself to professional critics; it might destroy a dream. And a vanished illusion is a mighty uncomfortable thing to live with – or without!

Prissy's propensity provided us with an hilarious highlight. On our first visit to Vancouver we were delayed by a stripped

---

[2] That fabulous device, deep within the bowels of the ship, where inquisitive lady visitors were inveigled to follow their host, but then taken advantage of, with no hope of rescue.

main engine bearing. We were towed out to a safe anchorage where the engineers beavered away down below to dismantle the offending bearing and send it ashore to the dockyard for relining. It provided the rest of us with an unscheduled holiday. Amos had relations on Victoria Island and he promised us that they would organise a shindig to beat ancient Rome. Once again visions swam before our eyes of regiments of sun-kissed, voluptuous ladies cavorting against a background of mountains of barbecued steaks and chops and oceans of drink. It turned out to be an absolute fiasco for poor old Amos. His relations barely welcomed him and spent the whole time criticising his grandparents, who had died before he was born, and making scarcely veiled criticisms of his parents.

Gus and I went ashore with Amos and when he departed for his family reunion in Victoria we hit the tourist trail. I was suffering from a poisoned insect bite; my arm, supported in a sling, felt hot and heavy. Alcohol was out because of the drugs I was taking to fight the infection. Near the Hudson Bay Company's department store we saw a broken tailor's dummy being dumped and it gave me an idea. I put it to Gus. He agreed so we entered the shop and asked to speak to someone in authority. We were eventually shown into the office of a beautifully dressed, middle-aged lady sporting purple framed spectacles on a golden chain and possessed of a very attractive if rather contrived voice. We explained Amos's predicament as a model for the old man. Her reaction was odd. She became more and more frosty and seemed to shrink into her chair. But we were polite, reasonably dressed and spoke fluent English, so she eventually concluded that we weren't mad and did not intend to molest her. She let us go through our story again.

'Do you often have damaged dummies to dispose of?' we asked. 'If so, would it be possible to buy one to relieve our friend of his onerous and unwanted duties as a dressmaker's model?'

She considered this proposal for some time, obviously not knowing quite how to react. Eventually she decided to take our request seriously although she remained a little leery of us; the situation was clearly quite outside her experience as a store buyer. 'I honestly don't know if we can help you. I don't think we have the mechanism to sell anything but goods purchased for sale...' Gus and I exchanged glances and she caught the thought behind the exchange '... but I'll discuss it if you don't mind waiting. Would you like some coffee?'

'Thank you very much, that would be most welcome.'

She spoke briefly on the telephone to someone and after a few minutes a girl brought in a tray and sat down at her desk; our lady left. The implication was not lost on us. The poor woman didn't want to risk leaving us alone in her office but was too polite to ask us to wait elsewhere or simply tell us to buzz off. The girl stared at us as we drank our coffee and we stared back. Not a word was exchanged. I was beginning to feel a little embarrassed, wishing we had not started the exercise. It had all seemed so simple. Gus was feeling the strain; he was fidgety and kept flicking imploring glances at me.

I was on the point of standing up and beating a retreat when the buyer walked in accompanied by two men – one an obvious colleague and the other a porter carrying a window dummy. 'Would you mind repeating your story to Mr. Scrivener', she said. 'He is the editor of our staff magazine.' Whether he was or not I don't know. He took no notes and demanded no photograph. It occurred to us later that he may have been a security man. On reflection it was an unusual experience for the poor woman and she was right to be cautious. We told him of Amos's travail and how seeing the dumping of the broken dummy had fathered a thought that we were now trying to flesh out. He had a hearty laugh and the story tickled him immensely. After a few questions and a check of our identity cards he accepted it totally. 'Well boys', he said, 'is this too badly damaged for your purpose?' She was perfect. Her nose was squashed flat and there was a deep indentation on her arm. Other than that, apart from an inked-on bow tie, a scribbled hairy chest and an anchor drawn on her forearm, she was in good condition. We were delighted. 'There is no charge', he said. 'Please accept it with our compliments.'

I am probably the world's premier authority on trying to wrap up a tailor's dummy in wrapping paper. It can't be done, especially with one arm in a sling. Somehow it's a difficult job to delegate; it's like watching someone play Patience – there is an irresistible urge to join in. Eventually we stopped trying. She came apart in the middle so Gus took charge of the top half and I carried her hips and thighs tucked under my good arm. We came in for a few curious stares as we left the store and strolled along the sidewalk. The further we got from the shop the more people were beginning to take an interest until they were turning openly in their tracks to stare at us, elbow each other and giggle. I was beginning to feel like the Pied Piper, but it was not until we were separated by traffic – Gus electing to beat a car across the road while I waited it out – that I realised what an extraordinary picture we presented. I looked across at the huge, black-bearded figure in the ginger corduroy suit and the Shanghai boots glowering at me from the opposite pavement, clutching in his arms half a nude, hairy-chested, bald-headed woman and I curled up; the more I thought about it the funnier it became until I was almost helpless. Gus strode back across the road, furious and embarrassed. 'What's s-s-so bloody fuh-fuh-funny?'

'You, you daft bastard; you look like something out of a Boris Karloff film. All you need is a bolt through the neck.'

'P'pack it in', he growled, 'or I'll d'd'dump it here.' I realised suddenly that he was horribly embarrassed and couldn't see the funny side of it at all. He was obviously very uncomfortable. 'Look,' I said, 'let's get a cab.'

'Right. And you can p'pay for the damned thing. It wuh-wuh-was your idea.'

Back on board we reunited her two halves and put her in Amos's bunk. When he came back the next evening rather the worse for wear after having tried to drown the memory of his miserable visit, he went to climb into his bunk and nearly had a seizure. What was even worse, he told us later, was that his cabin steward had seen it in his bunk on the Saturday morning and thereafter for several days walked warily round Amos, giving him nervous, sidelong glances.

'Hermione' served her purpose very well and the old man was delighted with her. We didn't tell him that we had actually acquired her for Amos's sake, not for his, so we basked in his benevolence for some time. To Amos's disgust, however, Prissy still called on him for the odd special modelling assignment. As we told him, 'a plaster and linen-scrim facsimile woman is no substitute for the real thing.' He remained stubbornly unconvinced and uncomforted.

CHAPTER THREE

We left Vancouver bound for the Philippines and for me the achievement of a boyhood ambition. On arrival in Manila I had circumnavigated the globe. I had previously accumulated several times the requisite mileage, but I had never before departed from a spot on the planet and sailed due east or west to arrive at the back door of my starting point.

The trip took eleven days longer than it should have done as we were plagued with a multitude of breakdowns – the longest of which enabled the mate to get a couple of boats over the side and tidy up his paintwork. It also enabled us to do some shark fishing. We hooked a couple of monsters but they straightened out the hooks and escaped. As we were winching up a seven-footer there was a swirl and a flurry in the water and we were left with about five foot of severely truncated shark dangling from the winch cable, spewing a multi-coloured spaghetti of entrails into the bloodied water. Whatever took it must have had an enormous gape, and the painters in the boats, who earlier had been sky-larking and deliberately falling overboard to cool off, were very happy to get back on board.

The engineers worked miracles with the old engine but something was seriously amiss and we proceeded for the rest of the trip at about fifty per cent revolutions. Anything more ambitious resulted in severe vibration. During the leisurely extended voyage we discovered that Gus was inclined to 'feyness', a legacy of his Highland forbears. We accused him of believing in spooks, and although he was reluctant to admit it and wriggled shamelessly, there was no doubt in our minds that he was a believer. As a result we played a very cruel trick on him that backfired badly and taught me a lesson I have never forgotten.

Ships are very atmospheric and can be quite spooky at times, especially ships as old as *Bellatrix*. She was over forty-years-old when I sailed in her and had survived two World Wars. At a conservative estimate some two thousand men had lived in her on and off for periods of around two years each. It was hardly surprising that she had a 'lived in' aura. By any estimate she must have seen deaths and sickness, sadness and anxiety, injuries and madness among her crew members during all those years with all those men. Some essence of their suffering and experience of life must have soaked into her personality. Gus believed it firmly. Others were more sceptical, but on cool, quiet nights at sea, with the ship asleep and the old engine snoring gently beneath our feet driving her massive blunt bows through the water at close on thirteen knots, it wasn't difficult to believe that the shades of her past companies were standing watch with us and looking over our shoulders.

Merchant ships don't keep dog watches[3], watch keepers always stand watch in the same time slot. The master doesn't stand a watch; the mate's is from four to eight and the second mate's from twelve till four. As third mate Gus stood the eight to twelve watch night and morning. One night about eleven-thirty we entered his cabin, unscrewed all the light bulbs and replaced them with green ones which threw a horrible, dim, sickly light. We took an old uniform and stuffed it with rolled up pandanus mats (mats woven from the dried fronds of a type of palm tree) and old clothes, with socks for hands and a pillow for a head. Having strung it up by the neck to the beam which ran across the cabin deckhead we turned out the lights,

---

[3] When the four to eight evening watch is split into two watches of two hours each. Watch keepers remain in their sequence but their time slot advances each day to ring the changes. The practice was discontinued in the British M.N. in 1936.

then switched them on again. The test was so alarmingly realistic as almost to make us abandon the project. There was a lumpy sea that night and the ship was pretty lively. In the ghastly green light the pseudo-corpse suspended by its neck looked gruesomely real as it swung eerily to and fro.

Amos went on the bridge at midnight to relieve Gus. The rest of us hid in Amos's cabin just across the alleyway and peered through the crack in the modesty curtain to observe Gus's moment of truth. Half asleep, he completed his rounds, ambled along the alleyway, entered his room and switched on the light. He was momentarily frozen with horror then gave a shuddering cry of shock and disgust and leaped bodily backwards out of his cabin into the alleyway, banging his head badly on the doorframe. The illusion was only momentary. He was shocked almost instantly awake and rapidly regained full control of his faculties. He gave a bellow of rage, tore the dummy from the deckhead, threw it into the alleyway and slammed the jalousie door so violently that it jumped off its hinges. Dumbstruck with shame and guilt at the overwhelming success of our nasty little game, we knocked repeatedly on his door. He refused to answer at first but eventually told us in very pungent terms to go away hurriedly. We did. Gus wasn't a sulky man but for days afterwards he would have nothing to do with us and would listen to no apology. He stood his watch, ate his meals then disappeared into his cabin. It was most distressing.

A long time later, when he was able to discuss it, he told me that he had once sailed as quartermaster in a ship where his shipmates had ribbed him mercilessly about his acceptance of the supernatural. That was why he had been reluctant to admit it to us, fearing to expose himself to another campaign of ridicule.

One night two of them, rather the worse for drink, went on the monkey island[4] while he was on the wheel. One of them had smeared his face with flour, filled in his eye sockets with lampblack and reddened his lips. The other seaman held him by his legs and suspended him over the forward end of the monkey island so that his head gradually came into view in the wheelhouse. It was late at night; Gus, standing relaxed at the helm, was focusing alternately on the compass and on the dark sea some four or five miles ahead of the wheelhouse window and slipping his mental clutch slightly. A skilled helmsman, he was functioning in automatic mode and responding only to the stimuli of his duties. The ship was rolling and heaving in a lively manner and he was having to work at it to maintain her course in the muscular, quartering seas. Out of the corner of his eye and on the edge of his consciousness he was suddenly aware of movement a few feet ahead of him and high in the window where no movement should be. He refocused just as a hideous, upside down caricature of a human face floated into view and grinned noiselessly at him.

He was so shocked at the apparition that appeared to be hanging in the air some eight hundred miles from land that he took an involuntary step backwards and slipped off the helmsman's grating. The combination of this stumble from the grating and his shocked reaction made him release the wheel just as a curler thumped against the ship's quarter. She slewed violently, throwing the anchor man off balance. After a short desperate struggle the white-faced man slipped from his grasp and fell some thirty or so feet onto the winch below and died instantly. The anchor man was 'luckier'. He followed his mate over the precipice but missed the winch and somehow made a softer landing – still hard enough to shatter every major bone in his body. They were days away from port, and,

---

[4] The deck from which bearings are taken, which forms the roof of the wheelhouse/chartroom.

having no doctor on board, did what little they could with advice over the radio. They ultimately made rendezvous with a Dutch naval vessel and he was accepted into their sick bay. It seemed likely, Gus said, that the man would never walk again or, at least, would never recover sufficiently to be able to follow his calling. Gus felt guilty about it and it had taken him years to shake off the oppressive feeling of responsibility for the double tragedy.

She must have been a desperately unlucky ship. There were several deaths among her crew during Gus's nine months in her. His first captain had been killed in a freak accident arising from circumstances which many seamen have experienced and which normally would have produced a few bruises quickly shrugged off by the victim with an embarrassed grin. The master's wife had been travelling with him and he was taking her ashore to fly back to the UK. Going down the gangway he was in front of her when she caught her stiletto heel in the matting on the top platform and lurched into him. He lost his balance and tumbled from top to bottom of the steeply angled gangway fracturing his skull on a stanchion. He died en route to hospital. It was nine o'clock in the morning and they were as sober as judges. It was just a tragic accident arising from a simple, fairly common incident.

Early in Gus's service in her, the cook – a devout homosexual – was heavily involved with one of the galley hands. The couple fell out and the scullion transferred his affections to another member of the crew. The cook sulked and took to drinking heavily. One afternoon when the lad came into the galley to prepare vegetables for the evening meal, the drunken cook abused him and threatened him with an enormous knife. The terrified scullion pushed the cook away and he fell on the galley stove. In agony from his burns and enraged at the double injury, as he saw it, he picked up a pan of simmering stew and threw it over the boy. He came quickly to his fuddled senses and, horrified at what he had done, locked himself in a storeroom and slashed his thighs, wrists and throat with the butcher's knife. He was dead long before they could break in. The boy was blinded and in agony. He screamed for three days and nights, and died before he could be landed in Valparaíso.

Our miserable little game had struck deep into Gus, much deeper than we could have foreseen. It taught me how dangerous it is to assume that we know all there is to know of someone and to assume further that he will react to an event in a predictable manner. I have hated practical jokes ever since.

Bellatrix was reputed to be haunted. She was said to have had her bridge party wiped out by a wartime South Atlantic raider's shell. Which war was not specified. Stories were told and retold about the dead captain being seen years later, standing on the wing of the bridge in tropical whites during howling winter storms in the high latitudes. I never met anyone who could claim first-hand experience of this phenomenon and I personally never witnessed any cold spots or heard or observed any of the traditional manifestations of unquiet spirits. We occasionally had ultra-susceptible oddballs who protested that they had detected some presence or aura and consequently would not go unaccompanied into the chain locker or steering engine flat or whichever space to which they had become sensitised. But I think it more likely that the slightly spooky character of a darkened, sleeping ship sliding smoothly over a silent sea in the cool, dark hours removed in time and space from normal, noisy, warm human activity, worked a special sort of magic on over-active imaginations. There is no doubt that the sea in certain moods and at certain times exerts a strange influence that is particularly effective on a sensitive mind in its more introspective moments. We called it being 'moonstruck'.

CHAPTER FOUR

After discharging in Manila we proceeded at half speed to Singapore for engine repairs. While we were there we had our second 'medevac'. Our second radio officer was sent ashore with a virulent form of dermatitis. It was horrible to see; the poor chap swelled up before our eyes and appeared to be rotting. He thought he had been bitten by something to which he had an allergic reaction, and was seriously ill for several weeks before the doctors got to grips with his condition. Once they had made a connection his recovery was rapid and complete, but, sadly, too late to rejoin *Bellatrix*.

His replacement came to us purely by chance. Peewee had paid off his previous commission in Hong Kong and was waiting for a passage home when he bumped into someone who told him about our owners, the Sikkim Brothers, and their complicated maritime operations. Being at a loose end he called on them just as they received the message that our chap had been sent ashore to hospital. Before he could draw breath he was on a plane to Singapore and joining what he thought was the scruffiest ship afloat. Peewee (he had a complicated Polish name with more consonants than vowels; his nickname was derived from a phoneticised transliteration of the first and final syllables) had never been in the Far East before.

He had spent a couple of years with one of the large radio companies which sub-contracted staff to the shipping lines. It wasn't a very good arrangement for the men concerned although it led to a very varied life. The pay was bare-bones agreement rate, and they hardly ever seemed to get the leave to which they were entitled because there was always a shortage of men. It was not unusual for Peewee to get back from a three or four month trip to find, when everyone else was going home, that he had to lug his gear round the dock to join a ship which already had steam up and was waiting for him before departing to South America or other foreign parts. He resented this exploitation and decided to freelance; although he was a little worried about going foreign flag, he felt he had nothing to lose.

It does give one a slight feeling of insecurity, or it did then – especially after having sailed with one of the old blue-blooded British fleets. Now some of the fleets sailing under flags of convenience are almost as secure and dependable as the old dignified British shipping companies – and certainly the pay is better. More and more UK shipowners have withdrawn from the cut and thrust of union skirmishing and the endless, niggling battles, and have replaced the Red Duster with newer, more gaudy and certainly less honourable colours.

In the British Merchant Navy the seaman is protected by various Acts of Parliament augmented by the NMB (National Maritime Board) Agreement of 1898. The Agreement, which everyone legally accepts when they sign the ship's articles witnessed by a shipping master, lays down rules of service and the basic standards of life for every man aboard under the absolute, magisterial authority of the vessel's master. It really is basic stuff. So much hard tack and preserved meat per day, when he is entitled to fresh milk and how much tinned milk when sailing outside a specific zone, etc. It would probably be impossible for a modern seaman to accept under normal circumstances – it's really just a subsistence diet stated as a legal minimum. In respect of food, no shipping line would dream of imposing the NMB standards on its men, but I have heard someone threatened with it. A persistent and unreasoning complainer about the quality of the food once had the base requirements read out to him by the old man. He was told that any more complaints and he would be put on the NMB scale. There were no more complaints.

The British seaman knows, too, that if he has to sign off in a foreign port for any reason he will not be cast adrift to make his own way. He will be cosseted by the local Consul, who usually resides in the offices of a shipping line or agent, and if he is not repatriated by his company – which would be unusual – he will ultimately travel home 'DBS' (Distressed British Seaman) in a British vessel back to his original port of signing on. I'm not sure how we would have fared. Obviously as British citizens, we could claim protection of the British Embassy, but presumably British shipping lines have a sort of 'knock for knock' agreement about repatriating members of each other's crew when necessary, the distressed seaman signed on for a nominal shilling a day, simply to make him a legal crew member of the carrying vessel. In arrangements like we had with the Sikkims, so much seemed to be agreed according to the force of the personalities involved and to their relative worldliness. I have no doubt that had Amos needed to be repatriated he would have negotiated a first class ticket in the 'Chusan' or 'Himalaya', while Peewee would have had to travel steerage in an Arab dhow.

Another disadvantage of sailing on a voyage-by-voyage agreement as a sub-contractor was the sense of isolation it engendered, although it led to an extremely varied life. You would rarely be in a ship long enough to work up relationships with the other officers. Peewee told us that he had often felt very much the outsider. Everybody else seemed to have been ages in the ship, but his next trip might be anywhere in the world on any ship from a dredger to an ocean liner and he would probably never see these particular men again. His own curious personality couldn't have helped matters much. His shipmates probably never had time to get to know the rather interesting young man who hid behind the oddly diffident but spiky manner.

Initially he was rather hard to take. He was pathetically anxious to be accepted as 'family' and irritated everyone with his overenthusiastic good fellowship. Amos rather cruelly told him one day, 'Look here, Peewee, pipe down or we won't let you be in our gang.' It found my tender spot. I giggled in my coffee for days afterwards whenever I thought about it. It seemed to point up exactly Peewee's juvenile delight and his naïve expression of it. What was a relatively long-standing and normal way of life for us, was for Peewee a recently achieved ambition and he just couldn't help commenting on it. What was even funnier, in retrospect, was the owlish way he goggled round at us, struggling to detect what there was in Amos's off-the-cuff remark to make me collapse with mirth. Poor old Peewee could only take it at face value and it meant nothing.

The Christmas he joined us was spent at sea, so festivities were rather restricted, but by New Year we were loading tobacco in Belawan on Sumatra, and could let our hair down. It was his first experience of the social life of *Bellatrix*. We had been given a box of festive novelties by the agent in Singapore. Lord knows where he got them, they must have come from a carnival or a rather ambitious fancy dress supplier. In place of the usual flimsy Christmas paper hats we had proper three-dimensional beauties made from felt, cardboard, canvas, cloth and plastic. There were tri-corn and pirate hats, Stetsons and bishops' mitres, straw boaters and little cloches, top hats with windows in them and bowler hats clad in colourful tinfoil segments with a child's windmill growing out of the crown. It was an extraordinary collection of odd and exotic headgear. I expropriated a magnificent tri-corn hat with a trimming of tinsel round the rim in place of gold braid. It changed my personality; I felt like Long John Silver.

Work finished about nine in the evening and jollities got underway at once. We had saved some time-expired distress rockets and at midnight we loosed them. Peewee, as the youngest man on board, had the time-honoured task of ringing in the New Year with twelve strokes of the ship's bell, while Amos upset the chief engineer by bleeding off most of his steam with inordinately long blasts on the siren. The food on board was abysmal and we decided to go ashore en masse for a rijstafel (literally 'rice-table') at a local restaurant that catered for stevedores during the day. The food was authentic and fiery.

The establishment consisted of a rudimentary hut and an open-air galley where the food was prepared and cooked in woks in front of the customers, who sat at tables distributed beneath the trees. A huge paraffin-powered Coca Cola fridge assured us of a supply of cold beer and the place was within staggering distance of the dock. Perfect.

It was a momentous night for Peewee. The proprietor welcomed us enthusiastically and the party got underway. I glanced round the assembly gathered about the rough-hewn table, their faces lit from low level by the flickering pressure lamps. The black tropical night pressed in all round them and the splash of harsh, green light from the lanterns threw their faces into sharp relief, emphasising the black hollows of cheeks and eye sockets. Combined with the exotic hats it gave them an oddly conspiratorial, medieval aspect. In a moment of whimsy I rapped for attention; Long John Silver (by Walt Disney out of Robert Newton) rose to his feet, tri-corn hat clasped to his chest, and with a 'Newtonesque' roll of the eyeballs intoned solemnly, 'Gen'l'men, the cause ah-harrr!' Their reaction astonished me. In one of those rare moments of subliminal accord resulting in simultaneous action, they all rose instantly to their feet as if they had been rehearsed, removed their hats and held them to their chests, heads bowed. 'The cause, ah-harrr!' they chanted in reply, rolling their eyes at me.

During the course of the meal, at odd times, all of us continued the childish game, much to the puzzlement of the proprietor and his aides, and each time got the same solemn responses as if we were conducting an obscure religious ceremony. Eventually Peewee decided it was his turn. He stood up and removed his hat. 'Gentlemen, the cause!' he said primly. Spontaneously and with no collusion at all we all said, almost in one voice 'Sit down, you daft bastard, ah-harrr!'

'Gen'l'men, the cause – aharr!'

Peewee was shattered. He blinked round at us, then sat down glumly, muttering to himself and wondering how he had got it wrong this time. It was very funny if a trifle pathetic. It was impossible to explain to him, and he obviously felt aggrieved, but he put us all firmly in our places a very short time later.

We had a magnificent meal and Peewee initially enjoyed it although he kept asking us to identify various bits which is not always the wisest thing to do! In the middle of the table was a sort of 'lazy Susan' laden with a staggering variety of pickles and condiments. Indonesian food is very spicey and the hottest additive is Sambal Oelek – a compote of peppers and chilllies. It sears the mucous membrane of the mouth lining and should be added in minute quantities, if at all. The unpracticed European palate should sample it with caution. We had warned Peewee that it would be safer to take up fire-eating but he insisted that he enjoyed hot foods. 'My mother always makes our curry hot', he told us. We tried to explain that he was not comparing like with like. A Maidstone Mum's lamb curry made with even liberal quantities of 'Ventacachellum's Original Prime Curry Powder' has no reference point in common with an Indonesian meal prepared by Indonesians for Indonesians in a roadside restaurant in Sumatra. He took a handsome spoonful of the Sambal Oelek and mixed it with his base rice. He didn't survive the first mouthful. He leaped to his feet, eyes bulging, and spat it out. It was too late. The condiment was burning into the membranes of his mouth, throat and nose. He tried to swamp it with cold beer but the relief was illusory and only momentary. Then, taking little gasping breaths and in considerable discomfort, he went into a sort of hyperventilation and frightened the life out of us. It was some fifteen minutes before things returned to normal.

At night, when the clientele had departed, rats scavenged the ground under the tables. Rats are ubiquitous in the Far East and occasionally augment subsistence diets where there are no religious objections. It wasn't hard to see why[5]. They are a ready source of protein and surely no more objectionable than some of the hideous things we drag from the sea and eat. The flesh of a grain-fed rat can't be so far inferior to the meat of a scrawny chicken, especially when it's been marinated in curried oils and cooked till the fibres separate. Rats didn't worry us much – we shared *Bellatrix* with a lively throng of them. Somebody was watching them when he saw a long, slender, sinuous shadow glide from the humpy grass onto the bare, packed earth. There was a confused scuffle, a squeak, then silence. It didn't register at first what he was looking at, then the penny dropped and he croaked an alarm. In a flash, we were leaping onto the tables, squealing like a Victorian virgin accosted in the dairy by a randy ostler, figuratively clutching our skirts about us. All except Peewee.

'What sort is it? he asked.

'Does it bloody matter?'

'They're not all dangerous you know. This one is probably just a rat snake. Hang on a tick.'

He grabbed a besom leaning against the wall of the hut, and to our astonishment strode confidently over to the far shadows, poked around for a moment or two, knelt briefly then came back carrying a snake. It was about four or five feet long and rather thin, the blunt head not much thicker than the body girth. In the guttering greenish light cast by the pressure lamps it looked pretty nondescript and seemed to be silky and of a uniform, slatey-brown colour with clearly defined scales. Eyes glittering, it lay looped and still, supported carefully in his hands. We stared at him in awe.

'As I thought,' he said with authority, 'it's only a ratter. I should think these people are delighted to see them about. Rats spread disease, snakes don't.'

This was a new and entirely unexpected Peewee; he had established his superiority in one stupendous stroke so far as

---

[5] In French Indo China they were called 'rice-rabbits'.

we were concerned. I know not everyone shares my personal nightmare with regard to snakes, but most people I know regard them with repugnance and avoid them, given the opportunity. Peewee was the only person I had then met who thought they were creatures of superlative beauty and grace, and enjoyed handling them. His father was a reptile keeper in one of the major zoos, and Peewee had been used to snakes and lizards all his life. He'd had them as pets, nursed sick ones and raised babies. He was altogether as happy with them as I would have been with a stray baby squirrel. The snake temple in Penang was a fascination for him and he spent hours there whenever he could. He became friendly with one of the administrators who was happy to show and discuss his charges. It would have taken a team of Clydesdales to drag me through the door. He was an odd chap – certainly odd enough to qualify for a place in *Bellatrix*.

CHAPTER FIVE

My affair with Loretta Young began inauspiciously enough in Sumatra. We were loading enormous peeled logs of a close-grained hardwood that gave me a painful rash if I touched them. Several of us were sitting on the after end of the boat deck one day when the coolies knocked off for their eleven o'clock break and opened their leaf-wrapped lunch packs. One of them was expressing an unusual interest in us, smiling up at us and making incomprehensible signals, indicating a parcel beside him wrapped in banana leaves. Eventually curiosity got the better of me and when he had finished eating I went down to him. We had for some time been studying Malayan for the Haji[6] run (which was rumoured for the next season), and I was anxious to try out my new skills.

'Hey, Boong,' I greeted him.

'Hey, Tuan,' he replied then leaned over and opened the parcel. I thought it was a dead cat at first. A small body with clumps of silver-tipped black fur was curled up inside. It had long, skinny arms, longer than the legs which were pulled right up, folded against the abdomen like a baby's. It stank. As I turned it over parasites ran over my hand. The pathetic little face came uppermost; the black mask, bearing the imprint of the leaf wrapping, was dried out and the lips – wrinkled clear of the teeth – were stuck firmly to the gums. A crust of dried mucus had cemented the lids together over the deeply sunken eyes. The tragic little beast looked dead except for a fluttering

---

[6] The annual pilgrimage of Mohammedans to Mecca via the seaport of Jeddah on the Red Sea. It was a very lucrative trade and is now almost exclusively carried out by charter flights from the major population centres of the religion.

in the throat which could hardly be described as breathing. Gus had followed me down. 'It's a gibbon. Poor little bastard needs a knock on the head; just look at its arse.' The tailless rump was one huge running sore, and as we examined it more closely I drew back in horror. Plump, glistening, pearly-grey maggots writhed grotesquely within the open wound. When I pinched the wrinkled skin in a bald patch on the shrunken belly, it peaked and stayed erect like a well-whipped egg white. I grimaced at Gus. 'What a mess. She's a goner I should think.'

'It'd be a mercy, I'll fetch the quack.'

While Gus went for the doc I questioned the coolie. 'Dia umur berapa? (How old is she?)'

He shrugged his ragged shoulders. 'Dia ada di ketorang tigga minggu. (We've had her for three weeks.)'

'Kau dapat dia dari nana? (Where did you get her?)'

He swung his arm to encompass the dense, tree-lined slopes that encircled the bay. 'Dia punyah ibu di bunuh dalam kabon pohon pohon. (Her mother was killed in the trees.')

It was a story that we had heard many times before. Either the mother was accidentally killed when her home was felled or, as sometimes happened, she had been deliberately killed in order to capture her baby. Gibbons were highly sought after as pets. This sorry little scrap had been taken too early or had been kept in appalling conditions. Gus returned with the quack, who examined the mite with a wrinkle of disgust on his face. 'What d'you reckon, Doc?' I asked.

'Well, she's alive, but only just. She's badly dehydrated and in a poor state. If we could plump her up a bit we could get rid of the maggots easily enough and probably cure the infections. I should think pneumonia would be the big risk, but I have no idea of what sort of antibiotic dose to give her. I might poison her.'

'She'd be no worse off then would she?' Gus said. 'Let's give it a try.'

I gave the coolie a tin of State Express 555 cigarettes for her and she became a major interest in our lives. Her effect on the quack was astonishing. His normal state was a precarious equilibrium between partial and intermittent sobriety and a total alcoholic daze. He was rarely staggering drunk but nor was he ever crisply sober. He lived most of his life in a sort of twilight world where he functioned in automatic mode at a reasonable level, but any emergency or unexpected demand on him would have blown all his fuses simultaneously. With the arrival of this tiny mite who was totally dependent on him for her very life, he changed dramatically. He focused completely on her. Either he made a conscious decision to eschew booze for the time being, or he became so engrossed in the problems of resurrecting the little creature that the need for his alcoholic crutch was sublimated.

We took her to the sick bay where Doc plucked the maggots from her rear end (and fed them to the Java sparrows who lived in a cage in the officers' smoke room) while I gently bathed her eyes clear with a warm solution of bicarbonate of soda. She hardly stirred and made no sound at all. He cleaned her wounds and sores and sprinkled them with Sulfa powder while I wiped her lips and gums with glycerine to separate them. After spraying her tongue and mouth with atomised water – achieved by filling his mouth with water and spraying her with the fine droplets he blew from between his lips – he set to ridding her of the parasites that colonised her patchy but surprisingly dense fur. It was a terrible job; I doubted that she would ever be free of them. He worked out dosages and gave her a course of injections that, he said, would have cost a hundred pounds in the London Clinic. I don't know what he gave her but it worked. Day by day she grew stronger and plumper but she remained in a deep, unhealthy sleep, almost unmoving, as if she were in a coma. Her weak state persisted for an age, her eyes sunken, her black cheeks gaunt and dry and scaly.

In Singapore the quack went ashore to consult a vet. He brought back reams of notes together with tubes, bottles and jars of vitamin supplements, creams and unguents to rub into her scaly cheeks and anoint the scabby, bald patches that disfigured her. Her horrible tail-end wound granulated. Almost as we watched she plumped up and her fur grew thicker, filling in the bald patches. But she remained without vigour, her eyes sunken. 'It could be that she's still very young,' Doc said, 'babies always sleep a lot.' But he was obviously concerned, so we didn't really believe him. She had too good a set of teeth to be very young.

The babysitting was shared among us now she was no longer a medical case. We fed her with a baby bottle or spooned gruel into her when she would not suck. She coughed and gurgled without becoming really conscious but she swallowed most of what we gave her. I kitted out a large bucket with gauze and cotton wool where she spent most of her time curled up asleep, and we noted with delight that she changed position a lot and was sometimes very active. The bucket was passed from watch keeper to watch keeper, so she always had attention.

She spent one night in my cabin. The weather was rough, so I had rigged a strop to the bucket handle and suspended it from the deadlight hook by the porthole a couple of feet from my head. There it dangled and she slept the sleep of the dead, swinging within inches of my head as *Bellatrix* rolled heavily. I awoke the next morning to curious, birdlike noises. I rolled over to look at the bucket and there, inches from my eyes, was the loveliest and most welcome sight in the world. Peering at me over the bucket rim was a tiny, black face dominated by two huge, shining, mysterious dark eyes. She appeared to be supporting herself with her mouth with her tiny knuckles on either side of her head like a miniature Mr Chad. She looked so enchanting and the sight was so unexpected, that I laughed aloud with delight and the tiny head disappeared abruptly, leaving the two skinny hands gripping the edge of the bucket.

It hadn't occurred to me that she would be frightened. She wasn't. She was just momentarily startled; within seconds the head slowly rose again above the bucket rim like the rising of a tiny silver moon, and we stared at each other in mutual wonder. I held out my hand; she craned forward to sniff it, then tested it with her lips. Her eyes were beautiful – round, intelligent and wondrously clear. I could think only of the eyes of that loveliest of screen ladies – Loretta Young. And so she got her name – Lorrie for short.

After her shaky start she never looked back; she grew to full strength and agility with extraordinary speed. Within days she had enchanted everybody and was always a welcome visitor. She had the run of the ship. We rigged aerial ropeways for her and her acrobatics were a constant diversion and delight. Her agility and speed of reaction astonished us, she could catch birds on the wing and could change direction in mid-air. An incorrigible show-off, she rapidly developed habits and tricks that never left her.

She was phenomenally seductive and I never saw anyone who could resist her soft and intimate approach. You would be sitting on the hatch or in a deckchair and would suddenly become aware of a long, furry arm draped round your neck or tucked through your arm. On looking down you would encounter the tender, submissive and infinitely mysterious gaze which would penetrate the hardest heart. Within seconds she would be scooped up to lie like a baby in your arms. Her greatest thrill was to have her stomach knuckle-scrubbed, and she would go into a transport of delight if you blew hard into the thick fur under her chin. In order to expose her throat and neck to the delicious draught she would arch her back, giving deep orgasmic groans, arms dangling overhead almost to the deck, until she was in danger of slipping out of your arms. If you stopped she would fix you with a steely upside down squint and make curious, explosive little sneezy noises. She loved to touch and groom her particular friends and she became extremely attached to Gus. I once saw her give him pieces of orange which she tore off with her teeth then passed to him with her fingers. It was a very touching display of affection. She never did it for anyone else.

Lorrie was a natural clown and exhibited a robust sense of humour. One irritating habit she had was to jump down out of the blue on to someone's head or shoulders, spring instantly to others in the group as if they were stepping stones, leap out of reach then turn and chunter at us. It was no joke if you weren't expecting it, and a ten-pound gibbon leaping without warning onto your head when you were about to sip from a cup or glass was potentially dangerous. It didn't happen often and we could never gauge exactly the mood which prompted her to perform the exercise. She would have occasional flurries of biting. It wasn't vicious but her teeth were sharp and it hurt. I cured her of biting me by snarling at her and biting her arm quite sharply. It staggered her. She squealed in astonished rage and avoided me for some time, but we became friends again quite soon. She never bit or threatened me again.

An endearing habit she acquired was to sit on my lap with both arms wrapped round one of mine. She would push her face under my arm and sleep peacefully for ages. It induced a very fatherly feeling and I would go to great lengths so as not to disturb her. Her voice was extraordinary. For a long time she had been relatively mute and seemed to find it unexpectedly; I think she surprised even herself. She did not often make much noise but she could let rip a howl of astonishing intensity and volume that swelled and warbled. Otherwise she restricted herself to coos, snuffles and various birdlike utterances. The one I liked best was a rapid clicking she made with her lips when she was being cheeky. She would pout at you and make a rapid chewing motion to produce the clicks with her lips. We came to recognise a wide range of expressions and sounds and we communicated on a very high level.

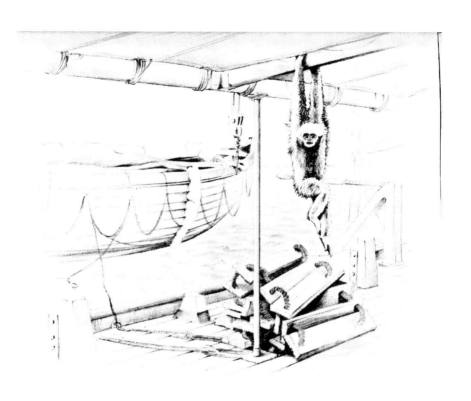

Lorrie was an elegant creature, gay and affectionate, an enchanting companion. Gibbons are the most vocal of the great apes; in the wild a gibbon's song is still audible at up to a mile-and-a-half to two miles. When we were in Sumatra or Borneo or round the islands, she would sometimes respond to the song of wild gibbons. For a reason I don't understand, it always chilled me.

Lorrie's voice was extraordinary, she could let rip a howl of astonishing intensity.

Her curiosity was insatiable and everything new to her was thoroughly examined and if possible pulled to pieces, sniffed, tested with her lips, then either eaten or discarded. This self-catering was not always sociably acceptable. We had a good many praying mantis on board – not so much as pets but to keep the cockroaches from taking over. *Bellatrix*, like all old steamships, was infested with 'steam beetles' – small, toffee-coloured cockroach-like insects. They got into everything. We became quite blasé about them and it was commonplace to spread curry on a white plate, flick out the steam beetles then add the rice. I still serve myself curry this back-to-front way today. Although they were harmless, when they became very numerous they gave me an itchy, unclean feeling.

They were almost impossible to eradicate. We were all supplied with 'Flit' guns – a half-pint can attached to a gadget like a bicycle pump – but the fluid supplied, while lethal to geriatric and semi-invalid flies, made no impression on cockroaches and steam beetles. We concocted our own supremely effective killing cocktail – 50% fluid supplied as a carrying base, plus 10% turpentine, 20% Dettol, and 20% pyrene (a fire extinguisher fluid). This was totally effective. The technique we evolved was to strike after dark. The ports were clamped down on strips of papier mâché to seal them completely, all vents were closed, the heat turned to maximum and a saucer of condensed milk was prominently displayed. After a suitable interval during which the heat in the cabin peaked at equatorial temperatures and the scent of the conny onny saturated the air and tempted the creatures from their nooks and crannies to track down its source, offensive action was initiated. The door was flung open, the 'Flit' gun pumped rapidly for as long as the operator could hold his breath and tolerate the blast-furnace temperature, then the door was slammed shut and the noxious vapour got to work. It was extremely successful but should only be used in emergencies we discovered. It took the gloss off varnishwork, polluted the cabin for hours and was almost as lethal to humans as it was to 'roaches.

Praying mantis were not so effective in liquidating roaches on a quantifiable basis but they were interesting and attractive. I think mine was the most successful. He was voracious and highly competent, and exhibited a degree of cunning that put him in a class of his own. A steam beetle that came within his considerable reach was snatched so quickly that you had to be looking directly at the creature to see the movement. Normally you saw only the effect of his action. He decimated my enemies in no time at all and I christened him Atilla. Gus was called Popeye because of its prominent eyes; Amos reckoned his looked like a Jewish grocer he knew who was always dry-scrubbing his hands – a characteristic action of the mantis – hence, Shylock. Edward lived with the chief engineer, and was named for Eddie Cantor of the saucer eyes.

They were weird creatures and not very rewarding pets in terms of personal relationships but they were fascinating nonetheless. They were grasshopper green and four to six inches long with huge eyes set in the top corners of their enormous, triangular heads. Two large, thick legs (or arms) were held up in front in an attitude of prayer. The legs ended in thick hooks and the two parts of the leg (corresponding to the femur and the tibia in humans) were lined with spikes which engaged when the leg was bent, thus trapping and holding the victim firmly. When a prey came within range the 'arm-legs' would flash out and then bend, trapping the prey and holding it where the formidable jaws soon made short work of it.

Praying Mantis – about four to six inches long and grasshopper-green – were interesting but slightly alarming to live with. I found their cold, watchful stance and their lack of unconsidered movement a bit disquieting. The face was clearly visible and lacked any expression; they were a bit spooky and seemed to be not wholly of this planet.

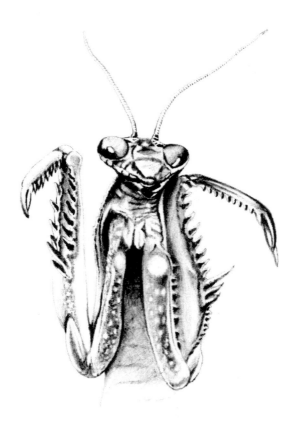

Attila was voracious, highly competent and a cannibal – as poor Edward discovered to his cost!

They were such alien creatures and the biggest insects I have handled that I was never completely comfortable with them. The face was clearly visible yet was so strange and expressionless that it made me feel ill at ease. I have no doubt that the only thing that stopped them from attacking human beings was the realisation that they were too big to hold and eat – it was a question of logistics, not ethics. They did not seem to be wholly of this world. They are cannibalistic, we discovered. Or rather, poor Edward discovered it in a terminal manner and was never able to put his knowledge to good use.

The chief engineer had suffered a small fire in his cabin and there was considerable smoke damage. He moved out while the cabin was cleaned and redecorated and lodged Edward with me while his home was out of action. Edward survived the move for about fifteen minutes. I couldn't believe it. I had placed him on my compendium top about a foot away from Atilla. I turned away to do something and when I looked back he was firmly in Atilla's deadly embrace and had already lost his head. Atilla gazed myopically at me in his usual absent-minded manner, as if he were not quite sure who I was, and continued to chomp on his compatriot with a steady, unhurried motion. It was horrifyingly cold-blooded and I felt as if I were the guilty party. The chief was quite brusque with me for some time, as if I had been remiss in training Atilla in basic etiquette and he had consequently committed an unforgivable social gaffe. 'Silly old sod', said Amos and offered him Shylock, but the Chief declined the offer.

'Do you think Atilla would like him?' Amos asked me, and I discovered that he had the same slightly wary attitude to the mantis that I had.

Their curious stance and lack of unconsidered motion, together with their cold, watchful attitude, were the characteristics I found most unsettling. They were rarely seen to move and this could be quite unnerving if you were engrossed in reading or writing. You would shift them out of harm's way on your dresser top and they would stand as motionless as a candlestick while you were looking at them. Divert your attention, even momentarily, then look back and they would have moved but were again motionless. It was as if they were playing a rather spooky game. Once or twice Atilla startled me when I thought he was elsewhere. While engrossed in a book, I would suddenly become aware that he had moved like a ghost up to my elbow and was apparently reading over my shoulder. With Edward in mind, I always suspected his motives and if he did it simply to tease, my inevitable and disproportionate start of surprise must have been most gratifying to him.

They were like sticks to handle, and so far as I know they never struggled or gave any indication of independent life, except when they were feeding. None of them lasted long and most met their deaths by accident. They were not robust. Moving silently and being in unexpected places led to a high mortality rate and a premature end for most of them.

Atilla met his end in an episode of poetic justice that must have had the ghost of Edward chuckling wryly in the shades. Lorrie was an inveterate thief and normally we did not allow her in our cabins as she could be destructive and had a taste for toothpaste which she would guzzle until she was sick. I had gone to my cabin one afternoon to collect my camera with her riding on my shoulder. Atilla was sitting thoughtfully on top of my compendium doing nothing in particular, just gazing into space and idling away the afternoon. It hadn't occurred to me that he would be at risk from Lorrie. She spotted him instantly even though he was still, leaped from my shoulder in a flash, grabbed him and bit off his head, then proceeded to eat him like a stick of rock. It must have given her a taste, for she polished off a couple of other mantis over the next few days. Sadly, she would never tackle the cockroaches of which there was an abundant supply, and which would have been socially acceptable.

I long cherished the dream of teaching her to drink from a cup but failed dismally, although she was highly intelligent and imitative. Her method was to dip her hand in the liquid then lick the drops from her knuckles. I suppose wild gibbons derive most of the moisture they require from fruit and leaves. She was polite at table and would take her place and eat quite daintily, like a vicar's wife, using her thumb and forefinger. But she was soon bored and, unlike a vicar's wife, would abandon her meal to investigate the ears or pockets or the dishes of her fellow diners, or anything else that attracted her. Lorrie was gay and affectionate, an enchanting companion and we loved her.

CHAPTER SIX

It suddenly looked as if we were going to have a fairly settled life. In Hong Kong we discovered that we had won a long-term charter by a Philippine/USA consortium and would have a nominally regular run encompassing Indonesia, the Philippines, Hong Kong and Japan to the West Coast of America, through the Panama Canal, up the East Coast then the reciprocal journey to complete a round trip.

A transit of the Panama Canal is an interesting experience. Where Suez is a scooped-out ditch between dull banks of sand and rock in a fairly bland landscape, Panama connects up a series of lakes, traverses lush jungle terrain and negotiates three sets of stupendous locks. In combination these locks raise the vessels some ninety feet at three or four feet per minute to cross the Continental Divide, then lowers them again to sea level on the other side. The canal is about 45 miles long and takes around four or five hours to transit. At the time it was built (at a horrifying cost in human lives – some estimates are as high as 20,000) it was hailed as the greatest civil engineering project since the Great Wall of China. Probably only the channel tunnel is a comparable feat.

The Gatun Locks at the Atlantic end hoists ships about ninety feet vertically. They proceed through the Gatun Lakes following a fixed channel which was once the course of the Chagres River, through the Gaillard cut to Pedro Miguel Locks which drop them about thirty feet to Miraflores Lake. They continue through the lake to the double locks at Miraflores which drop them finally a further fifty or so feet to sea level on the Pacific side. In the locks the ships are positioned and held steady by little mechanical trams called 'mules'.

Gatun Locks at the Atlantic end of the Panama canal. Ships are hoisted ninety feet to cross the continental divide and are then lowered again at the Pacific end. The canal is some 45 miles long following the course of the old Chagres river and traverses lush jungle terrain through a series of connected lakes. It was constructed at a horrendous cost in human lives – some estimates suggest over 20,000. It takes about six hours to traverse.

*In the Panama canal, ships are held steady in the locks by little
mechanical trams called 'mules'. This is a necessary precaution as
the ships are hoisted aloft by an enormous surge of water and
could easily be damaged if not restrained. The speed of the
operation is mind-boggling, it's like going up in a lift.*

The most amazing thing about the operation is the speed at which the ships are hoisted. The pumping system must be of phenomenal size and efficiency and the imagination boggles at the amount of water that must be displaced. Still, there's no shortage of it in Panama – the rainfall is tremendous and the humidity uncomfortably high.

We had frequent stopovers in Cristobal during the several years that I was running via the Panama Canal, but oddly enough I have never stopped in Balboa at the other end. Cristobal is an unremarkable city. The people are a curious hotchpotch of races and the climate is dank. At one time there was a bar there named the 'Doghouse Bar'. Externally it was built in the form of a huge kennel and inside was a replica of a Hollywood 'Wild West' saloon with a single enormous bar shaped like a hockey stick. The bar surface was constructed of four-inch thick, highly-polished mahogany planks and the beer was dispensed by a barman positioned at the pumps in the bend of the hockey stick. Girls were stationed along the length of the bar to take your money and call out your order to the barman who drew the beer into enormous glass jugs and skated them down the slipway at you. He was extremely skilled and the pot would stop directly in front of the customer, usually with the handle in the correct alignment. I never saw him misplace a pot.

However, when I first visited the place I was unaware of the impetus the barman had to impart to the huge jugs of beer, which I suppose must have weighed two pounds with contents. I ordered my drink; it was acknowledged and when a jug of foaming brew came skidding up the counter at me, I assumed it was mine and grabbed it as it flashed in front of me. The order had been intended for an earlier customer further up the bar. When I grabbed the missile I felt as if I had tried to stop a runaway horse. I managed to hold onto the jug but the intended customer got his beer. I was sitting on a tall stool and in the confusion it toppled, throwing me to the floor at the feet of the irate customer. The next few minutes were fraught indeed, but I was able to convince them that I was of feeble intellect and a novice to boot, and that no offence had been intended. It was a costly apprenticeship.

The 'Ladies' and 'Gents' toilets in the 'Doghouse' were designated 'Setters' and 'Pointers'. The subtlety escaped me for some time until I became au fait with American pronunciation.

On leaving Cristobal for the Caribbean, if you turn right you will come to Colombia, that sad country perched on the shoulder of the South American continent, now riven by drug wars and soaked in blood. It was a regular stop for us and in those days with its relaxed, slightly raddled air, it was quite popular with us. Cartegena in Colombia, like Macau, reminds me of an old film set. Unremitting, high-angle sunlight throws the crumbling, Colonial-Spanish buildings into sharp relief and the dense, black shadows have edges that might have been cut with a scalpel.

On our first visit, Amos and I were strolling round the ancient town when an incredibly dilapidated limousine of early 30s vintage pulled up alongside us. It had three rows of seats and was quite the longest car I had ever seen. It looked as if it might once have belonged to a Chicago mobster. If so, it had evidently fallen on hard times and wheezed and banged dramatically even while it was standing, panting, at rest beside us. We couldn't see the driver clearly and were astonished at the beautifully modulated, Etonesque voice that hailed us. 'I am a dragoman, gentlemen. I can show you the sights and escort you to the most interesting places in town for a very moderate fee which includes transport.'

Amos and I exchanged glances. It wasn't a bad idea, depending on what he considered to be 'a very moderate fee'. We were standing near a pavement café and were about ready for refreshment. 'Come and have a beer,' Amos said, 'and we'll see if we can do business.'

As we turned to make our way to the café the driver turned off his engine, we heard the door slam followed by the clip-clop of his footsteps following us. We sat down at a table under the awning and turned to greet the driver. I felt my jaw drop and Amos's astonishment was almost comical. Our reactions were unforgivably obvious and could have caused extreme offence, but the man took it in good part. He was evidently used to it. He was a diminutive, cadaverous albino Negro and quite startlingly ugly. The beautifully cadenced voice with its deep, mellow, English upper-class tones and pronunciation flowed over us. 'Please don't reproach yourselves. I'm afraid I take most people by surprise.'

It was incredible that a voice of such quality, such authority and timbre could be generated by so puny a man, and its refined 'Englishness' compounded the incongruity when viewed against his stature, race and physical defects.

Solomon was an enigma; he was forty-three years old, a Trinidadian and had lived in Colombia for ten years. That was the sum total of the information we gleaned from him, although he was frequently in our company over the next few days and we contacted him whenever we were in Cartegena – a regular stop for us. He was fascinating. His force of personality was such that within a very short time in his company his odd appearance ceased to register. He was erudite and extremely well read; his knowledge of the English poets was encyclopedic. He spoke Dutch like a Dutchman, according to our Belgian baker, although he claimed never to have set foot in the Netherlands Antilles or in Holland. His singing voice was magnificent. I never tired of listening to him whether he was singing huge chunks of the Latin Mass or giving us a rendition of 'Smoke Gets In Your Eyes'. He was very jolly and a thoroughly good companion but the strangest dragoman or guide I've ever met. The enterprise could have shown him no profit at all. For a ludicrously small 'fee' he accompanied us on our binges ashore, took us wherever we wanted to go and stood with us round for round.

One night we drove out into the hinterland of Cartegena. There must have been about ten of us because his enormous car was bulging at the seams. I can't remember now why we went so far out but it was a beautiful night and the journey through the countryside was a beneficence after weeks at sea. We stopped at what, I suppose, would be described as a hacienda, built round three sides of a courtyard. Coloured lanterns were hanging in the trees and exotic blooms hung like tangled ropes from the branches. We ate spicy food washed down by gallons of lightly flavoured, ice-cold beer and danced frenzied Spanish-American dances coaxed by the slim, dusky girls who swarmed round us with flashing smiles.

The mate on that trip was a querulous man who never ceased to complain about everything in a miserable, whining manner. He wasn't popular and we called him 'Mona Lot' after the depressive ITMA character. He was in top form that evening. He didn't like tacos, why couldn't they serve decent food? The beer was weak and far too cold. He didn't like 'wog' music; if they called themselves frigging musicians why couldn't they play the frigging foxtrot? He went on and on and became very tiresome. We had several engineers in the party and they showed him no deference at all, unlike the rest of us who had to be rather more circumspect. We had to work closely with him and ultimately he was in authority over us. 'Mona Lot' had an egg-shaped head and the illusion was heightened by the band of rusty, graying hair from which the shining, bald, pointed end protruded like an egg sitting cosily in a furry egg-cup.

The toilet facilities of the place were primitive in the extreme. The Gents consisted of a chest-high concrete block wall which decanted into a glazed brick channel running on an incline into a drain in the corner. The floor also sloped into the drainage corner so when it rained the place was left reasonably dry. Customers could relieve themselves and remain dry-shod – given reasonable competence – even in the wet season. It was a much cheaper arrangement than roofing the establishment. On this occasion the drain was blocked by cigarette ends and dead leaves, and the floor was awash to a depth of two or three inches. The proprietors had struggled manfully to clear the blockage and a large plunger with a huge rubber cup – some six or eight inches in diameter – was still in position over the drain hole.

One of the engineers returning from the loo brought with him the plunger and without warning clapped it on Mona's head. It was a perfect fit. Mona went rigid with shock for a moment then cussed blue murder, seized the handle and tried to drag it off his head. With tension applied vertically, the rubber stretched upwards and its transverse section accordingly contracted, clinging more stubbornly than ever. Try as he might, he couldn't budge it; the harder he tugged, the tighter it clung until he became incoherent in his rage and disgust. He glared round at us demanding, then pleading for assistance to remove the loathsome object. As he jerked his head round indignantly the three-foot handle protruding from the rubber cap wagged sternly to and fro like an admonitory finger and completed our disablement.

The place was in an uproar. Draped over tables and rolling off benches, we were all in a state bordering on helplessness. The more he cussed and struggled fruitlessly to remove his ludicrous helmet, the closer we came to total paralysis. The girls were close to hysteria, squealing with laughter and clinging weakly to each other, calling all and sundry to come and witness this extraordinary event. The courtyard gradually filled as customers left the restaurant and the kitchen staff crept from their duties to see what all the fuss was about. They too became infected and the mate's bellows of impotent rage interspersed with terrifying threats completed the descent into bedlam.

Eventually our host's inherent good manners and sense of decorum triumphed and a semblance of calm was restored. Two of the girls, still shaken by little internal eruptions of uncontrollable mirth, went to Mona's assistance and peeled off the cap. He spent the rest of the evening demanding that we return to the ship immediately. When we refused he sulked in a corner, massaging his head with handfuls of whisky to disinfect it until his pate glowed a dull, throbbing red.

CHAPTER SEVEN

On our first visit to New York on the new charter we arrived on my birthday – August 18th – and docked in Atlantic Basin in Brooklyn. It was hot and humid, and Amos had pestered me since late afternoon to go ashore with him. I really wanted nothing more than to shower and sit on deck in the gloaming with a cold beer and watch the lights of Manhattan across the teeming harbour. But he was relentless; so rather than generate a row, I eventually agreed that we would go to the British Merchant Navy Officers' Club in the Hotel Astor in Times Square. As we left the ship and walked to the subway through the hot, sleazy dockland streets, I became increasingly morose and determined not to enjoy myself. I would be as thorough a bad companion as possible to make Amos pay for his intransigence.

The subway train smelled as usual of greasy kitchens and overheated, moist, not very clean humanity. The shock wave of hot, foetid air that preceded it out of the tunnel had already sent my spirits on a sharply descending spiral. However, on the journey to Times Square my mood lightened. On pulling into Union Square a childish urge made me turn to Amos, look him straight in the eye and say lugubriously and with great deliberation 'O-n-i-o-n Square'. I was not prepared for his reaction. It was as if I had touched some hidden spring deep within him. He looked at me blankly at first, followed by a hint of mild alarm, then his lips quivered into his lopsided smile which degenerated into a giggle that he tried to suppress. The more he denied it utterance, the more it convulsed him until he was helpless. At first I found it vaguely amusing to see the dignified and imperturbable Amos making such an ass of himself. But I became progressively irritated then embarrassed by his spasms, hissing at him out of the corner of my mouth with my teeth clenched, 'Shut up you idiot', as more and more people turned to see what was causing the disturbance. This served only to increase the severity of his paroxysms until I had to hold him on the seat, red-faced and gasping, with tears running down his face, until the spasms subsided.

Sitting opposite was a girl I had noticed earlier – tall, slim and rather sombre-looking with needle straight, glossy brown hair cut square on the jawline. She had been watching Amos obliquely for some time. His extraordinary display coupled with my disgusted reaction must have struck her as very funny indeed, for presently she caught my eye and an enormous grin crept over her face, completely dispelling her sombre, rather intense expression.

By the time we reached Times Square, Amos had regained control although he was still shaken occasionally by little internal eruptions of mirth. On the way to the Astor I nagged him to tell me what was so funny, but he couldn't or wouldn't articulate the reason for his near hysteria. Consequently by the time we arrived at the club a measure of constraint had grown between us. We went straight to the bar and sank a couple of cold beers but they did little to alleviate the near heat stroke we were suffering. I felt very resentful towards Amos; I could have been sitting cool and comfortable on deck in a lungyi,[7]

---

[7] The lungyi – a wide cylinder of printed cotton – was the invariable relaxing/sleeping rig we used in the tropics. Worn as an ankle length sarong for lounging, it is folded round the waist to reduce its circumference and length. If the wearer is to be active the back hem of the 'skirt' is drawn up between the legs and tucked into the waist at the front so as to form a sort of baby's nappy. It is perfect hot weather sleeping gear when it is too hot and humid for even a sheet. In the early morning chill you unwind the waist and pull the cylinder up to cover your shoulders. The thin cotton is just substantial enough to reduce the impact of the fresh morning air to a comfortable coolness.

sipping better beer and enjoying whatever breeze was stirring on the Atlantic and being funnelled up the Hudson.

One of the big Cunarders was in and her dance band was filling the guest spot at the club; a few wilting couples were rotating desultorily on the pocket-handkerchief dance floor. Amos went off prospecting among the hostesses, and I stood at the window overlooking the Square, watching the huge animated Camel cigarette advert opposite blowing its gigantic smoke rings. As I turned to go back to the bar for a refill I almost bumped into the brown-haired girl from the subway. It took us both by surprise, She arched her thick brows and widened her eyes. 'Hello,' she said, 'has your friend recovered?' Her voice was crisply English and attractively modulated. That surprised me. I had pegged her as American-Jewish.

'My friend is a terminal imbecile,' I replied. 'He will never recover.'

'Whatever did you say to him to get that reaction?'

'Onion Square,' I said, wondering what on earth she would make of it. She waited, expecting more. But there was no more.

'Is that all?' she asked at last.

''Fraid so.'

'Well that's not very funny!'

'No it isn't, is it?'

We stared at each other solemnly and in silence for some seconds, then simultaneously burst out laughing. Her laughter, deep and husky, was as unexpected and enchanting as her curiously wide grin. She was resting her hand lightly on my forearm as she leaned forward to ease the tension of her laughter. I don't remember formally asking her to dance. The band struck up 'Tennessee Waltz' and there we were, tripping among the other couples on the dance floor. Dancing had been the furthest thing from my mind, but I was desperate to maintain that tenuous physical contact and dancing was a good excuse. Amos swept by with a statuesque blonde who topped him by a good three or four inches and I noticed my partner's eyes following them. 'Here we go again', I thought, 'old Amos has made another killing.' My heart sank and I lost interest in treading meaningless measures round the floor. 'It's rather warm for dancing, don't you think? Would you like to sit this one out and have a drink?'

'Mmm,' she said. 'Good idea, I'm melting.'

We found a spot where a fan oscillated across us, made ourselves comfortable and sipped at tall, icy drinks. Amos swept by once more, his partner totally engrossed in him. My partner gazed after them then turned back to me, 'He reminds me of someone, you know, but I can't think who.'

'Humphrey Bogart,' I said glumly. She looked at me in disbelief.

'You're crazy, he doesn't resemble him in the least.'

Vaguely irritated I replied, 'Well, I've had this conversation with dozens of women and I can assure you, they all agree. You're the odd one out.'

'Does it annoy you?'

'Not in the least. He can resemble whom he will and exploit it as he can.'

'No. I mean does it annoy you to have women talk to you about him?'

'Of course not... well, yes, I suppose so in a way. He's a very good friend but I must admit if we meet two girls I usually wind up with the lumpy one.'

'Thank you. That's most chivalrous but not very accurate. My mother says I look like a clothes peg.'

She laughed at my evident puzzlement. 'He's dancing with my friend,' she explained.

I looked at her anew and found her studying me, examining me with long, shiny turquoise eyes. I felt foolish and ill at ease, realising she had detected my flash of jealousy. I was anxious to make amends. 'Would you like to meet him?'

'I expect I shall, shan't I? Eventually, if he's your friend. I'd sooner dance.'

I took her on the floor in a happy haze. With those few words she had picked up my deflated ego, dusted it off and hung it high. She danced a little closer than before and it seemed to me that she gave me her undivided attention, looking up at me with those long, lustrous eyes and accommodating my every movement with ease and grace. The more I thought about it, the more I was delighted with her perception and delicacy. She had seen right through me and had rescued me from my own boorishness with a few simple words. I danced in silent contemplation for some time, then she brought me back to earth.

'Penny for them.'

'I was thinking what a kindly soul you are.'

'Humph. Makes me sound like Margaret Rutherford.'

'You're anything but – and you know it. Look, I'm sorry I was so tart about Amos. He's one of my favourite people, but sometimes I feel like the president of his fan club. It can get a bit wearing.'

She puckered her lips in contemplation and stared after Amos and his partner. 'He is **very** attractive,' she said at last.

I pinched the gentle swell of flesh on her slim back created by her bra strap. 'Ouch,' she smiled.

The music stopped and I looked round for Amos. He was standing in the corner furthest from the band, holding two glasses in the air and waggling them at me as a signal. As we walked towards him I realised that she still had hold of my hand; I felt like a schoolboy with an unexpected half-day holiday. With his customary efficiency Amos had acquired a table near the emergency exit which was open and provided a welcome, if slight, draught. He stood up again as we arrived and looked at my partner in frank appraisal – his invariable technique on meeting a woman. 'Let me introduce you,' I began and trailed off. I turned to her, feeling slightly foolish 'I'm sorry, I don't know your name.' Before she could reply Amos interrupted, smiling his most winning, lopsided smile. 'Allow me', he said, 'I'm Amos. Blair, you've been dancing with Tottie and this is Andrea. Ladies meet Blair. You may one day be allowed to call him Bic.'

I glared at him, but he hadn't finished.

'Andrea and I swapped your biographies while you two were lasciviously entwined.'

I ached to do him a long, drawn-out and painful mischief.

The table was crowded with brimming glasses; Tottie exclaimed and asked Amos was he expecting company. 'Amos is super efficient,' I said, 'and he has decided that it's too hot to dance, that the trek to the bar is hazardous and as we have ensnared the two most attractive girls and the coolest table here, the great thing to do is to stock up and defend all these assets with our lives. Or at least, with **my** life.'

Andrea smiled up at me as we shook hands. 'You two know each other very well, don't you?'

'We should', I replied. 'I've been his keeper now for nearly five months.'

Tottie, who was sipping daintily from a frosted glass of Tom Collins, snorted and wound up with a coughing fit. After we had patted her back and dabbed her dress dry, she wiped her eyes, thanked us and asked Amos had he quite recovered? This oblique reference defeated both Andrea and Amos, so I explained that Tottie had witnessed his extraordinary performance on the subway. To my delight this revelation momentarily dispossessed the normally imperturbable Amos, but despite our appeals we never discovered the reason for his disablement. I danced once with Andrea and once more with Tottie, mostly to remind myself how she felt, then the band struck up the last waltz and we beat the crowd to the door.

The next morning I had to visit the ship's agent in The Battery. On the way there the taxi passed the Cleveland Building where Tottie worked She had tried the previous night to describe the location of her office, but not knowing our way around at all, it had not registered; so it came as a pleasant surprise to find myself so close. Having completed my business, it had been my intention to spend the rest of the day sightseeing until meeting Gus in the late afternoon, but finding myself so close to Tottie I called her on impulse and received a very friendly reception.

'Lunch? Lovely, where had you in mind?'

'I've no idea. Suggest something.'

'Why not come to our commissariat? It's pleasant, the food's good and it will save time and precious dollars.'

'About one o'clock?'

'Perfect, can't wait. Bye.'

'Bye.'

I got there about twenty minutes early and wandered up and down in front of the building, lost in thought. She told me later that she had watched me for some minutes before interrupting, but the first I knew of her presence was a cool hand slipped into mine. It instantly and completely rekindled the gentle intimacy we had established the previous night. She had on a candy-striped dress in silver and bronze colours which complemented her tan and accentuated her slim figure.

'You look like a mint humbug,' I said.

'Thank you very much.'

'I'm very fond of mint humbugs.'

'I'm afraid that doesn't help a great deal.'

'Oh Lor.' I meant, of course – cool, sweet and tasty.'

'Too late, too late! You must be punished; I shall embarrass you by paying for lunch.'

'How awful. I suppose there's nothing I can do?'

'Afraid not; we have a voucher scheme here. It simply means that I shall have to go without food for a few days, depending how hungry you are.'

'You're in luck. I shall let you off lightly, I'll just sit and feast my eyes on you.'

She gave me her megawatt grin. 'Are all sailormen so soppy?'

The commissariat in the basement of the Cleveland Building was a splendid place. After the savage August heat of the Manhattan pavements, the air-conditioned restaurant struck with the chill of the Arctic. It was decorated in pale lemon, white and ice-blue; false windows looked out onto enormous coloured photographs of magnificent lake and mountain scenery giving a convincing impression of air and space. We lined up at the self-service counter and I leaned close to whisper in her ear. She smelled of sandalwood.

'Let me get lunch.'

'No, really. It's not possible. They don't accept money here. Honestly.'

'You're a useful girl to know.'

'Don't worry, you won't get away with it for long.'

Our arrival caused a little flutter of interest among some girls at a nearby table. Tottie smiled at them, then arched her eyebrows at me and rolled her eyes heavenwards in mock despair. 'They already think I've got two heads and webbed feet because I'm English. Whiskers and a tropical suit must seem very exotic to them, most of the men here are grey flannel suits, buttoned-down collars and crew cut hair.'

I nodded at the girls and smiled exotically. Tottie turned back to me. 'You meant Dirk Bogarde,' she said.

That threw me. 'Where does Dirk Bogarde come in?'

'Last night. You **said** 'Humphrey Bogart', you **meant** Dirk Bogarde.'

'Ah! Amos! Yes, you're right. He does a very good impression of Bogart and I always get them confused.'

'Andrea was full of him. She's quite smitten, I think. They're going out tonight.'

'Does that mean you'll be alone?'

'I hope not. I've got two tickets for Columbia University – 'Music Under The Stars'. Andrea's not coming now, and I was wondering how to get in touch with you when you called this morning.'

'Did you get those with vouchers too?'

She gave a little explosive laugh. 'No. You can pay for them if it will make you feel any better.'

I studied her across the table. She was like no girl I had ever met before – perceptive, direct, amusing and buoyant. She was very feminine and attractive yet thought like a man. A staggering combination. I wanted to know more. 'Why do they call you 'Tottie'?'

''Cos it's my name.'

'Really? I've never heard it before.'

'Well, it's my childhood attempt at 'Titania', actually.'

'What a gorgeous name. There must be a more apt short form.'

'Go ahead and try.' She gave me an enigmatic look. 'It'll have to be polite, mind – Daddy was a chaplain – and I don't like 'Tania'.'

We made plans for the evening and fired the first shots in the campaign of establishing a relationship – the gentle probing that slowly uncovers the true self, peeling off the onion skins of social veneer that mask the real person beneath. The gentle mechanics of enmeshing our personalities disguised the passage of time. It was not until a kitchen helper, anxious to clear our table, said pointedly, 'It's twenty before three', that the time registered with us at all.

'Good Lord', Tottie said, 'I'll get shot.' She leaped to her feet. 'I finish at four thirty, see you outside?'

I watched her walk to the lobby, her movement crisp and confident. She did not look back and I felt curiously deflated.

CHAPTER EIGHT

'Look, Amos, you ask him. He thinks I'm a thug and will say no on principle.'

'Well, he thinks I'm a poof.'

Gus looked up, interested, 'Why?'

'I dunno,' said Amos. ''Cos I've got clean fingernails I suppose.'

Gus spread his thick brown fingers like a fan, palm down. 'So've I.'

Amos grinned like a dog at him. 'Mmm yeth', he simpered, 'I'd notithed.' Gus scowled ferociously at him and returned to his book.

'If Father thinks you're a poof', I suggested, 'it might do you some good to ask him. Andrea is such a fine example of female fleshly virtues and seeing that you can't keep your hands off her the old man couldn't possibly question your hormonal balance. He'd have to change his mind about you.'

Amos looked at me thoughtfully. 'There may be something in that... all right, but what do I ask him?'

'Can they come on board for drinks tomorrow about eleven o'clock? We'll get the girls to bring a picnic, have a few snorts here, show 'em the ship, then off for a sail round the bay. I've booked the dinghy.'

'Righto', said Amos and disappeared. He was back within a few minutes, shaking his head and muttering to himself. My heart sank. 'No go Amos?'

'Au contraire, my Old, he's all for it. Enthusiastic even. 'About time you young buggers behaved as if you were in a civilised ship and not a bloody landing craft', he said.'

'Was he sober?'

'Yup... well, reasonably.'

Gus snorted, 'I bet the old sod changes his mind.'

'Shut up, Gus,' I said and raced to the phone to call Tottie.

Sunday dawned hot and humid. The skyscrapers in Manhattan propped grey, lumpy clouds, and thunder growled incessantly. The air was scarcely breathable. Their taxi arrived just before eleven; Amos and I strolled along the littered wharf to greet them. Tottie turned from paying off the taxi and stopped dead, staring at me. Amos and I exchanged glances. 'Anything wrong?' I asked.

'It hadn't occurred to me that you would wear uniform. You look very pretty.'

Amos snorted. 'You look pretty too,' Andrea said sweetly.

'The Yanks think we're a bunch of perverts,' he said. 'They're not used to seeing men in shorts.'

It was to be a day of surprises. As we turned to retrace our steps to the gangway we were astonished to see a line of heads hanging over the wall. It seemed that every man on board had gathered to witness the unnatural phenomenon of two ladies being escorted aboard *Bellatrix* as guests. When we reached the main deck an even more astonishing sight met our eyes. The old man was dressed in full Number 10's,[8] complete with scrambled egg cap. We had never seen him in a uniform cap before. The only hats he ever wore were an enormous Filipino straw sombrero in hot weather and a Red Army tank-crew fur hat which he had acquired as a survivor of a Russian convoy casualty. This made its appearance in high latitudes in winter. None of us even knew he had a uniform cap. Teeth clenched, jaw jutting to iron out the chins, he was striding nonchalantly up and down the wing of the bridge from where he had watched us come aboard. It was a little pathetic.

Amos looked at me quizzically, whistled silently and gestured with his chin towards the old man. 'Hang on a tick,'

---

[8] The formal, long-trousered, mandarin-collared white tropical uniform worn by officers of the Royal and Merchant Navies.

I said and leaped up the ladder to the wing of the bridge. 'Morning Sir,' I said brightly, 'would you care to have a drink with us?'

'Where? In the smoke room?' We had actually intended to start off in my cabin which was large and relatively airy on the after end of the boat deck, but I didn't say so. 'Yes, Sir.'

'Right. I'll be down in a minute. Thank you, Mister.'

I returned to the others and explained the development. Amos made a puzzled grimace and led the way to the smoke room. The sight that met our eyes staggered us and I wondered fleetingly if we had boarded the wrong ship. *Bellatrix* was quite well kept internally considering her age. She had been built in 1913 in excellent materials which, apart from a few blemishes from her hard life, had matured into a comfortable shabbiness but now the smoke room had been transformed. Every piece of visible wood gleamed as if wet. The bright work sparkled and the panelling glowed with a soft patina. New buff-coloured settee and chair covers, straight from the stores, disguised the rather worn furniture and the whole atmosphere was redolent of an English country house. Glasses and an assortment of bottles glinted on the sideboard and the piano, usually disfigured by sticky, ash-shrouded glass marks and overflowing ashtrays, beamed glossily at us. Little dishes of 'machan ketchile' – cocktail delicacies – were distributed about the room. As we entered, Piedad Fernandes, the butler, stood up. Instead of baggy khaki shorts and a shapeless T-shirt, he wore blue trousers and a crisp white jacket with brass buttons. Amos recovered first. 'Morning, Fernandes,' he said then turned to our guests. 'We have most things that live in bottles – see if you can catch us out.'

Amos and I had a quick conference. We were stunned by the implications and agreed that we should play our part. I sent a steward post haste to find Gus. When he arrived his huge black beard was split from ear to ear by an enormous grin. 'Bloody marvelous, isn't it? The old man said it would be done properly or it wouldn't be done again,' he whispered to me. We despatched him with invitations and soon the smoke room was full and we couldn't get near our guests for the press of bodies each trying to impress.

When father appeared our astonishment was complete. We hadn't really known him. The persona we had seen varied between that of an unreasonable martinet and a pathetic, shaking, semi-alcoholic wreck who had literally soiled himself when the engine failed in a tide rip while we were transitting the Bali Strait. Perhaps, this day, we saw the shades of the man he had been. He was courteous, impressive and utterly charming; his manner fitted exactly to the occasion. He was the ultimate host, and the girls were honoured guests in his home. It saddened me rather and I wondered what had happened to submerge this undoubted charmer beneath the personality I had come to know and discount for the past few months.

He stayed just long enough to be polite and before he left he spoke to Amos. Were we going ashore later? Fine. When we went to change he would be pleased if the ladies would take tea with him in his quarters. We were to join them at 1700. Would that be convenient? Splendid. Were we going to show our guests round the ship? Excellent. Not wise to leave it too long though as the threatening storm looked likely to break soon. Then he left leaving Amos and me to sit for a moment staring at each other in consternation.

After a while we left the party and toured *Bellatrix* with our guests, visiting Lorrie in her cage en route. She was sulky. She ignored us, sitting hunched in the far corner of the cage with her back to us. It seemed incredibly insulting and quite hurt my feelings. Whether she was jealous of Tottie and Andrea or was out of sorts in the horrendously tense atmosphere of the gathering storm, I don't know but I had wanted her to live up to the occasion and I felt curiously let down. 'Perhaps you should have sent her an invitation,' Amos said, which didn't help much.

As we entered the wheelhouse the first huge, splashy drops fell, thunder opened up a ferocious barrage and flash after flash of lightning sawed through the lowering sky. It was very dramatic. With glass all around us and a splendid view of the docks and oily expanse of water, we waited out the downpour and watched squall after squall churn across the harbour, reducing visibility to only a few yards. It was extraordinarily violent and seemed never-ending. 'This will put paid to the sailing.' I said. 'Let's have our picnic up here.' The girls exchanged startled glances and Andrea giggled nervously.

'We left it in the cab; I thought Tottie was looking after it.'

'And I thought Andrea had it,' said Tottie.

Amos grimaced. 'Crikey! You've done it now. We'll have to eat on board – and serves you right.'

But the surprises were not yet over. Luckily we hadn't told father that we had intended to picnic and he had assumed our guests would be dining on board. We were summoned to lunch by the xylophone and the old man's strictures were more evident than ever. Whilst it wasn't five star it was clean and adequate and surprised the girls. They tucked into an astonishingly varied salad with boiled sweet potato, fried egg-plant, hot rolls and a seemingly endless variety of tinned fish, meats and cheeses, followed by jam sponge with ice cream. It must have broken the chief steward's heart.

After lunch we sat a long time over coffee and brandy and chatted. Gus broke everyone's heart with his tale of Lorrie's sorry condition when she had entered our lives. She was generally regarded as my property because my cigarettes had purchased her freedom. This consideration must have influenced Gus, because as he described how we had rehabilitated her pathetic, maggot-riddled little carcass, he inadvertently ascribed to me the major credit for her resurrection. I was not at all unhappy to accept the totally undeserved accolade in that assembly. It gave me an opportunity to shyly, but manfully, decry my contribution (thereby extolling it) and gain extra kudos by generously doling out credit all round. I could have hugged him. I was hugely rewarded by the soppy expression on Tottie's face as she leaned her chin in her hands, elbows among the litter of ashtrays and coffee cups, listening intently to the cross talk and gazing mistily across the table at the hero of the moment. Although, on reflection, that may have been partly due to the pre-lunch pink gins. Amos asked me tartly afterwards 'How long have you been writing Gus's bloody scripts?'

The storm had given way to a dispiriting overall grayness, gloom and penetrating drizzle, so outside pursuits were not attractive. We returned to the smoke room and for the next few hours played an hilarious and unprincipled game of Monopoly. In *Bellatrix* formalised cheating was de rigueur and complicated the game enormously. The third engineer, whose father was a parson, extemporised on the piano jazzed up versions of all the old hymn tunes we could remember. Gus brought in Lorrie. She was in a much improved frame of mind now the storm had broken and she looked enchanting. Her fur – thick and glossy – gleamed like well-polished, ancient pewter and her huge, bright eyes shone like lanterns in the tiny matt-black face. She adored Gus and when he fell asleep later, sprawled on a settee, she delighted the girls by sitting on his massive chest, peering theatrically into his cavernous mouth when he snored and carefully grooming the enormous, spiky beard. It seemed a wholly appropriate way to spend a wet Sunday afternoon in New York.

CHAPTER NINE

Bellatrix was working the Far East/USA run with a colleague ship, the *Betelgeuse*, working reciprocally. When the schedules were established we would normally expect to arrive New York outbound as *Betelgeuse* was homeward, departing 'Frisco for the Far East. In New York on this voyage, *Betelgeuse* had loaded the body of a murdered Filipino nurse which was being sent home for burial. The second mate, a Shetlander, had been horrified at the prospect of carrying the corpse and prognosticated dire happenings. He was nervous throughout the subsequent voyage.

When we arrived in New York we learned that his foreboding had had some substance. *Betelgeuse* caught fire off the Mexican coast on the north-bound leg from Balboa to Long Beach and was a total loss. Fortunately, although the crew had abandoned ship at night and in marginal weather, nobody was lost and there were only a few minor injuries. The wreck was towed to San Pedro and the crew repatriated. When we arrived in Long Beach homeward bound some six weeks later, she was still at anchor and was a horrifying sight. The crated coffin of the murdered girl had been retrieved from the hold where it had been badly charred and covered in condensed milk from a consignment that had exploded in the intense heat. The coffin had been re-crated and we took it aboard for onward shipment to Manila where we were proceeding after loading in 'Frisco. We weren't very happy about it.

The voyage across the Pacific was extremely rough but otherwise uneventful until a few days from Manila, when we inexplicably caught fire. We fought the blaze for three days and nights with great difficulty. We couldn't open up the hatch freely to strip out and jettison burning material and get to grips with the seat of the fire because of the dreadful weather. It was touch and go at times but we managed to contain it, though it smoldered sullenly, breaking out again if we relaxed for a second. We would have been in a sorry state had we not succeeded as the weather was ferocious. Had it been necessary to abandon ship I doubt that it would have been possible to get the boats away, and had we succeeded in launching and manning them they couldn't have lived long in those seas.

The old man said he'd seen nothing like it in over fifty years at sea. The notional 'one-hundred-year storm' had arrived in earnest; the racket was mind-numbing.

The Pacific is a lonely place. Away from the coast one rarely sees another ship in the vast ocean tracts. Yet now the ether was full of traffic. Ships were in trouble all around us, pumping out distress and emergency calls and securité messages.

Away to the north-east some five hundred miles distant an ore carrier, whose name I forget, sprang a welded seam. Within minutes she was overwhelmed, broke up and sank with the loss of all hands. North of us, off our starboard bow, *Memphis Flyer* whose lights we occasionally glimpsed through the flying spray and spume and the frequent violent rain squalls that hissed over us, reported two hands swept overboard by a sea surge as they struggled to secure deck cargo that had broken adrift. One was tossed back on board by a following wave but was carried away again before he could be rescued.

Half a day behind us the *Craiglas* – a tramp out of Cardiff – was calling for medical assistance for men who had been trapped and crushed in a cargo space by shifting cargo they had been trying to secure. And somewhere close by, *Santander Bay*, listing heavily, was making water in her engine room and asking for standby assistance in case she should lose power. Broaching to in those conditions would almost certainly have proved fatal. *Santander Bay* would have been in serious trouble had her engine failed. Without power she would rapidly have fallen off; listing heavily, lying broadside on to the wind and waves and no longer able to present her head to the mountainous seas, she would easily have been rolled over.

It was profoundly distressing; men in fear of their lives were calling for assistance but no one could help them. It was a battlefield, every man for himself. No master with even a single functioning brain cell would dare attempt a turn. Sinbad – our skipper – had decided to heave to and ride out the storm, turning off track to meet head on the huge seas which had been climbing all over us, denying us access to the seat of the fire. Glass in some of the portholes on the weather side had been smashed and our starboard lifeboats had been pounded into splinters hanging in the davits.

The sea had broken into the galley and extinguished the fires. The cook and his gang performed heroically, skidding about in an ankle-deep slurry of broken crockery and shattered bottles, sea water, flour, tapioca, rice and varied ingredients which had burst out of the storage lockers. Yet throughout the emergency they managed to produce an endless supply of piping hot soup, thick sweet cocoa and mountains of corned beef and cheese sandwiches enlivened with curry sauce and mustard. Their dedication and professional pride was not without a price; several galley hands were scalded – one very badly.

In Manila the local fire brigade, being able to open up the hatch in safety with no threat of being swamped by mountainous seas, quickly extinguished the blaze. While the event was obviously a coincidence it spooked one or two people – including me.

Some months later I sailed with someone who had been in *Betelgeuse* at the time. He told me that he had abandoned ship by jumping into the rope falls of the motor gig which had already been launched, intending to shinny down the ropes into the boat. The scene was nightmarish and had burned

106

itself into his memory. The sea, black and heaving, was balefully illuminated by the flames that were consuming the ship. He jumped into the falls with the boat only a few feet below him then found it had moved away into the darkness on the swell. The ropes, though twisted, were running slowly through the blocks because of his deadweight and he found to his horror that he was being lowered slowly and inexorably onto the back of a large shark that was cruising between the boat and the ship.

He wasn't thinking too clearly and as the boat, alerted to his predicament, tried desperately to manoeuvre under him, he slid slowly towards what he thought would be a miserable end. It wasn't until he was inches from entering the water that he thought of grabbing the returning rope run on the other side of the davit block and thus arrested his descent. He hung there for several minutes half-cooked by the heat from the plates, his knees and arms bent to keep his legs out of the water, praying that the shark wouldn't look up. It didn't and a few minutes later the boat was directly under him and he stepped aboard without even getting his feet wet.

The saddest thing about the event, so far as we were concerned, was that we lost our most recent skipper – 'Sinbad' – our fourth and most favourite in seventeen months. He was a marvelous old man in both senses of the term. Throughout the emergency he had led from the front and for some seventy two hours had not laid his head on a pillow. He had been right in the thick of it. Smoke inhalation, a touch of hypothermia and exhaustion had brought on a disastrous asthma attack and probably ended his days at sea. He was a pitiful thing when they took him ashore. We were all cockeyed with fatigue and hunger, normal ship's routine had to be maintained of course and hot food in those conditions was just a dream – and we were on average about a third his age.

Of all the skippers I sailed with I remember 'Sinbad' almost with affection, and it was a pretty general feeling. He had that rare quality – natural authority – and was able to treat his lowliest subordinate as a human being without losing respect or his aura of command. Mealtimes were a delight. He was an East Anglian and had a dry, whimsical manner that invested even the most mundane pronouncements with humorous undertones. Only watch keepers left the table before him, reluctantly and not only out of deference. He was a natural storyteller and a piece of living history; his reminiscences were electric and humorous and not to be missed. We were like children at the feet of Hans Christian Anderson.

He had served his time and gained his mate's ticket in sail and as a boy had rounded the Horn in pre-Panama Canal days. There was an enormous swell, he told us, but the sea was calm and the weather was kind – the complete opposite of the Cape's frightening reputation for savage weather. (The last square rigger in the British M.N. – the *Gaunt* – was wrecked in 1925). The whole of his First World War service had been under sail.

His father had been a master maltster in one of the enormous malting enterprises that existed in East Anglia at the turn of the century. Sailing barges used to ply up and down the east coast carrying grain and one of his duties was to board them to check for contamination before the grain was accepted for processing. He came to know the skippers very well and one of them took on the twelve-year-old 'Sinbad' as a trainee and launched a career that must have seen close on sixty years at sea. He claimed to be sixty-four, but by computing his age from an accumulation of endless stories, we reckoned he was closer to seventy than sixty, yet he had led his crew in the fire fight in atrocious conditions for three long, weary days.

A wizard with his hands, he spent hours at marquetry and made some splendid boxes, chessboards and pictures. He gave me an exotic trick box that had no purpose other than to defeat the efforts of anyone trying to open it. Its six planes were decorated with a random and extremely complicated pokerwork pattern which camouflaged the joints and it required fifteen separate, strictly sequential movements before the lid would slide back. It was about the size of a brick and must have taken him days of work to complete. He was a sad loss.

CHAPTER TEN

We quickly christened Sinbad's replacement 'Stupor Mundi' under the illusion that 'Stupor' signified a dazed state or semi-coma, which it does in English of course. 'Stupor Mundi' seemed to be permanently drunk and on looking back now, I realise that he must have been very ill. He left us eventually with a drink-related medical problem which turned part of his digestive system to stone. I doubt that he survived it for long. An erudite passenger joined us on a short hop and after enquiring how father had acquired such an odd nickname, kindly pointed out that 'Stupor Mundi' translated as 'Wonder of the World'. Considering SM's alcoholic intake we thought the name was even more apt and it stuck.

Amos despised him, which I thought was a bit harsh. He was scathing about the old man's 'swinish' behaviour. 'How can a man who behaves like a pig be responsible for eighty-nine souls?' he once asked me. SM had appeared on the bridge at three o'clock that afternoon, clad in only a pair of filthy Y-fronts and engaged Amos in an aimless and inconclusive conversation about Cossacks. I had no answer but I felt sorry for him. Something had clearly gone wonky in his life; he was withdrawn and ill at ease with everyone. I thought it sad that a man intelligent and personable enough to qualify as a shipmaster should allow himself to sink to such a level.

The first port of call after SM took command in Manila was Mambagid, a primitive port in the Philippines where we loaded raw sugar destined for the refinery in Yonkers, upriver from New York. The port consisted of a sugar mill, very basic dockworks, a couple of rudimentary bars and a scatter of ramshackle huts where the workers lived. Peewee hadn't been to the Philippines before and plagued us to go ashore with him and ultimately wore us down. We knew Mambagid had nothing much to offer us but it was his first stopover and he was anxious to see what it was like.

The rate of exchange was crippling and made the dollar-based peso very expensive; arriving in the islands straight from the Yankee coast with only the Pacific crossing behind us to build up money in our accounts, we were always tight for money. In consequence we would augment our disposable cash by barter. Cigarettes were an obvious medium of exchange, and even more lucrative at the time were cosmetics. In the States lipstick and perfumed soaps were cheap and plentiful. A few dollars spent in one of the major chain stores would provide sufficient capital to see us all round the islands and back again.

There are tricks to every trade and the Filipino purchasers were very slippery customers, while initially we were straight and innocent. Caveat emptor certainly did not apply in our dealings. We were robbed blind when we first started trading. It took a long time for the Filipino economy to get back on its feet after the war and even longer for new currency to be issued. For some time bank notes issued during the Japanese occupation, overprinted with the word 'VICTORY' in black, were legal tender. We had accepted these in payment, went ashore for the evening and tried to spend them. The barman gave us a shrewd look, wet his finger and rubbed it over the black lettering. It smudged! We had learned a painful lesson. Whoever had doctored the notes had been an incomparable typographic artist. His lettering was indistinguishable from the official printing. The only way to tell the bona fide from the fraudulent was to rub the letters with a wet finger. The ink of the counterfeit was very unstable.

On arrival in Mambagid we were faced with a considerable wait before they could work us. It was a very small port with limited facilities. Berthing was on an enormously long jetty ending in a 'T' alongside the crossbar of which only one ship at a time could lay. The bagged sugar was brought from the mill to the ship by a tiny 'sugar-cane-trash' fired locomotive which seemed straight out of a Wild West film. It lacked only a cow-catcher on the front.

The wait wasn't onerous. We were contented enough; we fished and swam and sailed while the old man continued to destroy himself. When he wasn't sleeping he was drinking and became an absolute misery. He was normally a reasonable man but his benders changed his personality and while they lasted life on board was purgatory. He found fault with everyone and objected to everything we did, personally and professionally. Even 'Amos the Impeccable' came in for criticism of his paperwork, which was a bit like accusing the Pope of cheating at strip poker and Amos resented it bitterly.

'Especially,' he said, 'when the night order book[9] looks as if someone had tipped a bottle of ink over it and tried to mop it up with wire wool.'

The old man's 'swinish phase,' as Amos termed it, had gone on for so long and produced such violent discord that we were all jumpy and depressed, checking and double-checking everything and even then not really confident that it wouldn't be bitterly criticised. At that time father was detested; it was a very unhappy time. Shortly after we arrived in Mambagid he was very evidently deeply depressed and took to his bed. 'A bout of malaria,' he said. But we diagnosed it as a bout lost to the bottle. With the old man immobile, possibly for days if recent history were to be repeated, some of the tension that had built up was released. The mate, whose philosophy was 'anything for an easy life', was happy to have got rid of the monkey on his back and was very amiable.

---

[9] The 'Night Order Book' is a captain's means of passing on his orders while he is asleep. Most masters made a fetish of it as it had been known for the book to form the basis of a court action in a contentious issue regarding culpability for some ship-born disaster.

Masinloc P.I. Locals had assured us that swimming was safe, but when the agent saw this photo, he told me there were crocodiles in the river.

Scavenging dunnage (scrap timber used to pack out and stabilise awkward cargo during stowage) in Isabella P.I. Children as young as five or six could be seen handling outrigger canoes with consummate skill. In the water even younger tots were as confident and competent as otters; they were a joy to watch.

He was an elderly man for a mate and we supposed that somewhere in his past he had committed a heinous professional blunder that had robbed him of command in due season. Elderly mates hardly ever get promoted; the stigma of past misdemeanor – real or imagined – stays with them for life.

Against our better judgement we took Peewee ashore. One evening we put the motor gig in the water, loaded it up and set out for the village which sprawled down to the high tide line. We stepped from the boat practically straight into the door of the first bar and decided to stay there on the grounds that it was indistinguishable from the others. Above the door an over-painted Coca Cola sign proclaimed grandly in hand-painted, slightly wobbly lettering 'Reignbowe Bar' (sic). Imperfectly schooled in the lore of exchange and barter we made a strategic error and displayed on a table all the goods we had for trade. The mama-san's eyes lit up. Two other bars closed and the girls and guitarists transferred to our venue so as to complement the numbers and provide equity as between staff and customers.

It was a cheerful evening to begin with. They were pleased to have our custom and we were pleased to give it. The guitarists played complex Spanish-American music modified by Filipino idiom and every now and then were spelled by a wind-up gramophone which cut swarf from ancient records of Deanna Durbin and the Andrews Sisters. It didn't seem to matter that Miss Durbin's soaring and piercingly-sweet voice suited songs that didn't suit our fumble-footed attempts to match her rhythms with our rudimentary knowledge of the three basic dance steps. But we managed. Peewee rapidly became glass-eyed. He had foolishly become hooked on the local aniseed drink which tastes innocuous enough but has a spiteful streak, and he was soon in a state of suspended animation, staring sombrely into the middle distance, oblivious to all external stimuli.

Our enthusiasm for the dance gradually died. The records became repetitive and boring, and the guitarists, though highly skilled, had nothing in their repertoire except energetic, esoteric numbers that defeated our clumsy foxtrot footwork. One by one we faltered and eventually sat glumly beside the disconnected Peewee, wondering what to do next. We had been right to have avoided coming ashore in Mambagid in the past.

There was still a considerable credit balance left on the table in the form of barter goods when Gus stood up and stretched. 'I've had it,' he said. 'Let's go back.'

Amos was busy instructing the musicians – with only marginal success – in a series of basic tunes suitable for the Palais Glide and the Hokey-Cokey. They had matched us drink for drink and could now function only in automatic mode. This was adequate for their programmed repertoire but rendered them incapable of sequential thought and therefore totally immune to musical instruction in a foreign language. The mama-san realised that her guests were on the point of departure and that she had nothing left with which to tempt them. She began to gather up all the goods we had brought. Gus leaned over and placed his huge hands over hers.

'Hold hard,' he said and turned to me. 'Surely she doesn't expect to collar all this for what we've had?'

I agreed. 'Hey, Mama-san. This too much. Pricey pricey!'

She shook her head. 'Dis t'ing alllasame belong me now Joe. You have happy time, now you pay.'

Amos's little band struck up a caricature of an English dance tune and he seized a plump, dusky girl in a highly coloured print dress and waltzed her round the floor with exaggerated courtliness. Mama-san's face had become set and her eyes were like bullets. She beckoned to one of the girls and whispered to her. The girl left. Gus and I were trying to talk sensibly to mama-san and strike a reasonable deal with the barter goods, but she arrogantly slapped our hands away and snarled.

'You makee turruble then pulenty turruble for you bime-by.'

She wouldn't listen to reason and tempers were beginning to flare when Amos, who was dancing on the spot without music cheek-to-cheek with his dusky siren, gave an exaggerated cough.

'We have company, gentlemen.'

So we had. Two muscular cane cutters, barefoot and wearing tattered singlets and shorts, stood uncertainly inside the door. The muscles of their shoulders and forearms were corded and separated like those of an anatomy model. They stared at us with blank, handsome faces, their enormous cane knives dangling from sinewy hands.

'My number one, my number two son,' mama-san announced. She beamed at us and once again began to gather the goods together. The cane cutters placed their knives ostentatiously on one of the tables. Their first mistake. Gus didn't care much to be bullied, it made him irritable. With no warning he suddenly crossed the tiny bar in a couple of enormous strides. So unexpected was his action and so forceful his apparent aggression, that the two cane cutters shrank from his approach and actually backed away from their weapons.

Aggression is not simply a question of well-developed muscles and sharp knives; it lies much deeper than that. It is a function of confidence and a deep-seated, tappable reservoir of irritability. I realised later that mama-san's sons were little more than boys and the whole situation was beyond them – they wouldn't have lasted five minutes in the 'Bridge House' in Canning Town. They were simply gentle, bovine creatures who were magnificently developed physically. Gus picked up the knives and swung them experimentally; the locals all huddled against the wall and there was a spatter of apprehensive conversation between them as they wondered what would happen next.

I was delighted to see that mama-san was tense and very anxious; she had precipitated the crisis with her unreasoning greed and had then threatened us. She wasn't to know if she had read us correctly. We might have been gibbering lunatics under our apparently civilised exteriors and all their lives might have been at risk. Our boat was only a few feet from the door, and there would have been no time to call for help. It was late and most of the villagers were asleep; she was right to be anxious. She steeled herself, 'OK Joe, we talk now.' Gus shook his bull-like head, hefted the knives and swung them experimentally again.

'No need Mama-san, this number one knives.' He indicated the goods on the table. 'You take, belong you now. This knives belong us.'

The two boys understood instantly what he was proposing and there was an anguished outcry in which all the locals joined. I suppose the knives must have been worth several day's pay for them and they couldn't work without them. Amos ambled over, his arm still round his girl. He grinned appreciatively at Gus.

'You crafty old sod' he said, then turned to Mama-san and smiled his most winning smile at her. 'Look here, you old bat, we don't want your knives...' He pointed at the goods, '...this too much for beer...' then he held up a bar of soap, '...belong Manila one piecee buy maybe two beer. How much beer you speak for one piecee?'

She relaxed visibly and grinned her surrender at him; there was no harm in trying, she seemed to be saying. We all relaxed and Gus returned the knives to the boys. Mama-san signalled the band to strike up, the girls brought out more San Miguel and the earlier goodwill lurched into motion again. She was still reluctant to let the goods pass beyond her considerable grasp, but she had a tough adversary in Amos. All smiles, he sat opposite her and argued her to a standstill until he got his way. She shrugged. 'OK, I give you rum, some fruit, some fish.' She was completely unrealistic.

Gus grimaced, 'I couldn't stomach another drop of this rotgut', he said.

Amos shook his head. 'No deal, me beauty. What else you got?'

She shook her head pathetically and shrugged. 'Thas all Joe. I don't got not'ing. You want, you speak what t'ing you want.'

Peewee had been sitting slumped over a table, staring uncomprehendingly from a range of about three inches at the litter of glasses and bottles covering it. He suddenly raised his head and waggled it unsteadily round at the assembly, trying hard to focus.

'You can tell a man who boozes by the company he chooses, and the pig...' he mumbled, then lurched abruptly to his feet, stumbled to the door, and was violently and noisily sick outside. The deadly aniseed had struck again. All the girls trailed after him to help and we could hear them clucking sympathetically.

Peewee's truncated quotation had sparked a mad train of powder in Amos's disordered brain which could have blown us all sky-high, but it seemed a good idea at the time.

'Peewee's hit on it,' he said suddenly after examining the underside of the hut's roof for some time. Gus and I stared at him, trying and failing to extract some meaning from his pronouncement.

'Hit on what?' we said almost together.

'We'll have a pig.'

Gus and I exchanged glances then stared at Amos again, this time in blank admiration. He had solved the problem of the credit balance in one stupendous leap of the intellect, one imaginative stroke. Of course, a pig! What else? The very item we lacked. Amos turned back to Mama-san just as Peewee reappeared in the doorway.

'We'll have a pig, Mama-san. OK? Can do?'

She puckered her brow. 'A pick? What t'ing?'

'No, a pig. P. I. bloody G. Pig.'

Peewee returned and sat down weakly at the table, perspiring freely. His eyes were sunken in his grayish-green face. He looked terrible. 'When are we going back?' he asked plaintively.

'As soon as we've got our pig.'

He nodded absently then did a double take, staring boozily at Amos. 'Did you say pig?'

Amos nodded brightly. 'Yup'.

'What for?'

'That doesn't make sense. You can't ask what for. A pig isn't **for** anything.'

Peewee shook his head as if to clear it. 'I mean where're you getting a pig and why?'

'Here and because we haven't got one.'

Having ejected the contents of his stomach, Peewee by now was undoubtedly the most sober person present. He stared around at us, gathering his scattered wits, then turned back to Amos.

'Man, you're drunk...'

Amos laughed sarcastically... 'By God, a virtuous whore!'

Peewee was embarrassed and mumbled... 'Well, I mean it's crazy. Nobody keeps a pig...'

'There was a music hall turn once where this chap had a sow that could count...' Gus interjected helpfully.

Peewee turned on him. 'Shut up.'

Gus was considerably taken aback and offended by this most un-Peeweelike utterance. He glared at him for a chillingly long time then continued, speaking loudly and with great deliberation.

'He used to ask it questions and it would tap out the answers...'

'SHUT UP!' Peewee almost screamed.

'WITH ITS FOOT,' Gus bellowed back.

The Filipinos had been watching this byplay with amazement and total incomprehension, and were obviously enthralled in the contemplation of it. When Amos spoke to the mama-san she jumped visibly.

'Well, old thing. What d'you say?'

'Pick? Pick? No savvy.'

It took an elaborate pantomime with all of us, except Pewee, participating before they understood what we were proposing. They stared at us in disbelief then discussed it among themselves with much giggling, then stared at us again, seeking confirmation.

Mama-san turned to us. 'OK. Pick... you want, can do.'

She gave instructions to her sons, then piled all the goods on the table into a sarong and took them away before we could change our minds.

Pigs roam freely round Filipino villages. There is no shortage of them and they don't seem to belong to anyone in particular. We probably paid an exorbitant price by local standards. The two boys were soon back, covered in mire, laughing and joking together. They carried a skinny, strident piglet between them, one holding the forelegs and the other the hindlegs. When they put it down it bolted behind the bar, scattering the girls who fled with shrill cries. The boys' jocularity spread to everyone and they all talked at once, giggling together. Every bit of the mama-san's spare flesh was jiggling with jollity and her eyes were squeezed tightly shut. She rolled back and forth in her chair wheezing with laughter and flapping her handkerchief in her face. She turned to us in disbelief.

'This is pick? You want? For sure?'

She settled back in her seat still quivering comprehensively, as if a small motor were running deep within her bulk, and watched us as we inspected our acquisition. Amos was a little disappointed. 'It's not quite what I had in mind. I'd rather wanted a plump and pinkish sort of pig. This'uns skinny and black and it stinks.'

I thought he was being excessively finicky; all Filipino pigs are black. 'A pig's a pig,' I said, 'and there's nothing wrong with a pig smelling like a pig.'

'But it's filthy,' Amos protested.

'No problem,' Gus said. He seized a water jug and dashed the contents over the little beast. Alarmed by the sudden cold douche, it hurtled from its haven behind the bar and knocked over a table full of bottles and glasses, sending it crashing to the floor.

Amos was being untypically defeatist and I wondered if he was losing enthusiasm for the project. 'How will we get it back?' he asked. 'It seems exceptionally energetic.'

Peewee had decided to become associated with the project. 'Why don't we give it a noggin?' he suggested. 'That'll quieten it; it's what they do with babies.'

Amos remained unconvinced. 'That won't stop it leaking all over the place. Look what it's done to the floor.' We sat and pondered this for a while, then Amos himself came up with the answer. 'Peewee's right. We'll treat it like a baby and stick a nappy on it.'

And that is how we resolved the problem. The piglet seemed to enjoy the Canay rum that Amos and Gus administered, then we wrapped it in the hessian sandbag in which we had brought our barter goods. We returned to the boat, leaving the bar staff gazing after us in evident relief that we were going.

The pig being Amos's brainchild, we voted that he should carry it. With the little creature nestling like a baby in his arms we stumbled down the beach, embarked in the boat and pushed off. At first all went well. Whiffling its nose the pig lay completely still making little muffled grunts, staring up at Amos. Then we discovered that hessian sacking makes a poor nappy – it has no absorbent capacity at all. The beast, grunting with relief, suddenly drenched Amos's immaculate shirt front. Discomfited by the sudden enveloping warmth and unnerved by the pig's unwinking gaze, he gave vent to a strangled curse and holding the animal at arm's length looked wildly about him. Peewee – assuming that the pig's continued existence hung in the balance – stretched over, whisked the creature away from Amos and immediately regretted his action. He discovered simultaneously that the transfer from Amos to himself had disarranged the nappy and further, that the passing of water was but the prelude to a more ambitious and comprehensive evacuation.

He leaped to his feet with a cry of disgust and thrust the animal on Gus who jumped up, letting go of the tiller, and causing the pig to slide down his legs into the bottom of the boat. All was chaos. The boat rocked dangerously as Peewee balanced on one leg to strip off his soiled trousers, clinging onto Amos as he did so. At full speed with no hand on the tiller the boat careered out of control and Peewee fell, dragging Amos with him and they both cannoned into Gus who was trying to collar the pig. The four of them wound up in a tangled heap. I waded through the flailing limbs on the grid and grabbed the tiller but couldn't reduce speed or put the engine in neutral as the throttle and gear lever were completely buried beneath the thrashing bodies.

There were several ships in the crowded anchorage and a rogue boat was bound to come to grief; being overset in the dead of night was an alarming thought as we had spotted the odd shark during fishing trips over the past couple of days. I put on a tight turn and leaning back held the tiller hard against my chest to maintain a close circuit. This didn't help the stability of the occupants much but was the only safe manoeuvre in the circumstances. Eventually we regained control of the boat and recaptured the pig. Having sorted ourselves out we resumed course for *Bellatrix*, Peewee sitting in a pair of rather exotic Y-fronts, having lost his trousers overboard, Amos complaining about his ruined shirt and Gus growling to himself and rubbing his bruises. He had come off worst. When the boat went out of control and he had been felled by Amos and Peewee, he had fallen heavily and banged his head on the engine casing, then had his fingers trodden on first by Peewee then me in my lunge to grab the tiller.

When we arrived on board we were presented with a problem that strangely hadn't occurred to us before. Where was our new shipmate to sleep? Wrapped in alcoholic vapours he lay in the crook of Amos's arm, snoring gently, jaws agape.

The crisis, it is said, produces the man. Once again Amos rose magnificently to the occasion. 'There's only one suitable place,' he decreed. 'He'll make good company for Father in his swinish phase.'

Once again we stared at him in wonderment, lost in admiration of a man who could solve so monumental a problem with such ease. Where else indeed, **but** in the captain's cabin, could one put a drunken pig at half past two in the morning?

Breakfast that morning was a solemn affair. Gus was still smarting from his injuries and sporting a beautiful black eye where he had clonked himself on the engine housing. He sat glowering and silent and ate his own and Peewee's bacon and eggs one-handed – the other was all bruised and bloody. Peewee, barely recovered from the poisonous aniseed, was just managing a little dry toast washed down with coffee. He was pale and fragile, wincing at the banging from the galley and averting his eyes from the sight of Gus polishing off two fried breakfasts with evident relish. I was attempting nothing more ambitious than a bowl of shredded wheat, not from deference to a hangover but from sheer anxiety.

I had been on deck early, had seen the old man's tiger removing the piglet from Father's quarters and had barely survived a rigorous cross examination from the mate who had also seen it.

'You bright young bastards have overreached yourselves this time,' he told me with grim satisfaction. 'Someone's due for the bloody high jump if not all of you.'

In the cold light of day I thought he was probably right. We had clearly overstepped the mark and disaster seemed inevitable. When I had shaken Amos awake to pass on the morning's news and the mate's comments on it, he accepted it all with complete equanimity. I envied his impermeable self-confidence. Completely unrepentant he sat up in his bunk and itemised his reaction on his fingers.

'One. I don't give a damn. I've had it with that old bastard anyway. Two. It'd be no hardship to be booted out of this hooker. I'd as soon be away from the old rust bucket as in her. Three: If we all clam up solid they can't prove a thing. No one saw us come aboard and the old sod'll know nothing about last night anyway, he's been permanently pissed since we've been here.'

That was the obvious tack to take. There was no other way. We all agreed to deny any knowledge of the event no matter what pressure was brought to bear. The mate knew it must have been us but could do nothing without proof and he wisely decided to stay his hand until he found out the old man's reaction – anything for an easy life.

Amos sat drinking cup after cup of black coffee – the only sign that he had punished his system the previous night. Otherwise he was completely at ease, eyes clear and untroubled, his lean brown face showing no signs of the night's debauch. Stupor Mundi rolled into the saloon, his unshaven jowls wobbling, hair on end and his clothing in disarray. He fixed his watery, whisky-red eye on the mate. 'Who was duty officer last night?'

'I was, Sir...' he paused, '...the others all went ashore.'

'Sneaky,' I thought. The additional information was unnecessary – it was obviously the first stage in getting out from under. The old man did not pick it up, he sailed on with his inquisition.

'Did you read the night order book?'

'Yes, Sir.'

'Instructions were to beef up the moorings if the wind turned to come off the beach. I see no sign that it was done.'

'But the wind was off the sea all night, Sir, till it backed a bit at first light.'

Father's face went livid and we could see him working himself up to one of his notorious whisky-fuelled rages. 'Stuff and nonsense man. There was a disgusting smell in my room this morning. That stink came off the beach and it could only come off the beach if the wind was off the beach, eh?'

The mate stood his ground. He had no choice. 'No, Sir. It's in the log. Strong sea breezes till sun up.'

Unconvinced but having to accept the incontrovertible evidence of a log entry, SM relaxed slightly, waggled his head in puzzlement and winced. Amos's eyes flashed and his face assumed an expression of blank innocence. Knowing he was in one of his kamikaze moods, I froze with horror.

'Did you have a bad night, Sir? he asked. 'I found it unbearably close.'

The old man lowered his cup and drew a deep breath as if he was about to lambaste Amos for impertinence, then realised that it was just a sociable question. But he wasn't sure. He relaxed and studied Amos for a long moment before replying, 'I had a bloody awful night, Mister. I dreamed there was a pig in my room.'

CHAPTER ELEVEN

Before we left Mambagid we learned that our settled existence had come to a premature end within weeks of its beginning. The loss of *Betelgeuse* by fire off the Mexican coast had completely scrambled our projected schedule. A new colleague ship was to be chartered and we were to proceed to Europe (the raw sugar we had loaded had been reassigned to Tate & Lyle's refinery in Silvertown, London) via Suez, discharge, then dry-dock in Hamburg. After repairs we were to cross the Atlantic in ballast to New York, by which time we would be in correct alignment to conduct the Far East/USA run with our new colleague – an ex-Victory ship and at 15 knots a little faster than us.

In Singapore a welcome surprise awaited us. Sinbad joined us as passenger to the UK. Although he perked up considerably on the voyage home, he was a shadow of the man we had known. He had suddenly become old and frail.

In Ceylon (Sri Lanka) where we had a brief stop to pick up tea and desiccated coconut, I disgraced myself in a football match which the local Missions To Seamen padre had arranged. A scratch team thrown together from the ships in port played against a fairly integrated and experienced team fielded by the combined railway/dockyard. I had never played soccer before but was needed to make up the numbers. As a rugby fullback it was deemed that since I was accustomed to handling a ball I would perhaps do best in goal. It was a disaster. The trouble was, that in a dive for the ball which started in the best Frank Swift-style, instinct would take over in mid-flight and I would wind up executing a full, flying tackle on an unsuspecting winger. The resulting crunch was intensified by the unpreparedness of the eight or nine stone victim for a headlong assault from fifteen stones of flying beef. After a few such gaffes, when my penalty area was in danger of becoming impassable because of the litter of broken Tamils, I was sent off as a homicidal menace.

Some ten days later we found ourselves in Suez, swinging round the hook, awaiting our turn in the northbound canal convoy. We had no priority at all – passenger and mail ships get the top slots – and were the last ship in line. It was such a contrast to the last time I had made a Suez transit in a sleek passenger/cargo liner…

Passage through the Suez Canal always excited me. In truth there isn't much to see, except, perhaps, that a diligent Peeping Tom might be rewarded with a brief glimpse of army wives sunning themselves in their basket chairs and chaise longues on the shores of the Bitter Lakes. But there was endless fascination in gliding smoothly through the lilac and buff desert in a great ship on this ribbon of bright water under a permanent sun. Most passengers and off-duty crew felt the magic and many stayed on deck throughout the transit. Occasionally we might see a 'Glubb Pasha' camel patrol, bristling with guns, ambling along beside the canal like a vision of a bygone age. On the other side of the canal, the British army made its presence known by the frequent convoys that hurtled with whistling tyres along the road that parallels the canal's course.

On that previous canal passage homeward bound, two separate incidents brought home to me the diverse and entertaining nature of expatriate Britons. I was standing on the boat deck chatting with the nine-year-old son of a rubber planter who was returning home on leave from Malaya. We were watching the gently unfolding panorama when an army convoy, tyres singing on the tarmac, swished by.

'Hmph,' said my tiny companion disapprovingly, 'those lorries are much too close together.'

Thinking I was rather more knowledgeable in road craft than he, I disagreed. 'They're not going all that fast. I should think they could stop safely enough if they had to.'

He turned wise eyes to me in gentle reproof and explained patiently, 'A good Bren gunner could get two easily in one burst, or even three perhaps, and the rest would quickly be in a muddle.'

All this was delivered in the matter-of-fact tones in which a home-grown child would have discussed the latest Rupert Bear Annual. The implications made me look more closely at him, his twin sister and his parents, both about forty-years-old. The father was heavily scarred and partially deaf – the result of a grenade attack made on him while he was inspecting his estate. The mother, a pretty woman but desperately thin, was only now – after a six-week sea voyage in absolute safety – beginning to lose her tense, edgy expression.

I learned that their bungalow was sandbagged and concrete reinforced, that their compound was wired, mined and floodlit and that they shared their lines with a section of Gurkhas. Richard told me that he and his sister went to school in a Green Howards scout car. He told me with the absolute authority of a tried and tested expert that in the stands of rubber trees in a typical plantation, it was more effective to attack with grenades – especially at night. The technique was less likely to give away the attackers' position with muzzle flashes and there was a better chance of inflicting more damage on more people than by using guns.

This tragic child and his elfin sister had endured life under siege for three years but happily would now be released as they were going to school in England. His parents would be returning after a few months. For the rest of the voyage I couldn't look at his balding father or his thin, faded mother without a feeling akin to awe. I have met few genuine heroes or heroines in my life and if they read this they would be embarrassed, but that is how I came to regard them. Somehow, despite the appalling strain and impossible conditions, they had contrived to raise two children indistinguishable from youngsters raised in happier climes. True, they had a watchful quality and they bore a burden of knowledge and experience that should be imposed on no child, yet it seemed not to suppress their childish enthusiasms. Within days the veneer applied by the brutalities of their frontier existence had cracked and fallen off and the real child had emerged bright and cheerful, like a butterfly from its chrysalis.

My association with the Planter family touched wells of patriotism – even jingoism – in me that I never knew existed. They were Yorkshire people and as unlike the caricature of the public school empire builder as it is possible to be. Yet they displayed a doggedness, independence and gritty courage – highlighted by their simple, matter-of-fact attitude – that can only be matched by the gungho characters of Victorian 'Bulldog Breed' fiction. They were splendid people.

If the Planter family represented one side of the coin of English expatriates, we quickly had a sample of the obverse. We had, on that voyage, perhaps ten or twelve ladies between sixteen and sixty. Most of them were on the boat deck during the canal passage, leaning on the rail enjoying the passing scene. The bridge near Ismailia had been damaged by a passing ship some days earlier and a horde of Arab workmen were busy on both sides of the canal, dismantling the damaged parts and restoring the works. As we passed, a bunch of degenerates, on seeing the ladies, hoisted their filthy clouts and waved the distinguishing marks of their sex at the astonished onlookers with a great deal of catcalling and jeering. The ladies' reactions were interesting: a few embarrassed laughs, some sucking of teeth and a couple of outraged exclamations. Then in a body, chattering and giggling among themselves, they left the starboard side where they had been insulted and moved to the port side. They walked straight into a trap. There on the other side was another gang of workmen doing exactly the same thing.

It might all have ended without undue embarrassment if the mate on the bridge hadn't witnessed it all. He was a blunt and rather tactless Scot and his bellow of delight froze the ladies in their flight. What would have been endurable among themselves now had another dimension. Someone had witnessed their shaming. To most of them it didn't matter. But one illustrious, lilac-haired, gray-silk clad dowager took umbrage. Lady Uppity-Passenger was incensed as much by the mate's lack of sensitivity as by the ungentlemanly behaviour of the workmen. Ignoring the ancient, sometimes unwritten, but absolute law that passengers are allowed on the bridge only on the explicit invitation of the master, she stormed up to confront Robbie and berated him for his unseemly conduct. He tried politely to point out that passengers were not allowed on the bridge – especially during a canal transit – and asked her to leave. She was an impossible and arrogant woman and refused to leave until he had 'done something' about the conduct of the workmen, now half a mile or so astern.

'What can I do?' he asked reasonably.

But she was beyond reason. 'That is not my concern,' she replied. 'I am making an official complaint and I insist that you act on it. I refuse to accept such an insult.'

It happened that Robbie was already seriously out of favour with the lady as the result of an incident that had occurred a week or so previously during the Indian Ocean crossing. On the outward and homeward runs we had horse race nights. They were usually organised on the Indian Ocean leg as the 10-day trek between Aden and Penang outward and the reciprocal journey homeward were the only relatively uncluttered parts of the voyage, so everyone could join in the fun. It also gave us time to observe the idiosyncrasies of the passengers which assisted us in the preparation of race cards and horses. The race cards were quite elaborate and contained a little explanatory verse in addition to the name of the horse and its owner.

Thus a passenger who was enraged rather too obviously in pursuit of another would have his indiscretion publicly noted by the traditional form of naming horses – 'Clean' out of 'Spare Time' by 'Crafty Chase'. I can't find this gentleman's verse but that of his 'quarry' was – 'A delicate question dear we know,

> But in your hair you have a beau'

Sometimes the verse was quite substantial. We had a passenger from the German Embassy in Tokyo who was going home to get married. He chose to go by sea in the hope that the six-week voyage would enable him to lose weight and spruce himself up for the wedding. He was very determined and quite successful.

His horse was 'Anorexia' by 'Diet' out of 'Control'. And his verse:

> 'Our Fritz was worried about his pot
> So Fritz he wouldn't eat a lot.
> At breakfast, luncheon and at dinner
> Fritz diminished and got thinner.
> At last, one day poor Fritz – minus pot
> Was... 'Fritz, hey Fritz! Where's Fritz?'
> "Mein Gott!"

Another I remember was concerning a passenger whose pregnant wife cut his hair and who left the care of the other two children to him in the afternoons while she rested. His horse was 'Bald Patch' out of 'Slip' by 'Scissors' and his verse –

> Chasing round the decks all day
> After the young 'uns while at play,
> Must make you thank your lucky stars
> That this job usually is Ma's!'

On this voyage homeward in Hong Kong, where we were moored at the buoys, the mate had spent a bibulous evening with friends ashore. On returning late at might there was a fair sea running; he missed his step and wounc up clinging to the gangway base platform with his bottom half in the water. He never lived it down. His verse was a masterpiece:

> 'Robbie really is a sight
> Swimming in the dead of night.
> But aquabatic first mates outghta
> Take more gin with all that water'.

His horse (and for a couple of voyages after that) was 'Big Splash' by 'Mis-step' out of 'Sampan'.

The game was really a king-sized board game with outsized dice. The course and its hazards were chalked out on the boat deck and two midshipmen were appointed as dice men – each in charge of a huge die, about a foot cube. There was a maximum of six horses in each race, numbered one to six. The first die cast indicated which horse was to progress and the second dictated the number of squares to move. We had a tote and a considerable amount of money changed hands. The prizes were substantial and the balance went to the RNLI or some other charity. We sometimes raised two or three hundred pounds a voyage.

On this trip Robbie and I ran the tote and we dealt in every conceivable currency. Usually we allowed only round figure conversions. It was for charity and only for a bit of fun, after all. Lady Uppity-Passenger had dug up some German currency from somewhere and insisted that we gave her the official exchange rate. She thrust a handful of coins at me and demanded to know with how much she would be credited.

I turned to the mate, 'How much is a pfennig worth, Robbie?'

'Pf--- all,' he wittily replied, unfortunately not realising that the harridan was standing so close. She said nothing, but with her nostrils dilated she glared at him for a good five seconds, quivering like a plucked guitar string, then stalked off to find the old man and demand that the mate be suspended. The captain calmed her down and gave Robbie a rocket.

It was unfortunate but only a storm in a teacup. Robbie was quite upset. Despite his bluntness he was a gentleman and would never have intentionally used bad language within earshot of a lady. The next day she gave father a copy of a letter she had written to the owner – a personal friend of course – suggesting that he look more carefully at the social attributes of men before appointing them as chief officers in his passenger ships. She advised him that in her opinion Robbie was not suitable for employment in that capacity and unless she received a personal assurance that he would be demoted immediately, she would never travel in the company's ships again.

Robbie had tried to apologise but she wouldn't speak to him, consequently he had no time for her. Her ludicrous protest over the Arab labourers and her illegal incursion onto the bridge was the final straw. He lost his patience. 'Well, madam, I can hardly fire a bloody machine-gun at them, can I?'

This latest evidence of his unsuitability for high office rendered even her speechless, and she gobbled and gagged as he led her firmly back to the ladder where he handed her over to me to make a note of her 'official' protest.

I have never had a more improbable ten minutes. She was beside herself with rage and frustration. She seemed to regard the Arabs' actions as deriving from the insolent connivance of all the officers and crew of the ship. She worked herself up into a terrible state. I was as 'official' as possible. I thought that by taking the matter seriously and making obvious notes, she would be satisfied and ultimately calm down. Having taken a second breath, I thought, she would realise how ridiculous she was making herself and would drop it. But it was not to be.

I made a record of the incident with date and time and asked what was her specific complaint. She told me. How many people were involved? She had no idea. Could she describe them? They were like all Arabs, dressed in rags. Could she identify any ringleaders? No, they all looked alike. I had run out of questions yet she seemed to expect more. I racked my brain, searching for the means to take the matter further. In desperation I asked, 'Can you describe any of the offending articles?' That blew her self-control into tatters. She held her breath for so long while she glared at me that I marvelled she didn't collapse. For a moment it looked as if she intended to attack me then she regained control and swept out. I hoped that was that. But, again, it was not to be.

Later that day, having cleared Port Said, the old man sent for me. My heart sank into my buckskin shoes. The old man was terrifying. He looked like a tall, slim version of Bismarck and had tremendous presence. His teak-brown, wrinkled face was topped by a cap of thick silver hair cut 'en brosse'; a severely trimmed silver, bristling military mustache matched a clipped 'chin' beard; and gleaming like shards of ice beneath his thick black brows were the clearest, palest, hardest eyes I have ever tried to look into. Because of his intransigence and imperious manner, we called him 'The Iron Duke'. As I walked along the prom deck and mounted to the boat deck, I doubted that even the 'Gallant 600' could have felt more insecure and expendable as they galloped towards the Russian guns than I did at that moment.

It was a beautiful Mediterranean evening. Only the breeze of our passage stirred cross the decks and the dying sun had stained the hazy horizon a deep rose. The old man's door stood open and as I approached, Lady Uppity-Passenger stepped daintily across the weather step with a flash of slim, white thigh and gave me a bright glare of triumph. I realised later that she had then lingered within earshot to enjoy my disembowelment. I knocked and entered at his instruction. The Iron Duke, standing with his back to the door, was gazing out of his window at the sunset, his hands behind him fiddling with an ornate paper knife. He swung round as I entered and fixed me with his unnerving stare. The simile of the Light Cavalry throwing itself on the enemy guns seemed even more apt as he continued to inspect me minutely without a word. I felt more and more as if I were naked and standing barefoot on an electrically-charged metal plate.

At last he spoke, not in the crisp, sharp tones of command that his appearance prognosticated but in his deep, resonant actor's voice that could carry from the bridge to the fo'c's'le head without apparent effort. 'The Company and I require my officers to deal courteously and reasonably with passengers. Nothing more, nothing less. Does that accord with your understanding of your duties?'

'Yes, Sir.'

'Kindly give me your version of events regarding Lady Uppity-Passenger.'

I passed him the sheet of paper on which I had recorded the substance of the woman's complaint, to which I had added my questions and her answers. He read it without comment and handed it back, maintaining his basilisk stare.

'That's all, Sir. She was offended by my last question and left to complain to you.'

'I see... do you consider you were being courteous and reasonable?'

'I believe so, Sir, under the circumstances.'

'Do you indeed? Do you consider it was courteous and reasonable to ask her to describe 'the offending articles'?'

He allowed me a few seconds to rummage for a reply then unexpectedly reprieved me. His teak-like face twitched into a grim smile which didn't reach his eyes. 'Good God, man, when do you think the poor old bitch last saw one in earnest? What do you suppose is wrong with the wretched woman?'

I heard the sudden clatter of elegant court shoes on the deck and ladder and realised, incredibly, that I had survived the cannons' roar but poor Lady Uppity-Passenger hadn't. She had eavesdropped the whole conversation and the final cruel thrust delivered in the captain's booming voice must have penetrated even her armoured hide. She had every meal in her stateroom until she left and never appeared in public again. Although she had been booked through to London, she disembarked in Genoa and completed her journey overland.

Robbie told us later that she had spiked her own guns when she adopted the same mistress/coolie attitude with the old man as she had with the rest of us. The Iron Duke was an autocrat. He radiated a cold, sharp aura of total command that seemed to affect even inanimate objects. A sputtering and uncooperative fire-water pump under test had suddenly brightened up and whispered silkily into action like a sewing machine when the old man appeared, according to an engineer working on it. It seemed not at all far-fetched to us. Even passengers lying at ease in deck chairs seemed to stiffen into attitudes of respect without opening their eyes when they detected the captain's presence.

Lady Uppity-Passenger had bowled along to father's stateroom and entered with only a perfunctory and authoritative rap on the door. He let that go and invited her to sit down. Having heard her story he took much the same line as I had done and asked identical questions (except the final one, which he told Robbie he hadn't thought of). He had hoped to defuse the situation, calm her down and then quietly forget the matter. But she was adamant, and irritated him with her arrogance and unreasoning demands. It was not sensible to irritate the Iron Duke. When she detected his increasing resistance and growing hostility she figuratively fired a flare into the paint locker by instructing him that 'Your duty, Captain, is to help me to instill a civil attitude in these people.' She had undeniable courage, but that lost her the battle.

* * * * *

The Suez Canal is only a week or so away from home and has a poignancy all its own. It is usually the first foreign stop in a Far East trip. On the reciprocal journey it is the gateway to home and sometimes signals the onset of 'Channel Fever' or 'The Channels' – the effervescent and slightly dotty behaviour of blue water seamen approaching their home port after going foreign. Although we were not coming 'home', *Bellatrix* would be in Europe for the first time in years. Most of the Brits in her took the opportunity of a flying visit home – my first in twenty-two months.

CHAPTER TWELVE

We were four days discharging in London. It had never crossed my mind that I could ever miss London dockies, but they had a sort of spiky charm that seemed missing elsewhere in the world. Maybe we were just lucky on that trip or perhaps having been away for so long even the mundane had acquired a spurious attractiveness due to its unfamiliarity. There seemed to be plenty of characters among the dockies who worked us; most days produced a chuckle or two when we regaled each other with reports of the day's work and related the often pungent but deadpan quips of the dockers.

On that stopover they had a foreman nicknamed Sabrina.[10] I asked one of the dockies how he had come to acquire such an odd nickname. His reply convulsed me and we thought it typical of the understated London humour.

'He does ---- all, he says ---- all, he just ----ing stands there.'

The chief remembered one night on a previous ship in London's King George V Dock when a stevedore foreman with a powerful, reedy voice threw the saloon into confusion one sailing night. There had been a last minute hitch and a gang was working in number three hatch just forward of the saloon. It was a sultry summer evening and all the portholes were open so the men's uninhibited conversation drifted back clearly. It was pretty salty. The mate stuck his head out of a porthole and politely asked the foreman if his men would moderate their language as there were passengers aboard and

---

[10] Sabrina was a voluptuous young lady who adorned the Arthur Askey show. She appeared in revealing, leopard-skin dresses of a startling design. Her impact was entirely visual as she was not required to sing, dance or tell jokes.

nobody wanted to embarrass the ladies, did they. The foreman was most accommodating. He bellowed down the hatch, 'Hey lads, watch your ----ing language, there's ladies on this ----ing ship.'

The toilet facilities for dockside workers in the KGV Dock were primitive in the extreme. They consisted of a row of cubicles with minimal weather protection. The seats were positioned over a slightly angled channel along which water flowed constantly to empty into the dock. It was almost mediaeval . One ganger had trouble with his gang who were always breaking off, repairing to the WC – ignoring his protests – to sit and smoke and read newspapers. He found the perfect answer one day and wondered why he had never thought of it before. The channel protruded beyond the end of the ramshackle building where it was fed by a constantly running water tap. The foreman crumpled up a newspaper, sprinkled it with lighter fuel, lit it and set it adrift on the stream running leisurely under the seats of his reluctant workers.

He regretted his ingenuity although the result was spectacularly successful. The progress of his fireship could be followed by the bellows of shock and outrage and the rapidly lengthening line of heads that shot into view, like a reversed film of falling dominoes. London dockers were not renowned for their submissive qualities nor for their forgiving nature. The owners of the barbecued rumps were typical of their breed and it was a long time before the pyromaniac foreman dared drink alone in the 'Pelican' or the 'Graving Dock', or walk near a swinging load.

The primitive loos were demolished some time in the early fifties prior to a Royal visit. The Royal personage was not expected to use them – it was simply that under the spotlight of so illustrious a visit, the Port of London Authority had a belated attack of conscience.

On completion of discharging we proceeded to dry-dock in Hamburg where we were to have a couple of weeks in the

Deutsche Werft yard (a noted builder of U-Boats such a short time before!). Hamburg was an interesting stopover. On the way up the Elbe from Cuxhaven there was a large riverside pub on the north bank. As ships passed, the pub would run the national flag of the passing ship up its flagpole and play the relevant national anthem over loudspeakers. The pub became quite famous but for some reason we were never able to find it on the ground. It was featured on German television and we were the ship chosen as focus. We never saw the finished product as the TV crew came aboard when we were outward bound from Hamburg. They took shots of us waving and calling to the untypical mass of people who stood on the river bank waving brightly as we slipped by. It was a completely phoney dramatisation of a simple and pleasing gesture.

Hamburg always seemed cold enough to crack your bones. I could never quite understand why we needed the assistance of ice-breaking tugs to get us alongside while a few miles away across the North Sea the Northern British ports had never seen pack ice.

In St Pauli the huge 100-foot-high statue of Bismarck brooded over the ruined acres of the city, which day and night throbbed and rattled to the rumble of cement mixers and the stutter of riveting guns. Nobody seemed to sleep and there were people on the street all the time. They certainly never slept in the Reeperbahn. I suppose the frenetic night life was a reaction to the devastation and the recently endured and lucidly remembered obliteration bombing, but the inhabitants seemed to bear no ill will. The Reeperbahn was bright, noisy and gay. There were brothels with an extraordinary variety of girls in shop windows but it did not suffer from the overweening concentration of pornography that disfigured it latterly.

Our favourite watering hole was the Hippodrome, a night spot whose focal point was a circus ring. The customers sat in booths radiating out from the huge ring and the management had cunningly devised a cheap and foolproof means of entertaining them. They entertained themselves. A standing prize was on offer to anyone able to ride a certain homicidal and demented donkey for longer than a specific period. It was only a minute or so but it seemed an age to a challenger. The creature was so maniacal that it made the bronco busting efforts of American rodeo riders look like a couple of minutes on a Harrod's rocking horse. Nearly everyone was seduced into an attempt on his first visit. It looked simple; the donkey was quite small and had a deceptively placid demeanour. They soon learned painfully that it was otherwise, and better by far to allow others to meet the challenge and sit back to enjoy the tyro's inevitable downfall.

I never saw anyone collect the prize but we did once see the donkey get his comeuppance. A bad loser, who must have been phenomenally strong, climbed up out the sawdust, picked the donkey up bodily and staggered towards the ringmaster – presumably to drop the beast on him. But even his strength failed; he dropped the donkey and collapsed in a heap to be dragged back to his seat by his colleagues. For a while the ass looked chastened, but not for long. It was an arrogant beast and totally unrideable.

Its first trick was to collapse abruptly onto its forehead with its rump in the air. If that didn't unseat the incompletely sober jockey – for none sober would have attempted it – it would suddenly flick its rump into the air until it was almost standing on its head. Few survived that. But if even that failed, as it occasionally did with those who were long in the leg, it would reverse the procedure with extraordinary violence. The unfortunate, leaning well back and congratulating himself on having survived the donkey's first manoeuvre, would suddenly discover that his stance had been turned against him. The ass would sink onto its haunches and sit up like a dog. Having ridden out the early acrobatics the rider would find himself sprawled in the beer-soaked sawdust.

If those three ploys failed the beast would abruptly perform a lateral roll and the wise rider would abandon his attempt, rather than risk being crushed or trampled when the animal regained his feet. Hardly anybody lasted long enough to be threatened with the death roll. The donkey usually celebrated his latest triumph by racing round the ring, kicking wildly with all four legs and having a quick snap at anybody within reach of his blocky head. Oddly enough, although the performance looked highly dangerous, we never saw anybody seriously injured. The event, which became funnier in direct proportion to the incapacity of the challenger, was an hilarious spectacle when the observer was ensconced safely behind the two foot high barrier and viewing the proceedings through the bottom of a beer pot.

The donkey was only the entrée, so to speak. The main course was provided by a series of beasts all trained to make an utter fool of anyone bold enough to accept their challenge. Donald, the mate, attempted to ride the camel one evening and became rather smug after sitting successfully on the enormous hump some eight feet above us for five or so minutes. I can't think why. The animal did nothing more energetic that stalk imperiously round the ring in time to the music. Normally the management could depend on drunks falling like autumn leaves, but Donald had a good head and was only merry and slightly incautious. So they put 'Plan B' into operation.

The music changed to cue the beast and it abandoned its stately promenade round the ring and ambled directly across it. Suspended in the centre was a revolving ball of mirrors used to reflect coloured spotlights during professional sequences. It caught Donald full in the face and swept him from his perch. Without changing his posture he slid down the stern of the camel in a sitting position and landed heavily on his backside in the sawdust, still in the attitude of a Touareg chieftain leading a trans-Sahara caravan. He sat unmoving for so long that we became anxious that he had, perhaps, done himself a mischief, so we ran across to help him to his feet. He was uninjured but completely disoriented by his sudden change in circumstances.

In mild shock at the unexplained and abrupt disappearance of a whole, live camel from beneath his rump, he could not figure out how they had done it or where it had gone. The camel compounded the insult by completing his stroll across the ring, stretching his neck over the low barrier and drinking the mate's beer. Donald protested that it was somebody else's, as his was the full pot at the other end of the table. But he was in shock and we weren't, so we knew best – although on reflection he had been sitting by the full pot.

There was a magnificent white horse in the show and we were invited to ride him. I considered myself no end of a horseman that evening and his splendid, glossy, fourteen hands rippling with corded muscle presented no fears for me. To the cheers of my compatriots I strolled nonchalantly across the sawdust arena, acknowledged the 'groom' with a lordly nod and accepted his bunk-up into the saddle. While the band played a rumpity-tump continuum, I coolly and professionally adjusted the stirrup leathers, took the reins and when the band struck up a horsey number I was firmly in charge. I sat loosely and well balanced with long, cavalry-style stirrups, the fork of my crotch solidly contacting the saddle and his barrel body gripped firmly between my legs. My back was ramrod straight, my feet correctly pointed and my body weight beautifully distributed as we walked, then trotted, then cantered in a smooth, fluid sequence on a left-hand circuit of the huge ring.

I had overlooked the fact that I was riding a circus horse and actually had no control or influence over its behaviour at all. I was forcibly reminded. The gentle ride went on for some time. I was enjoying myself and giving a masterful display of horsemanship although, on reflection, it was about as difficult and skilled as Donald's camel ride. The gentle motion and impeccable behaviour of my mount misled me and I became careless or overconfident. The ringmaster was on to it in a flash. At his signal the drum played a double beat and the horse abruptly changed direction with no reference to me and my counterfeit competence was exposed.

By then, programmed for a left-hand circuit, most of my weight was on the left stirrup. I might just have survived an unexpected left-hand turn which would have kept me in the same relative plane. But his manoeuvre took me by surprise – he turned one hundred and eighty degrees to the right, facing out of the ring. My stance was turned against me. My left leg buckled, I lost my right iron and all coordination. While I was floundering to find the stirrup and regain my balance, the music speeded up and the horse broke into a strange, jerky motion – a sort of spaced trot which I had never encountered before. I found it impossible to accommodate. A wedge of daylight appeared between my rump and his back. I began to bounce about like a sack of ping-pong balls, became unseated and finally collapsed over his neck, reins lost and all semblance of control dissipated.

I wound up hanging under his chin, arms and legs clasped in a desperate and panic-stricken embrace round his neck and my feet crossed on the saddle where my crotch had been cemented so firmly and professionally just seconds before. He cantered merrily round the ring on a right-hand circuit, snorting wetly in my face and looking down his Roman nose at me. His expression was faintly disapproving, like a Rabbi's, who has discovered something rather nasty in his beard and is not in a position to remove it but wishes to keep it in view until he can.

Another attraction at the Hippodrome was a little amphitheatre which featured women wrestling in mud. It was a curious entertainment and I found it neither particularly exciting nor erotic. The girls were certainly well endowed but I would have preferred them without the coating of yellowy-brown mud. The wrestling was decidedly un-athletic and lacked any recognisable technique. It consisted mostly of confused grappling with a great deal of high-pitched squealing through bared teeth and phony savage expressions. Every now and again one or other of the girls would spin out of a clinch to measure her length in the gooey mud. They seemed to take turns.

It wasn't very impressive as a spectacle, and soon became boring. Donald protested loudly that they were the worst wrestlers he had ever seen and challenged any or all of them to wrestle him and discover the meaning of life. They ignored him at first but he began to jeer sarcastically at their repetitive antics. As they were doing their best, they tired of his heckling, paused in their performance and called to someone standing in the shadows behind us. Suddenly a phalanx of tough-looking men with Neanderthal brow ridges and prognathous jaws, materialised out of the thick blue tobacco haze like a battle squadron of the Kreigsmarine breaking out of a smokescreen. They bore down on us, with their knuckles dragging on the ground, and ploughed through the sea of faces turned on the ring. I pointed out to Donald that the new arrivals more closely resembled wrestlers than did the embattled ladies and that now might be an auspicious moment to pipe down. But it was too late. They hove to beside us and invited us to leave. I was in instant agreement, but Donald considered the invitation for a full four or five seconds then wisely decided it was acceptable and we left with our tails between our legs.

CHAPTER THIRTEEN

The run from Hamburg to New York in ballast was very uncomfortable. *Bellatrix* made heavy weather of it, but the engine repairs done in Singapore and the more general refurbishment carried out in Hamburg stood the test. She came through with flying colours and we arrived on the East Coast with nothing worse than a leaking stern gland. We had a longish time on the coast and got to know more about America than on any of our previous visits.

GBS said that America and Britain are two countries separated by a common tongue. It goes deeper than that. In some respects America is almost as alien a place, say, as France. The visitor is seduced by the common language into believing that culturally and intellectually our two countries are closer together than is evident on closer acquaintance. The 'commonness' of the languages is often illusory. Englishmen and Americans can derive totally different meanings from the same words. 'I was mad about my flat', for instance. To an American this means 'I was furious about my puncture.' But translated into 'Americanese' from the English it would mean 'I was delighted with my apartment.' This is not a particularly wild example, but there is commonalty enough to make social intercourse effortless and enjoyable with occasional moments of confusion.

The country, though of course we saw mostly the seaboard, is magnificent. In general, outside the large conurbations, the people are kindly and hospitable but to an Englishman display an odd blend of the sophisticated and naïve. They contrive, somehow, to be materialistic and unworldly at the same time. They think nothing of exploiting sentiment for gross profit and yet can accommodate extreme religious sects within the community with no sense that they are different or in any way 'odd'.

The sophistication of the Immigration Service must have been severely tested by our Lascar crew when the McCarthy witch-hunt for Communist sympathisers was at its height in the early fifties. Everyone entering the States had to fill in an enormous form listing endless personal details. They were supposed to have been completed personally by hand. Most of our crew were illiterate and signed any documents either with a thumb print or an 'X', so we prevailed on the Goanese butler to fill in the forms for them. He had a splendid, flowery hand more suited to illuminated scripts than form filling. His imaginative spelling combined with the garbled grammar created an exotic patois and his magnificent penmanship imbued it with the authority of a long established language.

We often wondered what the bemused recipients of the information made of such gems as 'purtal hip on knec'; 'scare on noz betwin is' and 'operator whole on bely'. On enquiry these exotic distinguishing marks translated as 'purple heap on neck' – i.e a boil; 'scar on nose between eyes' and what might have been construed as a parasitic twin turned out to be nothing more dramatic than an appendicitis scar.

In Georgia we had a curious experience which was triggered by the butler and his men. We were carrying hazardous cargo and had been berthed on a remote and dilapidated wharf on the Savannah River miles from town. After walking for an age we came to an odd little local bar which seemed to have been built by odd-job men in an undisciplined moment. It was ramshackle and looked unstable although the materials from which it was constructed appeared to be in good condition and relatively new. Somehow the building contrived to look vastly older and sicker than its component parts.

The interior came straight out of a Norman Rockwell American 'folk' painting. The room was small with rough boarded walls. A huge old-fashioned, pot-bellied iron stove squatted on a brick pedestal in the centre of the room and beside it sat a wrinkled and ancient man, swinging back and forth in a creaking rocking chair. Occasionally, at the end of a forward roll, he spat a black gob of tobacco juice which flew across the room for some distance to plop with unerring accuracy into a wide-necked brass spittoon which stood by the rudimentary bar. He appeared to be asleep but when we filed past him he continued his metronomic rhythm and without opening his eyes, spat through the gaps between us as one by one we ran the gauntlet. It was masterly.

The lady of the house stood by the bar at an ironing board, chatting in a disconnected and intimate manner with two or three locals who sat nodding over frosty glasses of beer. The conversation had an odd, dreamy quality to it as if it had been progressing endlessly without prospect of development or conclusion; they seemed to be on a conversational treadmill. When we entered everything stopped instantly, except the old man in the chair, and they all turned to look at us in consternation as if we were from another planet. We wondered at first if we had walked into a private house by mistake.

Amos nodded politely at the assembly. 'Do you sell beer?'

'Beer?' the woman repeated dopily, looking round at her regulars as if seeking support to avenge an insult.

'Yes please,' Amos said. 'We'd like four beers please.'

The woman studied us for a moment then called to someone who could be heard rummaging about in the room behind the bar. A large fat man waddled through the door.

'Four beers please,' Amos repeated.

The man did not even look at us. He drew four beers from a tap out of sight beneath the counter and placed them on the bar top. Then he gave us a close inspection, peering myopically at each of us in turn.

'You Limeys or sumpen?' he asked eventually. We agreed that we were.

'I hear your history goes back t'ree, four hunnerd years,' he said and we thought that at last we might have a tenuous contact. But the brief comment had exhausted his reservoir of social awareness and he turned his back on us without further comment and returned to the back room.

We sat huddled together sipping our icy beers and talking in whispers while the locals stared at us. Reluctantly we came to the end of the first round and were steeling ourselves to start the extraordinary operation all over again when the door opened and in walked the butler and a couple of his men. The effect could hardly have been more startling had someone opened the door and emptied a sack of live cobras into the bar. One man knocked over his beer glass in agitation and the others all froze, staring horrified at the newcomers.

The woman recovered first. She bawled for the barman and he burst through the door into the bar in instant response. Before he could speak the butler wished us good evening. The barman turned to us. 'You know these guys?'

'Certainly, they're from our ship.'

'They cain't come in here.'

'Why ever not?'

'They's nigras and nigras ain't allowed.'

A very strange argument then broke out between the proprietor and his local customers. Fernandes and his men with their sleek, brilliantined hair and aquiline features were patently not 'niggers', although they were very dark skinned. This fact disturbed the more liberally minded customer. 'They ain't nigras, Josh. Nigras got woolly ha'r.'

'They's black, so they's nigras,' the barman said with unassailable logic.

'But they ain't got woolly ha'r man. Ah never seen a nigra ain't got woolly ha'r.'

'Ah don't give a mother. Black's black and black ain't allowed.'

Amos intervened. 'They're Indians,' he said quietly, 'not Negroes.'

'Indians?' bellowed the barman. 'Hellfire and damnation, thet's even wuss. They ain't proper God-fearing Christians, they's dangerous. They's all got knives.'

It was ludicrous. Goanese are the gentlest and least aggressive of peoples. We tried to explain where they came from but I don't think anyone there was aware of the existence of the vast Indian subcontinent, let alone its political divisions. Eventually we were able to persuade the barman and his wife that the inoffensive butler and his men were not Negroes or half-breeds. Nor were they renegade followers of a latter-day Geronimo, tanked up with fire water and liable to scalp any 'white eyes' they could hold still long enough, so they could be served without any qualms. We couldn't explain exactly what they were, so we settled for suntanned Portuguese or Spaniards who lived in the tropics, which was close enough.

So that, really, was that – except for the old man who gathered the tatters of his consciousness around him, peered blearily round the room, mumbled 'Goddamned nuh-nigras is like fuh-fuh-flies, then lapsed back into his dream world. We had another beer and left. It was a depressing place.

Georgia and South Carolina had an odd aura. Both were attractive in a raddled way but had a curiously unsettling feel to them, like the slight but pervasive sadness of a deserted army camp long after the last inmates have left. The outskirts of the towns had streets and streets of unpainted, dilapidated houses where the blacks lived in those pre-integration days. We were shocked to see notices like those in the buses 'Coloured passengers will be seated from the front to the rear and white passengers from the rear to the front.' It wasn't so much the segregation that appalled us, we had seen it in many places, but the cynical regard for profit that the arrangement denoted. Had the buses been divided into clearly defined white and black sections, it would have been possible for the companies to lose money. Theoretically, with such an arrangement, it would be possible for either section to be full while there were still vacant seats in the other part of the bus.

By this cynical manipulation however, the blacks could be ritually humiliated while allowing the operators to claim their pound of flesh – black or white. In theory it would have been possible for the entire bus to be full with black people except for four whites on the back seat and on the return journey the reverse could apply – a bus full of whites with four blacks on the front seat.

One of the more attractive and curious aspects of life in the Deep South were the fireflies. One bar we frequented in Savannah had seats and tables under an enormous tree in the garden. On hot summer nights we would sit for hours, listening to the cicadas and watching the countless fireflies zipping around us, glowing brightly like tiny cigarette ends in the velvety darkness under the tree.

We met a delightful little man who was generosity itself and the epitome of the 'Southern Gentleman' of fiction. He was rotund and energetic and beamed good fellowship and optimism with a permanent smile behind the cleanest, most sparkling pair of rimless glasses I have ever seen. It was in the Deep South and we were tied up on a dilapidated wharf some distance from town. One Sunday afternoon a large fawn and chocolate coloured Cadillac pulled up on the adjacent roadway. A little man in powder blue slacks and a blue checked shirt stepped out accompanied by an equally dumpy, middle-aged lady with sunglasses and a hectic lavender coiffure. Several of us were leaning on the rail surveying the rather dull countryside and waiting for the usual crop of sightseers to turn up to inspect us. The little man engaged us in a shouted conversation.

'Is this'n a Limey ship?'

'No. We are Bahamas registered.'

'But youse guys is Limeys, ain't yuh?'

'Most of us are.'

'Can I talk to someone then?'

We invited them aboard and had a cup of tea together. His son had been in England during the war and had been treated with generosity and courtesy, he told us. He would like to repay the kindness. Would we like to come to his house for a barbecue that evening or any time we could make it.

'How many of us?' we asked.

'All of youse,' he replied, 'I gotta big garden.'

So he had. An enormous garden. He lived in a sprawling, 'ranch-style' house that we would call a bungalow, but there the similarity ended. The house was huge; expansive open areas led into expansive open areas lit by picture windows the size of double garage doors. There were acres of carpet and endless vistas of natural wood screens fading into walls of hand-made brick and natural stone.

There by the swimming pool we had a barbecue that brought us to our knees. Amos and I lay at ease in chaises longues and discussed our good luck. He had just strolled round the estate with our host and was filling me in with some of the details.

'He must be worth a fortune,' I said. 'Any idea what he does?'

'Yes. I know exactly what he does. Noticed anything odd about the swimming pool?'

'It's full of piranhas.'

'The shape, idiot.'

I couldn't say that I had. Its shape was slightly eccentric but not excessively so; it wasn't a guitar shape or a motor car. It was considerably narrower than a conventional pool, but that could perhaps be accounted for by constrictions of the site or perhaps our friend was a speedy swimmer who needed the length. Amos gave me a knowing look.

'Walk up those steps in the rose garden and look back.'

The grounds were beautifully landscaped. Some thirty or so yards away a flight of riven stone steps climbed a bank of roses to open further vistas of exotic bushes and shrubs that led to a mock pagoda at the end of a needle-straight stone path. When I climbed the bank I looked back and got a considerable shock. It amused Amos enormously.

'It's a bloody coffin!' I told him when I got back. He grinned.

'Full marks! Now guess what he does for a living.'

Incredibly, our host was a successful undertaker with umpteen branches. I looked across at him standing in the barbecue pit wearing Bermuda shorts and a chef's hat and apron, piling food with profligate generosity on to the plates of total strangers. It seemed impossible that the shiny little man with the glittering spectacles and the bouncy, cheerful manner could follow such a profession. But he did. He showed us a current advertisement which featured in a whole page advert in the Saturday Evening Post. He was agent for a range of hermetically-sealed metal 'caskets', as he called them. The advert showed a young widowed mother surrounded by her fatherless brood. She was sitting on a window seat looking out into a rain-filled, stormy night and there in the corner of the advert was an insert. It depicted in end view the cross section of a coffin in a grave and even illustrated the position of the corpse with a circle representing the cross section of the head. The grave was waterlogged with the tide line half way up the grave space but the interior of the coffin was dry and cosy – thanks to the patented, hermetically-sealed bronze casket. The headline read something like '…On a night like this it's good to know your loved one is safe and dry'. It made me squirm.

Our host was currently embattled with the local administration over what he called 'a serious breakdown credibilitywise'. It seemed that the highway authority let franchises to sections of the nearby interstate freeway to various mortuary enterprises. Any fatalities in that stretch belonged to the owner of the franchise; he collected and arranged disposal of the victims. It was quite lucrative and so, inevitably, was occasionally subject to corruption.

There had recently been a major shunt which had resulted in several dead, and our friend's share of the harvest was less than he had expected. This was because the police had either misinterpreted the contract or had cunningly done a paper shift of the accident site, he told us. He was entitled to corpses on neighboring sections if the cause of the accident originated in his. It was a complicated story and was perhaps not so straightforward as I have set it out. Nevertheless, our friend had been short-changed one way or another and felt defrauded and irritated. He explained it all carefully in terms of profit and loss related to the cost of maintaining the franchise etc, etc. It all made perfect sense and we understood that all businesses have to protect their interests, but I never felt quite the same after he had given us an insight into the politics of his profession. But he was an exemplary host and we were grateful for his friendship.

Before we left that evening he invited us to tour his workshops and inspect his chapel of rest. Considering that the victims of the recent multi-vehicle, chain reaction accident were then being 'processed', we declined. He insisted that it would be very interesting and educational but understood our reluctance.

We returned his hospitality on board and had several return visits over quite a long period. I visited his son's grave in the American war cemetery near Cambridge some years later and sent them a picture of the site. I received a letter from his solicitor informing me that he had died earlier in the year. His wife was crippled with arthritis and was unable to reply personally to my letter but she thanked me for my interest and thoughtfulness.

The impromptu hospitality dispensed so generously by our mortician friend was by no means unusual, although I never again experienced it on so lavish a scale. It happened usually in the smaller ports of call where our arrival had a more noticeable impact on local life. We were frequently approached in bars, restaurants and parks when somebody overheard our accents. They wondered if we were English and followed it up because their forefathers were British or their husbands/brothers/sons had been in UK during the war.

Some traded on it shamelessly. We had one young man who was as English as muffins. On hearing that someone had gone ashore in a kilt and had been almost mobbed, he borrowed the kilt from its owner and went ashore several nights running. He walked up and down waiting to be noticed. When he was he made the most of it, muttering dark Hibernian sayings such as 'Och aye, the Sassenachs are abroad the nicht' and 'Lang may ye're lum reek', which defeated even the true Scots among us. But it got him a few invitations to American homes and his picture in the local paper.

CHAPTER FOURTEEN

Nowhere is the separation of America and Britain more obvious than in medical matters. It is possible, I suppose, that in pre-National Health days in the UK the system more approximated the extant American arrangement. I can't judge that, it's outside my adult experience, but I have given blood in both cultures and the experiences can't be compared.

The motivations for my donations could hardly have been more at odds. On my first blood-letting in Liverpool, I had just arrived back in the UK and was faced with an enormously long wait for my train home. I had exhausted all the recreational amenities requisite to the hour – mid afternoon. I didn't wish to eat, the pubs were closed and no cinema programme attracted me. I was strolling along Castle Street bored and fed up when I saw an extremely pretty nurse standing at the door of a blood donor station. I don't know if it was deliberate, but it worked. She smiled at me and I smiled back. Before I could catch my breath I was flat on my back on a bunk in a small dormitory and a tall, gangling, middle-aged lady with sinewy hands and tufted eyebrows was driving into my arm what appeared to be a gas pipe with a length of rubber hose attached to it.

When I left half an hour or so later I felt as if I had been raped. I never saw the pretty nurse again and all I got for my trouble was a sore arm, a cup of weak tea, a wholemeal biscuit, a barley sugar and a severely dented libido. Perhaps my memory of the experience is slightly distorted by my disappointment at not having got to grips with the enchanting little siren who lured me onto the rocks. I have given blood in England many times since and have found the extraction teams to be kindly, courteous and professional and the centres clean and efficiently run.

The same could not be said of the vampires of New York. It's probably unfair and misleading to compare all American blood banks with the one we patronised in Manhattan. It seemed like something dreamed up by Charles Addams during a deep depression. To be fair, it hid nothing. Its external appearance gave due warning of what it would be like inside. Had dollars not been so scarce and the price of $5 a pint so attractive, nothing could have dragged us in.

The street was a mixture of warehouses interspersed with dosshouses and what we imagined to be soup kitchens. The premises in happier days had probably been a shop. The big display window was painted an unprepossessing green on the inside to render it opaque so the gruesome activities carried on within wouldn't frighten any passing horses. It was the closest thing to a knacker's yard that I could imagine. You entered directly from the street into a reception area – a large room floored with dust-coloured lino. Here any number of dull-eyed men in various stages of dereliction would be standing, heads hanging, arms dangling, awaiting the call. When your turn came you shuffled to a desk where a pneumatically plump, shiny, very black male nurse asked a few questions – were you suffering from syphilis, malaria or hepatitis – and gave you a large numbered card and a small crate containing two bottles, one large and one small.

There appeared to be no controls at all. The derelicts, in the manner of the American panhandler, went straight to the nearest bar with their five dollars and presumably could come straight back and sell another pint of blood for beer money. Several of those present wouldn't have made a square meal for Dracula. We presumed that the staff were trained to detect the moment when the blood and alcohol in a potential donor's veins went into equilibrium and rendered them unsuitable as donors. We supposed they were then sent away to let nature take its course and convert the alcohol to potentially saleable blood.

When your card number was called you entered a wide corridor with double-tiered bunks head-to-tail down the entire length of one wall. The bunks were covered with bloodstained brown paper and you were directed to lie down on the nearest empty one so as to let your left arm dangle over the side. Almost immediately your arm would be seized and the connector stabbed into the inside bend of your elbow. My memory of the operation still gives me goose pimples and makes my toes curl. The implement that was driven into the vein was about as thick as a pencil and appeared to be made of aluminium. It was sliced at an angle and scolloped so that a sharp point was formed in the metal tube. The other end of the hollow metal spike was attached to a rubber tube which snaked down into the sample bottle.

When my turn came I lay down on the bunk with a crackle of brown paper and put my head on my hand to keep it off the pillow. The attendant grabbed my arm, slapped the inside of my elbow joint sharply with two fingers then pressed the point of the implement into the large, blue vein. My whole arm seemed to buckle and a large indentation appeared. Suddenly the sharpened tube penetrated my flesh with a 'plop' that I'm not sure if I heard or felt. The first trickle was directed into the small sample bottle which the attendant picked up, swished around and inspected. He was evidently satisfied that it was the correct colour or consistency, because he transferred the connecting tube to the glass tank that I was required to fill. I started off in full flow which rapidly declined to a puny dribble. Time was money.

'Pump, man, pump it!' the attendant said.

I felt sick and miserable. 'How?'

'Clench and unclench your Goddamned fist.'

It gave me a strange, uneasy feeling right down to my toes but I pumped away with a will and, thankfully, the foaming purple fluid gradually rose in the huge jar – I'm sure its capacity was more than a pint. After a while the patrolling attendant stopped by my couch, snatched the tube out of the bottle and capped it while I was still in full flow. I knew then why the brown paper was so bloodstained; I must have wasted twenty five or thirty cents worth of good blood.

He plucked the tube from my arm and the distended vein collapsed. He dabbed my wound with antiseptic, bent my elbow to clasp the cotton wool ball in place and bellowed 'next'. I glanced round to see what everyone else was doing, picked up my crate and presented it to a desk where it was placed in a racked trolley. The cashier gave me five single dollar notes then we filed past a nurse who removed the cotton wool pad from the puncture, flicked it into a dustbin, had a quick look at the wound and stuck a round elastoplast dressing on it. Next minute we were out in the street of sleazy warehouses enriched by five dollars and an unbelievable – and for me unrepeatable – experience. I was told later that in Boston they paid twenty-five dollars a pint. So far as I was concerned they could have multiplied it by ten before I would subject myself to such a degrading exercise again.

We had an odd arrangement with the company regarding dentistry. If we required dental treatment we could have extractions free but had to pay for fillings. The logic of that has always escaped me except, I suppose, that more people require fillings than they do extractions, so the arrangement would save the company money. But not a lot, I would have thought.

Americans who cannot afford or are not insured for dentistry can, if they live conveniently, go to a dental college for treatment – either free or carried out at a nominal charge to cover malpractice insurance. Presumably apprentice dentists have to practice on live patients at some time and the poor and uninsured make good forceps-fodder. Treatment is expensive and dollars were scarce, so we toyed with the idea of the college solution from time to time but it didn't appeal much. We'd heard horrific stories of people being dragged round the surgery by a muscular baby dentist who had latched onto a tooth that just refused to part company with the jaw. Or even worse, of the wrong tooth being drilled and filled because it was more in line with the last lecture the apprentice had attended than was the molar with the putrefying cavity.

I only required treatment once in America – in Baltimore. As a wartime child deprived of sweets I had managed to enter into my twenties before needing metal to plug up the ravages of enamel-destroying sugar. The agent had arranged an appointment and I duly turned up to find that all the dentists in Baltimore seemed to operate from the same building. It was a concentration of horror. Streams of people shaking with apprehension were entering and others, pale and trembling were leaving. I entered nervously but my surgery was warm and cheerful and my dentist cosily middle-aged. His competent, unforced manner reassured me. I lay back comfortably in the huge profiled chair and closed my eyes against the spotlight.

He began to probe and mumble to his assistant, then all went quiet and nothing happened for some time. It was warm and peaceful, the chair was comfortable and supported every curve of my body; I felt myself drifting gently into sleep. The fumbling and probing began again and I heard voices murmuring softly as if from a great distance. The hands felt different somehow, or perhaps they smelled or tasted different. 'It must be the assistant,' I thought dimly. Then it came to me that there must be a veritable regiment of assistants, for the identity of the hands seemed to be changing frequently but going through the same motions. I opened my eyes to find that I was surrounded by white-coated men and women, mostly young but with a sprinkling of hoary heads among them. I was startled at first then discovered that I was being used as an object lesson in the benefits of a sugar-reduced diet in the immature. In the privileged young patients with whom these relatively inexperienced dentists were dealing, a perfect set of teeth lasting beyond teenage years was rare indeed.

Despite allowing my dentist to use me as the subject of a lecture I still had to pay full whack for my filling.

Baltimore was a fairly liberal-minded city. In the days before pornography became mandatory for the public at large, commercial sex was available in most inland cities, I suppose, and certainly in every seaport I ever knew. It was usually fairly discreet and concentrated in a specific area where it could be easily found by the potential client, but wouldn't intrude on the daily life and sensitivities of the average citizen.

In Baltimore's main street, burlesque theatres stood cheek by jowl and the shows were carbon copies of each other, all based on the display of female flesh and rarely was it young and vibrant. One bar had a resident act with a lumpy lady and a large boa constrictor which was supposed to be a sight to remember. When I went, the lady, resembling a mummified wrestler, appeared swathed in multitudinous muslin veils and announced that 'Henry has a 'toomer' and is unable to appear'. Henry was the snake; I don't know if he recovered. As a substitute for Henry's performance we were treated to an interminable and inexpert dance of the seven veils. I couldn't help wondering how on earth Salome had hooked poor old Herod with so basic and naïve an exercise. But I suppose he may have led a sheltered life and Salome may have been a more shapely and accomplished stripper.

It was in Baltimore that I witnessed the most shameful display of racial hatred that I have ever seen. It was a simple act but the black's humiliation stayed with me for a long time. Gus and I were walking in the main street one bright, windy afternoon when a hat came bowling by us, rolling end over end, and we heard the clatter of the owner's footsteps as he came chasing after it. A man just in front of us trapped the hat, picked it up and turned to see who was the owner just as an elderly black man puffed past us. The middle-aged white who had picked up the hat watched the black approach and when he extended his hand to retrieve the hat the white man looked him full in the face and with a disdainful flick of the wrist flipped the hat into the gutter. He stood face to face with the black man, waiting for him to protest. No protest was forthcoming.

From about eight years of age, Gus's childhood had been almost Dickensian in its deprivation and he had swallowed more than his fair share of humiliation. It made him impatient with bullies. An odd rigidity came over him as he saw the black man's hat insolently tossed in the gutter. My heart almost stopped – Baltimore was no place for two white strangers to become embroiled in a racial brawl. Gus stooped, picked up the hat and in a couple of strides he was looming over the two men. He lowered his face to within inches of the white man's and said something low and savage. To his credit, the man didn't take to his heels as I would have done in the circumstances – Gus could frighten a squad of paratroopers just by looking at them. The man went very pale and looking slightly shocked, backed off a couple of paces and stared at Gus for a moment. Then in bravado, I suppose, because he wasn't to know how Gus would react, he gave him the obscene one-finger salute, turned on his heel and walked away.

I'm not sure what I expected from the black. I don't think I expected him to prostrate himself and place Gus's foot on his head, but I expected something. 'Thank you', perhaps. Instead he almost snatched his hat from Gus and rammed it on his head. He hesitated as if about to say something then nodded curtly and strode away. A few yards away he stood on the kerb waiting to cross the road and looked back at us for a long moment as we were strolling towards him. When I met his eye he turned abruptly and crossed the road.

'Bloody funny business,' I said. 'What did you say to the bully boy, Gus?'

'It's not important.'

'Well I think you might have got a 'thank you' from the darkie.'

'What for? For having someone witness his humiliation?'

He was pretty angry so I dropped the subject, but it made me see him in another light. Most things I learned about Gus made me like him more, especially in the early days.

America was certainly a strange and complex place, especially for a youngster raised in wartime Britain and entering his teens in the days of savage austerity. It seemed a land, not so much of plenty, but of witless extravagance. For example the range of sandwiches available from snack bars was almost too much to comprehend and made choice difficult. In England we would probably have had four or five basic choices if you discount minor modifications, such as cheese and tomato or cheese and cress – there would have been only one kind of mousetrap cheese. At the snack bar in Times Square subway station the board listed twenty-five or twenty-six varieties of sandwich on different types of bread and the range of pickles and condiments seemed endless. So did the choice of milkshake flavours. It made our pineapple/ banana/strawberry/chocolate/vanilla straight jacket seem very mundane. And what on earth was 'root beer'?

America for me is a land of contradictory attitudes. Their picnic grounds amazed me, they were so clean and hygienic, with rubbish carted away or stuffed in the receptacles provided. They were usually in isolated areas with no attendants, but the people who used them treated them with respect. In England they would have been vandalised and left in ruins. On the other hand it was often hazardous to drive along an urban highway at night for the beer cans that came flying from the windows of passing cars, and the hygiene evident at picnic grounds wasn't reflected in public toilets. The few there were, were disgusting.

It is incredible that one country can accommodate with no apparent sense of incongruity the lunatic, homosexual shambles of San Francisco and the strict Dutch and German religious sects which forbid drinking and dancing, yet seem not to lose all their youngsters to less rigid environments. What a strange nation it is that can spawn the twin improbabilities of Hollywood and Salt Lake City with their attendant cultures. They have managed to have simultaneously extant total licence and rigid conformation. They have invented AIDS and the Salk vaccine.

America was certainly fascinating but above all it was exotic. There were exotic murders. While we were in New York once, a girl was murdered in a cinema one afternoon by a man who stuck a hypodermic needle in her leg as she passed on the way to her seat. When she collapsed her boyfriend didn't know what had happened. The man slipped away and so far as I know was never caught for the brutal and pointless murder of an innocent stranger.

The weather was exotic. There seemed no end to the strange tales told, such as people freezing to death while standing at a bus stop; a coloured girl was found buried under snow and frozen so solid that even her eyeballs were hard, but she recovered. Tornadoes and floods, landslides and earthquakes; breathless, savage summers that actually killed people; rainfall that washed away bridges and drowned cattle in their thousands. All these strange occurrences happened, not to alien yellow and brown people whom you expect to get eaten by sharks, mauled by wild animals and frizzled in volcanoes, but to English-speaking people who were generally indistinguishable from men and women in any UK pub. It gave America, for me at least, an odd, slightly dreamy quality as if it were somewhere I had known long, long ago but on re-acquaintance had found that subtle and almost indefinable changes had rendered it an unsettling blend of the familiar and the alien.

CHAPTER FIFTEEN

There is a seamen's adage 'You can't know a man until you sail with him'. Like many an old saying it encapsulates a hard nugget of truth. Shipmates are more than workmates. Leaving aside any romantic 'Boy's Own' nonsense about 'one for all and all for one', or 'special bondings', men who sail together become utterly reliant on each other. In a merchant ship there is precious little overlap of duties and everyone is interdependant.

There is no shoreside equivalent that I can think of. Perhaps a fire brigade watch is the closest approximation, but even there the analogy fails. The fire team is just that – a team – a composite, multi-headed beast that can only function as a unit. At the end of their watch or shift they go their separate ways. There may be some socialising in off-watch periods or at the weekend, or on the occasional evening in the social club, but they are not totally reliant on each other for their social life in addition to their professional support.

Officers in a merchantman function consecutively or in parallel. The sum total of their labours – the passage of a ship safely from A to B in one piece with intact cargo and healthy passengers – may be considered the result of teamwork, but the individual members work independently. Their off-watch periods or shoreside jaunts are spent either alone or in company with their shipmates. Personal relationships are important – you just can't get away from each other. The closest analogy I can think of is the family. A well-ordered family respects the privacy of its individual members but it is a social unit. Its component members function individually but for the common good. What affects one affects all. A drunken and brutal father impinges on each of them in different ways and they can survive only by pulling together. So it is with a ship's company.

A happy ship is not dependent on creature comforts but on the way in which the crew shakes down together, subject to the vagaries of 'father' – the old man or captain – who can make or mar a happy ship. *Bellatrix* was severely deficient in creature comforts. She was built before the First World War and lacked all modern amenities. There was no hot water on tap. No drainage. Your steward delivered a large enamel jug of hot water for your ablutions when you were called for duty. As the temperature of the water depended on the thermal perception of the steward, the distance of your accommodation from the galley, the weather en route and the alacrity with which you sprang from your bunk, the water was rarely hot enough to shave comfortably so most of us wore beards. The water was used in a tip-up basin hidden away in a mahogany compendium which had a spring-loaded cold water tap. The contents of the basin were discharged into a bucket in the cupboard underneath by restoring the basin to the vertical and securing it with a little brass clip on the face of the fitment. The cupboard containing the bucket tended to be dark and damp and was a favourite breeding ground and hiding place for cockroaches and steam beetles. If your steward was idle or forgetful or not quick enough in heavy weather, the slops in the bucket were spilled and the place could quickly become smelly.

The accommodation was miserable in hot weather when your cabin fan burnt out its armature windings (a frequent disaster – the fans were about 30 years old and in constant operation). You would wake in a muck sweat and a sharp hose-down with sea water was beneficence.

Bellatrix had no air-conditioning. In the public rooms, horizontally mounted ceiling fans with large, brass-tipped mahogany blades created quite an effective draught but in the cabins and workspaces small fans, which frequently burned out their ancient armature windings, stirred the hot, stale air. As we spent most of our time in the tropics, prickly heat was a constant hazard. We constructed wind scoops which were placed in the portholes to conduct fresh moving air into the accommodation when we were under way. Unfortunately in port we had to suffer in silence; the scoops could not be used as the portholes were secured to defeat sneak thieves – an endemic problem in many sea ports. In cold climes the cabins were heated mostly by steam radiators which hissed and leaked and soaked the cotton waste wadding insulating the steam-carrying pipes. This created a perfect environment – damp, dark and warm – for even more wild life.

There was no ice water on tap and potable water was always a problem. We carried only a few tons which sometimes became contaminated. Although fresh water showers were available, they depended on the whim of the old man or chief engineer and mostly we had to make do with sea water baths using a special soap – which, as it happened, was an effective antidote to prickly heat. It's an ill wind…

But she was the happiest ship I ever sailed in. She had a 'tight' crew. There was no animosity between departments as sometimes happens and, by and large, misfits didn't last long. Most men stayed in her for long periods and were usually unmarried. For one reason or another we had a high turnover of skippers and even the most anti-social didn't stay long enough to do more than just bruise the corporate skin. She was virtually the permanent home of the chief engineer who was childless and had been widowed during the war. He was the Oracle, the Grand Master, our Guru and the fount of all knowledge regarding *Bellatrix*. He knew every rivet and dent in her hull and he seemed to remember every man who had sailed in her during his long tenure.

The Chief held Amos in high regard and could never understand what he was doing in *Bellatrix*. 'That lad is destined for higher things...' he once told me, '...mark my words.' Amos had very high personal standards and according to the chief within a very short time of his signing on, had an extraordinary effect on the ship. He was very 'correct' and, despite the occasional flash of a 'wild' streak, inclined to be formal and always wore uniform. He would never dream of entering the saloon improperly dressed, preferring to miss a meal if necessary.

Men who had become sloppy in a ship which paid no heed to uniform and insignia of rank, initially sneered, called him 'Admiral' or 'Captain Bligh' and poked fun at him. He ignored the jeers and gradually they began to conform to his standards. Proper tropical whites began to make their appearance again instead of rugger shorts, swimming trunks and T-shirts. And ships, like people, tend to feel the way they look. Amos was tremendously good for morale. With no sermonising, no real authority and with only the sense of his own worth and his self-respect, he was the catalyst in transforming the ship's self-image. This transformation was well under way when I joined and each new signing consolidated the new order. Most people are happy enough to accept the status quo.

Most of Amos's bad points were simply over extensions of his personal qualities. His confidence and sense of what was right could sometimes lap over into near arrogance. On one occasion somebody was relating the story of an impromptu polo match played on a football pitch in some outlandish spot. He rode under the goalpost frame, he told us, 'and was almost capitulated.'

'You mean decapitated,' Amos corrected him. The poor chap was covered in confusion and soon made an exit. I was furious at having been embarrassed.

'You're an arrogant sod,' I told Amos. 'Was that necessary?'

'Of course it was, he was using the wrong word.' He was convinced he had done the chap a favour and I suppose he had really, even if the doing of it had been a painful experience for the beneficiary. My cowardly approach would have been to use the correct word as soon and as obviously as possible, hoping the storyteller would pick it up – as a mental query at least. If not I guess he would still be using the word incorrectly to this day.

Many people thought Amos was mean. He wasn't, but he was meticulous with money – his own or other people's. If he asked you to carry out a commission for him and gave you money to do it, he would expect a perfect accounting and the exact change, down to the penny. In contrast he would throw money into a kitty with no thought of equity. If he lent you money he would agree a date for repayment and demand it at due date with no embarrassment or coyness. On the other hand being broke was no reason not to accompany him ashore.

'Can't, Amos, I'm all spent out.'

'Well I'm not, my Old. Get your pretty knickers on and we'll see what's doing.'

He would give no thought to what it cost him and would never remind you.

I commented on this odd attitude to Gus one day and naïvely remarked. 'It's a wonder no one has ripped him off.'

Gus chuckled. 'Rip off old Amos? You must be joking!'

He was right. I know of nobody who was less rip-offable. I suppose it was a question of compatibility. Reasonable people treat as they are treated. Money to Gus was there to be used and it didn't matter much to me either – so long as there was sufficient. We all tended to behave in the same way to each other; what we did was more important than how it was funded, so long as nobody took advantage.

We once saw Amos give an attempted ripper-offer his comeuppance. Several of us had gone ashore together in Saigon and it was soon apparent that one of the party was a

171

floater. When his round became imminent he would disappear for a few minutes and return when the threat had receded. It became obvious after a while that he was dodging the column and Amos faced him up.

'I can't afford to buy you bastards booze,' he coolly replied. 'I'm married.'

Even Amos was speechless for a second, but he got his breath back.

'Listen my tight-arsed friend,' he said. 'A round costs twenty francs, you've dodged two. Put forty francs on the bar or ---- off. Please yourself.'

In Japan musical instruments were cheap and of excellent quality; the guitar was the most popular and everybody seemed to own one. While most of us were struggling to acquire dexterity in the three basic chords, Amos experimented and within weeks was effortlessly performing calypsos and intricate, mannered pieces. Then he discarded the instrument. It bored him. He had an advantage over many of us – he was musically literate. He played the piano beautifully and occasionally performed on a silver flute. Had he focused on music I'm sure he could have achieved considerable success.

We had a mate who worked hard at being a 'character'. He wore bizarre hats and was deliberately and irritatingly 'eccentric'. One thing at which he excelled, however, was playing the tin whistle. He would perform with it at the drop of a hat. Amos got hold of it one day, sat fiddling with it, working out the musical logic, then played it. It was astonishing. In his hands it was transformed into an instrument of extraordinary versatility. It rippled and trilled, harsh and sweet, loud and soft, whereas in the mate's hands it had just produced notes monotonously in whatever sequence he decided – however nimbly.

Amos was a talented mimic. Nobody was safe from his acute observation and biting wit. He nearly always used it as a weapon, although he had a few party pieces that were as funny as anything I have heard from the 'professionals'. He seemed to make them up as he went along and they were seldom repeated. If you asked for a repeat performance he professed to have forgotten the item in question. My favourite was a just-about acceptable vignette in which he used the voices of Humphrey Bogart (indistinguishable from the original), Clark Gable and Donald Duck. Despite his usual 'throw away' style, he had obviously worked on this and it was very slick and professional. I never tired of hearing it. It's genesis was a grisly account we'd had from an old China hand about the (probably fabulous) goose brothels of old Shanghai.

It cast a drunken Bogart as a procurer for Gable and depended on the premise that only a duck can distinguish a lady duck from a gentleman duck. The action started with Bogart's husky, slurred 'Now listen sweetheart' and developed into an argument between Donald and Bogart, as the irascible duck tried to convince the befuddled procurer that he wasn't interested in a date with Gable – 'big movie star or not.'

Enter Gable. Donald becomes desperate and tries to explain that he 'ain't no lady.'

Gable (as Rhett Butler): 'Well frankly, Donald, I don't give a damn.' Donald emits a string of strangled and inarticulate squawks ending in a final explosive and indignant 'QUACK!'

I got on well with Amos from the first and although our humour was compatible and was the basis of our relationship, we didn't always see eye to eye. He was very conservative and could be rather staid. He believed in a rigid pecking order in every department of life. He was extremely conscientious and would never look the other way, no matter how much grief it may have saved him. I fancy his parents must have been diplomats and often thought Amos would make good administrative stock for the Colonies. At best he was meticulous, clever, unflappable, unbending, tough and humorous. I could just see him as a 19th Century District Officer in the Dark Continent, single-handedly quelling an incipient native mutiny by unconcernedly strolling among the brandished assegais, ambling to the throne of the vacillating chief and winning him over with a wisecrack in his mother tongue and a conjuring trick, before resolving the uprising by shooting dead the troublesome witch doctor.

He was an extremely good companion and we always seemed to stumble into something amusing or interesting. We shared a niggling curiosity so he never minded if I led him into a dodgy situation in the course of following up something that interested me and vice versa. He developed a very close relationship with Gus although they were as different as it is possible to be in almost every way – socially, intellectually and physically. Amos was invariably likened to the film actor Dirk Bogarde, to whom he bore an uncanny resemblance. Gus, on the other hand, resembled nobody I can think of other than Bluto – Popeye's arch-rival for Olive Oyl's hand.

He was a huge, slightly ponderous man with most of his inordinate height in his legs. Sitting down he didn't appear to be excessively tall. His dark-tanned face combined with the beetling brows, the deep set eyes and the dense, spiky black beard gave him an intense, glowering expression that made some people nervous of him. They derived entirely the wrong signals from his physiognomy. It didn't accord with his character at all. He was difficult to get close to but the effort was certainly worthwhile.

His insecurity made him quick to take offence where none was intended and, especially in his younger days, got him into a good many scrapes. Fortunately his sheer size, obvious strength and the contemplative violence that seemed to lurk in his hooded, honey-coloured eyes got him out of more trouble than it got him into. What the casual observer was not to know was that the brooding, tense expression denoted not restrained violence but a wariness of people, an almost pathological shyness stemming from the misery of an orphanage childhood. At sixteen he had his full growth but his deprived childhood had robbed him of the natural confidence of a tough, strong, intelligent youth. The sadistic, or perhaps merely the unthinking, had battened on the large, ungainly lad who couldn't or wouldn't stick up for himself. When he went to sea as a boy deckie in Scottish trawlers, his first couple of years were purgatory.

The normal pattern of a trawlerman's existence was three or four weeks at sea followed by a few days in port, often spent in an alcoholic haze. Gus had no home and hated the institutionalised comforts of the Flying Angel[11] hostel and similar refuges, so he lived on board when he could. It was often miserable and uncomfortable but he felt free for the first time in his life. After a couple of years fishing, growing financial independence boosted his confidence and he began to plan. Deep sea ships, he reckoned, would provide a more permanent home than the diesel-fugged, fish-tainted iron hulks in which he lived and worked. So he joined the Glasgow Pool.

Blue Water sailing was all he had hoped. The men were broader minded and somehow kindlier and he was no longer treated as the village idiot. As a young EDH[12] with his confidence kindled, he began to aspire to higher things and determined to sit for his tickets and make the leap from fo'c's'le to bridge. He did it, but not without a struggle and not without occasionally sinking into despair. When I met him he was a highly competent and experienced deck officer who knew the ropes better than any hand on board.

His background and experience of life could hardly have been more at variance with the rather privileged progress of Amos. I think his early traumas and setbacks and the effect of his unending and unsupported struggle to better himself had had a highly beneficial effect on his character. I think it would

---

[11] Flying Angel – The Missions To Seamen, named after its flag – a white flying angel on a blue background.

[12] EDH – Efficient Deck Hand, the rating below that of OS (Ordinary Seaman) and AB.

not be unfair to say that Gus was the nicer person but Amos the better companion, if only because we were on exactly the same wavelength. Amos and I had quickly but unconsciously developed a sort of intuitive shorthand that short-circuited nearly everyone else out and welded our compatible humour into a composite experience.

Gus was happy only with what was concrete and it infuriated him that Amos and I seemed to know instantly what the other was thinking without any obvious communication, while he was struggling to understand what was going on. Sadly we often made him the butt of our humour although I'm sure that he came in time to realise that it was without malice, and even signified a degree of affection for him.

If this makes him sound dim-witted or slow thinking, it couldn't be further from the truth. He was perceptive but loyal to the point that he was blind to the faults of his friends. His professional competence was unassailable. When Gus stowed cargo it stayed stowed. His sun sights were almost instinctive and if there was any real discrepancy between the claims of those 'shooting' the sun at the noon day sight, Gus's observations were nearly always accepted as likely to be the most correct.

Gus and Amos seemed almost to complement each other in a strange way and although we frequently struck sparks off each other, they were very congenial companions. I don't believe we had a serious disagreement in all the time we sailed together.

CHAPTER SIXTEEN

Gus was a pushover for gadgets and gimmicks. American newspapers and magazines are a rich hunting ground for naïve and gullible speculators; they are crammed with offers of fabulous artifacts and exotic services, which most people would regard with extreme scepticism. But not Gus. The more incredible the claim, the more he would covet the item and when, as invariably happened, performance didn't match the promise, he would sink to the depths of despair and grouse endlessly about charlatans and cheats. He never learned.

Amos and I concluded that his almost obsessive acquisitiveness was a legacy of his deprived childhood. At eight years of age, his sole personal possession was a battered Hornby locomotive with no wheels. He had carried it everywhere that he reasonably could, he told us, and even slept with it. He still valued it; it occupied pride of place on the top shelf of his bookcase alongside his pipe rack with his impressive collection of pipes.

One day in port we were having a pre-lunch tot in his cabin when I commented on a pair of enormous blue socks hanging on the washing line over his basin.

'Ah,' said Gus proudly, 'they're fireproof.'

I thought Amos would choke! After a moment's struggle with himself he managed to regain control enough to ask innocently. 'How much did they cost?'

Knowing Amos of old, Gus became wary. 'Why?'

'Just wondered,' said Amos. 'Were they expensive?'

'Reasonably, but they're fireproof so you'd expect them to be, wouldn't you?'

'But Good God, man,' Amos exploded, 'why would anyone need fireproof socks?'

'You never know,' Gus said darkly, becoming a little uneasy as the innate sense behind Amos's heckling began to dawn on him.

Amos sat studying Gus with a curious expression of fondness mixed with disbelief on his face. He winked at me. 'I mean, can you imagine a situation where fireproof socks would be a boon or even marginally useful?' Gus sat silently, glowering at us.

Amos pressed on. 'Did you get a certificate with them?' Gus shook his head.

'How d'you know they **are** fireproof then?'

'They wouldn't dare advertise them if they weren't.'

'Well, I think we should test them; we wouldn't want them to let you down in a hot spot would we?'

Amos leaped to his feet, fished his lighter out of his pocket and flicked it alight.

'Hey,' said Gus, 'cut it out. They're bloody expensive.'

'Not to worry, my Old. Little flame like this couldn't hurt 'em.'

He applied the flame to the toe of a sock. For a moment nothing happened. Then the sock came violently to life, withdrawing suddenly from contact with the flame, shrivelling into itself. Amos re-established contact. The tormented sock became galvanised; it writhed spectacularly and shrank vigorously from the flame. Covered with a barely discernible, shivering blue flame it contracted rapidly until a black crisp, about one tenth the size of its fellow, hung from the washing line. The speed of transition from sock to cinder was astonishing. Gus was sitting rigid as a pointer, impaling Amos with a ferocious glare. Amos seemed not to notice.

'QED, my Brave,' he said. 'I think you've been had.'

'It didn't really catch fire,' I interjected.

'True, true. But I'd say 'fireproof' was an extravagant claim. Flame retardant maybe.'

Gus rose slowly and ominously to his feet. He towered over Amos by nearly a foot.

Amos backed towards the door. 'Sorry, my good fellow, but the truth can be painful.'

'And bloody expensive. You owe me thirty bob.'

'Good Lord! Did they cost three quid?'

Gus looked puzzled. 'No, thirty bob.'

'But I only cremated one of them.'

'What good is one bloody sock to me?'

'Look here Gus,' Amos said, 'be reasonable. What were the chances that you would ever need fireproof socks in earnest?' Gus shook his head but said nothing.

Amos turned to me. 'Come on, Scribe, you're a clever sod. Can you conceive of a 'Boy stood on the burning deck' situation where Gus would need the protection of fireproof socks?'

I confessed that I couldn't.

'So it would be a pretty remote possibility?' I agreed.

With his thumbs in his armpits, Amos postured like learned counsel making a case-winning point in court. 'There you are then, my good man. Now you've lost fifty per cent of your protection you'll just have to be twice as careful, that's all. Then you'll have lost nothing. I owe you fifteen bob.'

He slid quickly into the alleyway before Gus could unscramble the spurious arithmetic.

* * * * *

Amos had a facility for avoiding trouble that we all envied. He wasn't glib or devious; he just seemed to bask in the unremitting favour of whatever gods oversee the fortunes of sailormen. At that time it was possible to buy in Japan ferocious fireworks which were subsequently banned in almost every country that had experience of them. They consisted of papier mache nodules about the size of a large acorn. They came complete with a tiny catapult and when fired against a hard surface exploded with a terrifying crack. They were not very stable.

Gus and I were taking one to pieces one day with a couple of pairs of pliers to see how it worked when it exploded, peppering Gus's face with little bits of grit. Although we had taken the precaution of wearing safety goggles, it scared him out of a year's growth; when Amos got to hear about it he gave us no peace. In our investigations we discovered that the slightly soft ones exploded under sharp pressure, while the rigid ones needed a smartish blow.

It happened that Amos had perfect watch-keeper's bowels. It was totally in character that they should function like clockwork either by rigid schooling or happy coincidence. They never prompted him at inconvenient moments and he never had to rush down off the bridge to pander to them. You could set a clock by him. He came off watch at four pm and his inviolable rule was a visit to the thunderbox ten minutes later. And 'thunderbox' was a true and accurate description.

It was a small iron closet about two feet six inches wide and four feet long; it vented just aft of the bridge by means of a large skylight. Self-interest had long since outlawed the intense, if juvenile, pleasure of dumping a bucket of water onto the victim below, but most hands kept a wary eye aloft when using it. In fact the quack had convulsed us one day by reading to us an hilarious paper he swore he was intending to send to the Lancet. It was a masterly exposition on 'Crapulitis Fenestris' – a dread condition occasioned by the need for the afflicted to sit bolt upright with the neck craned back to keep the skylight in view, when the satisfactory performance of the process demanded a totally different posture.

The string of complaints he adduced to this phenomenon made hair-raising reading. He supported his thesis with highly coloured and complex charts showing deformed parallelograms of force related to skeletal structure, normal musculature and the disposition of organs and orifices. The purpose of this tour de force was to prognosticate the probability of inner ear damage caused by diverted pressures and flattened capillaries. It was a glorious spoof.

The thunderbox was a dire place. If you inadvertently dropped the seat, the resulting crash was magnified a hundredfold and reverberated endlessly within the tiny iron confines until your head spun. Here it was that Gus intended to wreak vengeance on Amos for the cremated sock and for his endless ribbing over the firework incident. We gently massaged six of the vicious little balls until their structure was broken down, then just before four o'clock, we taped them carefully under the toilet seat. The scene being set, we retired to Gus's room just up the alleyway from where we could see the entrance to the shower and toilet. Gus didn't think it would work.

'He's far too light. I reckon he'll float down onto the seat like a feather.'

The millenium had arrived. At ten past four there was no sign of Amos. At four-fifteen the mate appeared and barged into the toilet. We were horrified. The mate was a rangy, pink man who never tanned. His head was large and bony with sparse, sandy-coloured hair; his eyebrows and lashes were of the whitest white. He looked like a farmer and was universally known as 'Porker'. He was also quite the nicest man I knew and a gentleman to boot. In the five months I had sailed with him I had never known him to swear or use a coarse expression. He was intelligent and energetic to a fault. His command of English was such that a tongue lashing from him could cut you to the bone and shame you without his drawing breath but without giving the slightest offence.

His energy was legendary. I had once seen him single-handedly beat a much younger pair at deck tennis. He did everything at the double; he raced up ladders two rungs at a time, he threw himself into chairs, he slammed doors, he bellowed and blustered. If anyone could detonate our booby trap, he would – with his weight – hurling himself onto the seat from his considerable standing height. And thus it proved. The result was beyond our wildest expectations. Seconds after he had crashed through the bog door there came a thunderous, sustained explosion. It roared and rippled, folding in on itself then expanding again before dying reluctantly in a series of multiple, tinny echoes. For a few seconds there was an eerie silence, then heads began to appear through doors and portholes; enquiring voices could be heard speaking in hushed tones. The thunderclap penetrated even the quack's whisky haze. Looking in his long johns like a pneumatic John L. Sullivan, he shuffled to the doorway and peered round his modesty curtain to see Porker emerge from the bog, clutching his trousers to him with shaking hands, hair in disarray and eyes revolving wildly, his head and shoulders covered in little rusty flakes of paint.

'Probably something he ate,' the quack mumbled unsympathetically and withdrew.

As Porker staggered unsteadily to his cabin a shaken Gus turned to me. 'God's truth,' he muttered, 'would you have believed it?'

My ears were still ringing. 'Bloody Amos, dodged the column again,' was all I could think to say.

'Hey listen,' Gus said. 'Porker's a good skin, we'll have to tell him. When he's got his head on straight he's bound to start asking questions; he'll think we're a right pair of prats if we don't own up first.'

It was the longest speech I had ever heard Gus make. But he was right. Porker was no dope. He'd soon work out who were the perpetrators – especially as our misadventure with the little bomb was common knowledge.

'What's his poison, Gus?' I asked.

'Dunno. Whisky I think.'

'Lookit, you hang on here. I'll pry a bottle of Scotch out of the poison dwarf and we'll go and make peace.'

The poison dwarf, more politely known as 'Pompey', was the chief steward who lorded it over the bar. Although it was only about half past four and the bar didn't open till five, I hoped to acquire a bottle as an olive branch. I should have known better. I rattled my finger nails down the jalousie door of his quarters and entered. It was normal practice. Pompey was a ferocious little man, permanently angry and at war with the world. He took instant offence at the most innocent actions by anybody, except father. He was on top form.

'Don't you ever bloody knock?'

'Sorry, Pompey, I thought I had.'

'Waddaya want?'

Sitting stark naked on his settee cutting his toenails with an enormous pair of shears, he looked like a garden gnome badly made in suet. His bald head gleamed white as he leered up at me from between his scrawny knees. As he wielded the huge scissors, shards of horny, flint-hard toenail zipped round the hot, tiny cabin like shrapnel. I stepped back out of range.

'Pompey, can you let me have a bottle of Scotch?'

'Certainly. Five o-bloody-clock.'

'But I need it now.'

He reached down his back and scratched between his shoulder blades with the point of the scissors and glared at me with his goat-like eyes.

'Bar opens at five.'

'It's a matter of life and death, Pompey; come on shape up.'

'Then you'll just have to bloody well die. Five o'clock. Now bugger off.'

I turned away, furious with him. 'Thanks a lot, Pompey. I'll pass your message on to the old man.'

He leaped to his feet 'You don't drink Scotch do you?'

'Nope.'

'You didn't tell me it was for the old man.'

'Oh, didn't I?'

I turned back. Standing up he was even more grotesque. His tiny five-foot frame was loosely draped with a mottled skin apparently several sizes too large. His breasts hung like ironing boards and a double pelmet of loose skin almost covered his shrivelled unmentionables. He looked as if he were slowly melting. He reached into a locker and withdrew a bottle of Bell's. I took it and picked up the chit book on his desk. 'Got a pen?'

'What're you signing a chit for?' He looked at me with sudden awareness. 'That's not for the old man is it?'

'No. I never said it was.'

His face went blood red and he trembled with rage. 'You crafty get! You conned me. I won't forget you.'

'Shouldn't be too difficult even for you, Pompey, you see me every day.'

Enormously pleased with myself for having outwitted Pompey, no mean con man himself, I made my exit. Gus was sitting anxiously on the end of his settee looking up the alleyway towards Porker's cabin. He looked at me with relief, then at the bottle in my hand.

'Oh, you got one.' He produced an identical bottle from under the settee. 'Didn't think Pompey'd cooperate, so I swiped one of the quack's. He won't miss it and he can have it back when the bar opens.'

'Come on,' I said. 'Let's get it over with.'

We rapped on the mate's door and at his 'Yes?' I pushed Gus in and entered behind him, peering round his protective bulk. Porker was sitting in his armchair. He was still in mild shock There was a telling rigidity about his stance and a touch of nystagmus still trembled in the protuberant blue eyes. He was clutching the arms of the chair with his blotchy, pink hands.

'Well?'

'We've come to apologise…' I began.

He looked suddenly haunted. 'So it was you. Why me? What did I do?'

'It was an accident,' Gus mumbled.

Porker's voice quivered noticeably and there was a slight rise in its pitch. 'Accident? Accident? How in God's holy name can you accidentally leave a bloody bomb in the bog.'

'Well we put it there right enough,' I said, 'but it was intended for Amos.'

He relaxed slightly and Gus took up the story. 'Amos always goes in at ten past four. We were after him. You were supposed to have been on the bridge.'

Porker shook his head slowly. 'How did you achieve it? I didn't see anything.'

Gus held out his enormous paw. The little yellow nodule looked like a mustard seed in his plate-like palm. 'We taped them under the seat – six of them. But only three went off.' Gus replaced the bomb in his pocket.

'Well you can thank your lucky stars that only three **did** go off. If they'd all exploded the seat would have flipped me through the skylight like a bloody mortar bomb. It was a damn silly thing to do. You both ought to know better.' He looked at us thoughtfully for a long moment, then continued. 'I should think that mining a toilet seat would contravene the Geneva Convention. I don't know what penalty that should attract.'

I held out the bottle of Bell's. 'What's that?' he asked.

'An antidote to exploding balls,' I said.

Porker nodded slowly. 'Something wrong here. I'm a navigator, a mathematician of sorts. I find my way round the surface of this planet by the happy confluence of numbers. Equity is exquisite. Imbalance offends.' He leaned towards us to emphasise his point. 'And I might tell you it often augurs ill for somebody. Has done throughout history. You might think it's superstitious. But I don't; I think it's a bad omen for you. For both of you.'

I looked at Gus. From his expression an onlooker would be entitled to assume that he had been set upon by a plague of lice. He was staring at Porker, struggling to grasp the meaning of the flood of words. Porker continued his gentle tirade, striking his fingers into the palm of his hand to emphasise points in his dissertation.

'This outrage was perpetrated by **two** cretins. There were **two** victims – one actual, one potential. I nearly lost **two** valuable bits of my esteemed person, and yet...' he paused and looked meaningfully at the bottle of Scotch.

'Ah, Mr. Prime,' I said obsequiously, 'you misunderstand us. This was intended only as a deposit; we wanted you to have it before you went on watch.'

I nudged Gus, gestured with my head and waggled the bottle of Bell's at him. After a moment's hesitation he understood and dashed off. Porker and I stared at each other, he now at ease and slumped back in his chair, arms folded across his chest and a rather smug smile creasing his broad face. Gus returned with the second bottle. Porker reached out for it then sat back with a bottle in each hand, his forearms resting on the arms of his chair. He nodded sagely and looked sternly at us down his considerable nose.

'It is possible – by no means certain – but possible, that by your prompt action in attempting to expiate your unprovoked, if unintended, assault upon my venerable person, you may have propitiated the gods who protect all-powerful chief officers from explosive emasculation.'

We salaamed and moved to make our exit. Gus was first out of the door and I was about to follow when Porker called out, 'By the by...' I stuck my head back round the door. '...it wouldn't have worked you know. Amos is far too light and delicate, he'd never have triggered them. You'll have to think of something else.'

He grinned at me and raised a bottle in a mocking toast. 'Cheers, you dumbell.'

I withdrew, closed the door and stood for a moment in the alleyway, smiling to myself and thinking. Porker Prime was a very nice man.

CHAPTER SEVENTEEN

In one context a sense of humour is simply a sense of proportion. The quality was singularly lacking in the officials of a minor port lying miles up a tortuous river, the colour and consistency of mulligatawny soup, in a Central American Republic. I shall call it El Panazuela – just in case I have to go back! The place was low lying and surrounded by fever-ridden, mosquito-haunted swamps. It must have represented a vision of hell to Stout Cortez, or whoever was responsible for placing it on the world atlas. Uniformed officials were everywhere. They were extraordinarily bloody-minded and arrogant and permanently on their dignity. Politically the place was a tinderbox. To make matters worse it was hot, steamy and extremely dull; the slightest movement squeezed copious sweat from every pore. The people wore a 'cooked-in' expression of ennui and sheer disenchantment and seemed to go in fear of their lives and liberty. Murder was a greater hazard than a road accident, often erupting suddenly from seemingly innocuous circumstances.

One of our engineers was in a bar one morning when an argument developed between two barflies and the barman. The barman settled the argument by drawing a gun from under the counter and shooting the less-favoured contender dead. Everyone else departed precipitately so it wasn't very good for trade. Trade hit rock bottom so far as the barman was concerned when the police arrived a few minutes later and poured a barrage of indiscriminate fire into the tiny bar. Our chap watched in disbelief as the police carried away three blood-soaked bundles on stretchers.

One of the problems was the proliferation of guns. They were regarded as casually as we would regard cigarette lighters.

It was not at all unusual to hear fusillades of gunfire throughout the night and often during the day as well. What they represented we never knew, but Gus did find out about one of them. For some reason that escapes me now, he wanted to buy a pair of maracas. The local version was very attractive; they were made from natural gourds, delicately coloured with vegetable dyes and decorated with poker work. Gus was tracking down a pair when he saw a dog lift its leg against a market stall. The stall owner walked nonchalantly round to the front and killed the dog with a single pistol shot. Gus was so close that he was splattered with the animal's blood and was nearly deafened by the muzzle blast.

Looking back I suppose it was not unreasonable that the permanently depressed population should seek to enliven their dreary lives by whatever means were to hand. But it seemed to us that they risked shortening them considerably by playing with guns.

On arrival at such ports – and there were several on our itinerary – there were strict rules to follow. Officials from an unbelievable number of government and quasi-government agencies descended on the ship for a day out. Customs, immigration, police, health, agricultural authorities, the criminal bureau, security services, coast guard and navy, port administrators and hordes of other unidentifiable semi-officials – all in uniforms festooned with gay, multi-coloured medal ribbons and sprinkled with brass insignia – came aboard in droves. Their invariable badge of office seemed to be an enormous revolver in a glossy leather holster, white gloves and mirror–effect sunglasses. They were accompanied by heavily armed, olive-green clad body guards or assault troops. The regiment of troops spread like smoke through the ship, looking for unsecured portholes or anything not welded down. The prime dons were escorted to the saloon where cartons of cigarettes, boxes of cigars, bottles of whisky, brandy and gin and plates of small delicacies were laid out.

These refreshments were designed to facilitate business by sustaining the officials in the onerous task of examining the ship's documents, filling in and rubber stamping mountains of forms and, hopefully, of ultimately declaring the ship, her crew and contents to be safe, clean and legal and fit to be exposed to the rigours of thirty-six hours in El Panazuela. Normally the ritual of clearing the ship inward took as long as was necessary to satisfy the appetites of all the officials involved. It often became apparent why they needed so many retainers to help them. It was not unusual to see two or three support troops helping their superior down the gangway. He would be eased into the back of his twenty-year-old, black, shiny American sedan to be whisked off to enjoy his alcohol-induced siesta in the privacy of his own secretariat.

This occasion was no different to scores of others. The ship was cleared and most of the officials had departed leaving the health inspector making his rounds – checking the galley, the storerooms and taking samples of the potable water. He had with him two young men, both of whom sported the ubiquitous pistol and both of whom were somewhat the worse for wear for having been exposed to the brandy bottle. Having completed their rounds with the inspector, the two guards were waiting by the head of the gangway while their superior made his final foray to the saloon. One was leaning against the gangway stanchion, idly picking his teeth, while his colleague sat rather dopily on the hatch, elbow on thigh and chin in hand, dreamily contemplating the middle distance through a brandy glow. His holster, low on his thigh in the best 'Wild West' tradition, was pressed against the hatch board and had gaped slightly, allowing the pistol to slide partly out. On the butt end dangled a gay, multi-coloured tassel and this attracted the attention of Lorrie. Before anyone could guess her intention and intervene she had sidled over to the guard and as slick as an Epsom pickpocket, snatched the pretty tassel.

Gibbons are tremendously strong in the arm; I was close on fifteen stone and Loretta could effortlessly pull me off balance if she braced herself. Nevertheless, she was astonished at grabbing a silk tassel to find herself custodian of one-and-a-half pounds of oily metal. She was nonplussed for a moment but quickly recovered her wits when the victim of her larceny yelled at her. Two things happened simultaneously. The second guard, galvanised by his colleague's shout of alarm, spun on his heel and drew his pistol while Lorrie, terrified at being bawled at, made a flying leap for the boat deck safety rail four or five feet above her. Unfortunately being encumbered by the pistol she made a botch of it, landed clumsily and dropped the pistol which fell onto the lower deck and went off with a fearsome bang. The bullet hit the boat deck fish plate above the gangway guard's head, ricocheted and howled across the wharf to shatter the windscreen of the health inspector's Studebaker. The somnolent driver went into a convulsion and the various guards and attendants still loitering on the wharf scattered for shelter.

The tooth-picking guard in his befuddled state, presumably convinced that he was under attack from a homicidal ape, started to blast away at Loretta and everyone on deck dived for cover. The first guard, not too sure what was happening, assumed from his colleague's aggressive reaction that there was, indeed, cause for alarm. He shouted to the men on the wharf and the next thing we knew an absolute barrage was whizzing over our heads from a variety of weapons. Sparks, soot, rust and paint chips were flying from the funnel, derricks and samson posts as they liberally hosed the only parts of the ship's upper works that they could see from their position on the wharf. Bullets shattered the wheelhouse and chartroom windows and the thick, heavy glass fragments burst inwards on the old man's tiger who was gathering up mugs and plates from inside, cutting him about the head and shoulders. He was fortunate not to have been more seriously injured.

After an incredibly noisy interlude, which to our later astonishment we found had lasted for only a few seconds, peace returned as the various pieces of ordnance ran out of ammunition or common sense took over. There was a long, embarrassed silence while everyone tried to unscramble the sequence of events and decide what had actually happened. Men came running up the gangway to stand sheepishly on deck; the health inspector, more tipsy than ever, stood in the saloon doorway swaying slightly and querulously demanding from his acolytes what was going on. They were in the worse possible position to advise him. The brief nightmare began to turn into farce as it became obvious that nobody really knew what had happened but tried to explain it anyway, at the tops of their voices, to everyone else.

No harm appeared to have been done except for the chipped paintwork and dents on the upperworks and the expenditure of a great deal of nervous energy. We didn't find Carreras – the tiger – and the damage to the bridge windows till later. We smoothed ruffled feathers with a few judicious bottles and everything gradually returned to normal except for poor little Lorrie – the unwitting cause of it all. Trembling pathetically she clung to Gus with her face buried in his hairy neck, her fingers entwined in his hair and clothing, and refused to budge.

Next morning the nightmare returned tenfold. The ship's agent accompanied by the port commander together with his usual armed entourage, appeared at the old man's door. They had come to 'arrest' Loretta. The animal had been declared dangerous because she might have caused injury or death to officials of the Republic of El Panazuela or to members of the ship's crew. Her continued freedom could not be permitted. Unfortunately father was not thinking too clearly. He had just received a report from the mate about the condition of Carreras and the damage caused by the storm of bullets to the bridge house and the ship's upperworks. He responded by blasting the port captain for the drunken behaviour of his men which had resulted in personal injury and great damage. He refused to allow them to remove anything, living or dead, from his ship and demanded an apology and compensation. His recalcitrance virtually signed Loretta's death warrant.

The port commander formally advised the old man that the ship would not be allowed to work, that no one would be permitted ashore and that no outward clearance would be possible until his dictum had been enforced. That was that. The ship was sealed off and virtually under arrest until Loretta had been handed over. The situation had suddenly taken a very serious turn indeed and the complications could multiply endlessly. Fortunately the ship's agent was also consul for several countries including the country of our flag and registration. Rasmussen was a sharp and canny man. He permitted tempers to cool and attitudes to slacken, then he got to work.

As a result of his diplomacy, some hours later a deputation of fairly high-ranking officials arrived on board to discuss the matter. It was virtually a trial with prosecution but no defence. The outcome was disastrous. Loretta must go, then everything would be back to normal.

'What will happen to her?' I asked. Rasmussen spoke rapidly in Spanish to the 'court' then translated for us.

'I regret very much that she must be destroyed.'

I felt as if I had received the death sentence. It was so unjust, the poor little creature had committed no crime. All she had done was to investigate a pretty tassel. The incident had arisen because of the indiscipline and drunken overreaction of a bunch of Central American cowboys. Now they were on their high horse and trying to save face.

'Why can't we simply lock her up until we leave port?' I suggested. 'She could do no harm to anyone then.'

Rasmussen conferred with the officials, turned back and made a 'hopeless' gesture with his hands and shoulders. 'I'm sorry. Their decision is final. The animal must be destroyed.'

'How will that be done?' the old man asked. A further exchange took place.

'No one seems to know,' Rasmussen said. 'It's outside their experience, but I suppose it will be shot.'

The mate was sitting frosty faced, thinking about his paintwork and this grisly business was the final straw. 'More likely they'll bloody kick her to death just for the fun of it.'

There was a frozen silence. Rasmussen went rigid and I wondered why. Then the senior official spoke in perfect English, although the entire proceedings thus far had been conducted in Spanish with the agent translating. Now I understood his reaction. The mate's outburst had robbed us of any goodwill at all. They had all undoubtedly understood the insinuation. The senior man's response removed any doubt.

'We are not barbarians, Captain. We understand the appeal of animals, my own children have a cat who lives like an empress. Nevertheless, our sad decision must be obeyed. Even in your country I expect that the owners of an animal are responsible for its action. The animal is dangerous and the ship will not be permitted to work or to leave until it is taken to our custody. I am sorry, but that is our decision.'

It was quite a speech and he was very angry. His face was flushed and his eyes were like dagger points as he glared from the mate to the old man. I thought his anger was partly due to embarrassment. It seemed an extreme attitude to take over what was basically a trivial matter. He was obviously an educated and sophisticated man. It seemed a faint chance. I caught his eye.

'May I show you this dangerous animal?' His colour darkened, he stared at me for some time then relaxed slightly. He seemed to be about to agree, but one of the other officials interjected something, there was an animated exchange and his expression hardened.

'That will not be necessary.'

My heart sank but I pressed on. 'If she is to be destroyed would you permit us to do it? We wouldn't wish her to be frightened, especially as she is innocent.'

The barb went home to the hilt. He looked hard at me for a long moment and then without consulting his colleagues gave his consent.

'This is permitted but it must be witnessed by my representative and the ship is under embargo until the matter is concluded.'

By lunch time the news had spread throughout the ship and the saloon was buzzing with indignation and exotic suggestions to resolve the crisis. But there seemed no way out of it. We put it to the quack 'There's nothing for it Doc; only you can put her down so she doesn't suffer. Those bastards would make a sport of it.'

He refused absolutely and it was not until Amos took him aside for a few minutes earnest conversation that he reluctantly agreed. We had told the authorities that it would be done at three o'clock and they agreed to have their observer on board at that time.

At two-thirty the quack came puffing up to the top accommodation, his face aglow, excited and conspiratorial. 'We must be bonkers,' he said. 'It's simple. I'll inject her with enough dope to knock her out so the bloody executioner can see its done, then we drop her over the side into a boat. We lock her up till she comes to and keep her out of sight.'

Gus was ecstatic. 'We'll only have to keep her quiet overnight. We'll be away by mid-morning.'

It was an uplifting thought but I thought it was too simple and too good to be true. I hated saying it but the idea was desperate and a non-starter. 'They're not that daft. What's to stop the observer from walking over as we drop her over the wall? He could hardly miss seeing the boat and concluding the obvious. They'd be sure to drag her off and brutalise her out of spite – and we'd all probably wind up in jug.'

Amos lit one of his vile lunkahs,[13] tilted his chair back and gazed silently over our heads, puffing clouds of pungent blue smoke into the fan suspended from the deckhead. 'I think Doc's cracked it,' he said at last. 'It could be done but not with a boat.'

Gus made a loud, explosive exclamation of disgust. 'Talk bloody sense, Amos. Bic's right, they're not stupid.'

'Shut up and listen,' replied Amos, 'we haven't got long. The organ grinder (**chief engineer**) has a damned great landing net with a handle than can reach the water from the well deck. I reckon if he leaned out of the sickbay porthole he could stretch forward far enough without being seen from the main deck. We drop Loretta into the net and he could haul her to safety quick enough for the observer to be allowed to check the water and convince himself she'd been dumped.'

We stared at him in admiration. 'Christ!' said Doc. 'It's perfect. If we can keep the bloody executioner far enough away for a couple of minutes, we'll pull it off.'

I felt hope and relief surge through me. 'That's simple. We'll just get Gus to glare at him while you're putting the needle in. That should gain us a few minutes. If we have plenty of weight to make a good splash, then insist he checks the water, we'll do it.'

It was a brilliantly simple solution. All it required was timing, a few minutes grace with the observer far enough away at the critical moment, and the will. Had we had time to digest it – to think and talk about it – our courage would probably have failed. But we had only a few minutes to set it up and we went along on the flood. We were committed before we had properly analysed what we were about to do, or

---

[13] A black, nobbly very pungent Indian cheroot. Amos bought them in tens bound with a raffia band. They never seemed to dry out and always tasted hot and musty. I much preferred the green Filipino cigars – a box of 25 could be bought for a tin of 50 English cigarettes – then 1/9 (approx 9p) for 50.

to consider the only two possible outcomes and the consequences of either.

Luck was with us; the observer was the health inspector. I suspect it was a little 'poetic justice' administered by the senior official. To make the man who was ultimately responsible for the fiasco witness the results of his lack of control was the sort of sophisticated touch I would have expected from him. It worked in our favour.

The inspector was anxious, embarrassed, very nervous and over-effusive. While we rigged the charade on deck, the old man – stern and icily correct (and totally innocent of the intended masquerade) – entertained him. It must have been an ordeal for the wretched little man. At three o'clock they came out of father's quarters and stood on the after end of the accommodation boat deck on the starboard side where they could overlook the action that was to take place on the hatch below.

Amos was frantic. 'That's no bloody good,' he hissed. 'If the silly sod stays there he'll see the whole thing. We've got to get him off the boat deck or on the other side.'

Gus was almost in tears. 'We can't tell the old man, he wouldn't allow it.'

'Damn and blast. It's the only way, Gus,' I said. 'We'll have to tell him what's going on and hope he won't blow the whistle on us. He's the only one who can get that damned fool out of the way. Doc, can you break a needle or something? Waste some time. We've got to tell father.'

A considerable crowd had gathered and I wondered for a moment if some silly rescue attempt was contemplated. They were intensely angry and their obvious hostility had begun to work on the inspector. Gus, with Lorrie in his arms unconcernedly inspecting his ears, was sitting on the hatch glaring up at him – and an angry glare from Gus had the penetrating power of a titanium-tipped drill bit. I pitied the poor little man. As I reached the top of the ladder intending to make the old man privy to our conspiracy, the Spaniard said something to him and they turned away. The old man called to me over his shoulder 'Let me know when it's done, Mister,' and led the way back to his quarters.

It didn't seem possible. I felt a tremendous surge of hope and disbelief. 'It can't be as simple as this,' I thought. 'It just isn't possible.' I returned to the lower deck.

'Crikey, that was quick,' said Amos. 'Whatever did you say?'

I smiled smugly and tapped the side of my nose with my forefinger, thereby gaining for myself an instant and totally undeserved reputation as a 'Mr Fixit'. Suddenly, easily, we had achieved the impossible. It seemed incredible. Doc put Lorrie to sleep and just below us and well out of view of the deck, the second engineer leaned out of the sickbay porthole with the Chief's huge landing net.

When all was ready I rapped on the captain's stateroom door on the port side.

'Come!' he boomed.

I entered. 'We're just about to drop her over the wall, Sir.'

They rose from their chairs, the health inspector avoiding my eye. I was staring hard at him; we had to keep the pressure on. The captain was heading for his starboard side door.

'Could you please come this way, Sir,' I said.

He was slightly taken aback; he looked from his port to his starboard door and back again. He didn't quite shrug but gave me a shrewd, sideways look that made me nervous, then he followed me out on deck with the inspector trailing unhappily. We walked aft to the ladder and at the top we stopped to look down on the scene on the other side of the ship, separated from us by the width of number three hatch.

Gus stood by the bulwark with a limp Lorrie in his arms. Everyone was glaring up at us, the hostility was palpable – I was glad I was on their side. When we were in position Gus took Lorrie by one arm while the third engineer held a bundle of old fire irons apparently attached to her leg. She dangled limply from Gus's massive paw. I felt my throat constrict and there came a stinging in my nose that made my eyes water. I had to swallow hard to keep control; she was such a pathetic sight. Gus and the third leaned over the rail... there was a splash and they straightened up, stood irresolutely for a few seconds then walked away. The small crowd dispersed rapidly.

At the head of the ladder the three of us stood silently, the old man and I staring hard at the inspector. If there was any doubt in his mind, despite what he had just witnessed, my genuine tears must have convinced him. I wasn't sure we had pulled it off. It had seemed so certain and final and utterly convincing that I wondered if the major players in the farce had backed out at the last moment without telling me. I was not surprised that the little man accepted the evidence of his eyes. He reached for my limp hand, shook it vigorously then turned to father and shook his hand.

'I regret very much this tragedy, Sir. I shall make now my good report for your ship.' He scuttled down the ladder, almost ran down the gangway and jumped thankfully into his car.

It had been impossibly easy. I was glad we'd had no time to frighten ourselves off the idea. The inspector had checked nothing. Although, as Amos said, his earlier foray onto the starboard side boat deck had been a blessing in disguise. He'd had a good view of the ship's side and the water from the break of the bow to the starboard quarter had been clear. He was completely convinced that Lorrie had been dropped into the water. Sadly, Lorrie took a violent dislike to the quack. The needle must have hurt her. She came round eventually but for a long time she avoided him. Although he was saddened he took the philosophical view.

When the old man discovered the conspiracy he was furious. I feared for his sanity for a while; we marvelled that he didn't have a seizure. He threatened everyone with the sack but reserved his particular brand of verbal violence for me as, I suppose, I had personally misled him. It was an accident that I had been cast in that role but there was little I could have said to reduce the impact of his assault. He wasn't a man easily convinced by excuses. The only thing to do was to duck your head and ride out the storm – which was easy enough when I reflected on what we had achieved.

He would never accept that the mate wasn't party to the farce, which was unfair. He gave him a savage dressing down in front of us, then stuck his hatchet-like nose right in Donald's face and bellowed at him, 'If anyone ever plays ducks and ----ing drakes with me again in my ship you won't see his arse for dust!' He relaxed and glared round at us, all in a state of semi-shock. Then he abruptly stuck his face into Donald's again and spraying him with little gobbets of spittle howled 'and I mean **anyone!**'

Some months later I found him sitting in a deckchair with Lorrie squatting between his feet. He was feeding her with pieces of chopped cheese, her favourite delicacy. Holding his clenched hand containing the cheese in both of hers, she was chuntering at him between morsels, wriggling on her bottom in excitement, her gaze flicking anxiously between his face and his clenched fist. He squinted at me over the top of his gold-framed, half-moon glasses and gave me his curiously boyish smile.

'Pretty little lass, isn't she? I'm glad we were able to save her.'

When I reported the encounter to the others later we laughed a lot over the 'we'.

'Cheeky old bugger,' said Donald in disgust.

CHAPTER EIGHTEEN

We had accommodation for eight first class passengers and by re-rigging the after centre castle accommodation we could carry thirty 'steerage' passengers in something less than luxury. Conditions were dreadful, more suited to cattle than fare-paying passengers. We only used the accommodation once in four years. There was no natural light; the iron cots were arranged in three 'dormitories' and there was precious little privacy. I can't remember now how catering was arranged, but they ate at a long refectory table centrally placed to separate the two rows of cots in the largest of the dormitories. Concepts of comfort for 'steerage' passengers had certainly left something to be desired when *Bellatrix* was built.

In contrast, the first class accommodation was quite luxurious. *Bellatrix* was built at the height of elegance in ship design in terms of early twentieth century shipbuilding. The door and porthole furniture was made in thick, chunky, solid brass and the cabins were handsomely wood-panelled This tended to make them rather dark but gave them the ambience of rooms in a stately home. The bunks were wide and, with forward-facing portholes and large side windows that wound down with big brass handles, the cabins were very comfortable while the ship was under way.

A good many people enjoyed travelling in her and we had some fairly regular passengers. The problem was that as there were practically no amenities for passengers, they were virtually integrated with the ship's officers. Presumably this was part of the attraction for certain people, but it was a pain in the neck for us. Cranky passengers were the bane of our lives. In general, we found that the more illustrious the status of the passenger, the more friendly and reasonable he or she was likely to be.

As an illustration, we once had as passengers a very senior administrator of an island group with his wife and daughter. They were with us for only a week or so. The circumstances were somewhat unusual I should think, as they would normally be almost certain to have travelled by other means, but I can't remember the details. They were the most delightful, unstuffy people you could hope to meet. We had a ship's dog and early one morning the husband appeared at my door and asked if I could find him a couple of sheets of paper or some cardboard. I rummaged around, found what he wanted and stepped outside as he walked away. To my astonishment he walked over to where the dog had committed an indiscretion, scooped it up and threw it over the wall. He could have ignored it, reported it, or summoned a sailor or steward to clean it up, but he chose to do it himself – certainly not the act of an arrogant man.

I played chess with his wife most nights. They asked the old man if they could use our smoke room (which was positioned thwart – ships on the after end of the prom deck with doors on both port and starboard sides, so was quite cool) instead of the dark and gloomy little box provided for first class passengers. We put it to the vote and nobody objected. They came and drank with us, swapping stories and playing at cards or Monopoly – their presence wasn't the least inhibiting or unwelcome.

In mainliners carrying twenty-four or thirty passengers at eighteen knots on a hundred-and-ten-day round trip (give or take a tide) to the Far East, passengers were tolerated as a necessary evil. They gave some priority in the Suez Canal transit. Some of them could be quite snooty. Lady Uppity-Passenger was perhaps an extreme example but there were some who could run her a close second.

In those ships, in those Imperial days, from time to time we carried a good many service personnel and colonial administrators together with their wives and families. We found the most insufferable ladies were usually those who had probably married their husbands during the war in fairly humble circumstances. The war and exceptional ability had carried the husband's career aloft; he had changed and gained the stature commensurate with his ascending status while she, frequently, was unable to keep abreast. The almost invariable result was that such a wife became either shy and withdrawn or loud and domineering – ladies we described as 'all mink coat and no knickers'.

'Do you know who my husband is?' one such harridan demanded of our raunchy Australian second engineer who had upset her somehow.

'No,' he replied, 'point the poor old bastard out and I'll go and sympathise with him.'

We had one passenger taken off in a straight-jacket. It was at the height of the Communist insurgency in Malaya and he was from upcountry, from a particularly dangerous and troubled area. He was going home on sick leave to recover from his experiences. The poor chap was in a very distressed and unstable state. He had survived several ambushes and grenade attacks and hadn't had an uninterrupted night's sleep for months. His nerves were shot to pieces. To make matters worse he had an insect bite in his groin which had gone badly septic and resisted all efforts to reduce the infection. After he had left the ship the quack told us that the poison had swollen his scrotum to the size of a small melon.

On the way home he began to drink heavily. I suppose the combination of all these factors and the sudden cessation of the pressures that had been oppressing him for month after terrifying month threw him into a mental spin. He began to act strangely. Mild madness is quite amusing to those not directly involved and his slight eccentricity was tolerated at first. Sadly he deteriorated rapidly. He thought poison gas was being blown at him out of the punkah louvre[14] vents; loudspeakers of the public address system were microphones picking up his every word and he tore several off the bulkhead. Assassins waited for him round every corner and the dark of the night was peopled with horror for him. He burst into several cabins – passengers' and crew's – in the dead of night seeking company and this frightened people. Our Chinese stewards were perceived as a threat to him and he abused several of them quite madly. He heard and saw things that no one else could detect.

Matters came to a head when he stole a cleaver from the galley one night, 'for protection,' he told a fellow passenger. When this development was reported to father, he had the poor chap moved to a larger stateroom where he was confined with a permanent watch on him. In Genoa – just seven days from home – he was taken ashore to hospital.

One of the most interesting passengers we had in *Bellatrix* was a lady etymologist and anthropologist. She was in her early middle age and had spent the war in counter-espionage. There seemed few languages she was not able to analyse for us, so presumably she was able to converse in them. From our speech patterns and pronunciation she was able to suggest our backgrounds and sometimes even the dialects spoken by our parents. It was remarkable. Sadly her thought processes took place at such a rarefied level that it was difficult for us to converse on equal terms. After working with the aboriginal Malayans – a shy and not very well-documented people – she was going to do field studies with a recently discovered tribe in the Philippines.

In those days, before relatively cheap transport was available to the masses, there were odd pockets throughout the world where strange characters seemed to roost. They flitted through a sort of twilight existence in far distant places and their life-styles seemed out of phase with modern living and

---

[14] Air circulation/ventilation system.

aspirations. As passengers or as brief acquaintances met on the beach their life may touch yours briefly and then they were gone like wisps of smoke, leaving you wondering if they really did exist.

The most memorable of the 'wisp of smoke' characters I ever met was Jake. He was a freelance charter pilot who travelled with us as passenger on the five-day run from Singapore to Hong Kong. He had come aboard briefly in Port Swettenham with an absolute mountain of luggage and aircraft parts, then travelled by train to Singapore where he rejoined us. He had recently irretrievably broken an aeroplane somewhere and had raw scars and a black eye to prove it.

Over the next few years it was almost as if we were stalking each other. We would meet in the oddest places, but always in passing, and I rarely saw him without an outstandingly pretty girl on his arm. He could hardly have been described as a matinee idol but he very evidently had enormous appeal for the ladies.

He was considerably older than us – probably mid to late thirties – and was inclined to portliness. Before the war he had been a professional civil pilot and joined the RAF in 1938. As a Blenheim pilot he had taken part in some of the earliest sorties of the war, dropping leaflets over Germany. He had been shot down on his second mission. At least, that was how we construed it. He had been chucking waste paper all over Germany, he told us, which irritated the fanatically tidy Hun. Some young men ascended to remonstrate with him and irresponsibly damaged his machine. From their boorish behaviour and lack of consideration for a stranger in their midst, he had judged them to be hooligans; in trying to avoid conclusions with them he had become lost in murky weather. After flying round for some time hopelessly lost, plane damaged and fuel running low, he saw flat, marshy ground dotted with black and white cows beneath him through a break in the murk. 'Ah, Norfolk,' he thought and set the plane down to find that he was still in the heart of the Third Reich.

We found out later that he had, in fact, been very badly wounded in the head, neck and arm. He had stuck with the plane and landed it because he was much too weak and badly hurt to bail out. His entire war had been spent in a series of prison camps and hospitals and in the final one, in Silesia, he had fractured his leg while playing football. It had mended badly and although surgeons after the war had managed to improve its strength and performance, his flying days seemed to be over.

The Berlin Airlift in the late forties reprieved him. Desperately short of pilots, the administration welcomed him and he put in an incredible number of hours. From thence he graduated into freelancing all over the world. He had flown in every continent on every conceivable sort of job in every known type of plane still airworthy – and several that were not. He had flown for governments, for rebels, for civil administrations and for private bosses. He had set up his own airline and had twice seen it crash in flames – literally. He had survived the most incredible adventures.

In South America he had been hired to fly some machinery into an isolated spot and had been told to land on a sandbar in the river. It was perfectly adequate for the aircraft he was flying and it had been done many times before. He set her down as instructed and as it came to a stop the machine began to sink. He was not sure if his employers had conned him into landing as an insurance fiddle on the loss of the plane and the freight, whether he had picked the wrong sandbar, or whether the sandbar was the right one but had changed characteristics due to wind or tidal effects.

He and his co-pilot had only enough time to run along the wing and leap frantically as far as they could to what seemed to be firm ground. Fortunately it was. The story of their struggle to return to civilisation with no supply of food or water, armed with only a pistol, a pocketknife and a dodgy compass, was an epic in itself.

For a short time he was private pilot to a film mogul and from that it seemed a short step to 'action flying' (he refused to call it 'stunt' flying) for various films. He loved the job and the benefits it brought him – mostly suntanned camp followers – but the attitude of his fellow flyers sickened him. They seemed to court danger, he told us, as if they got a sexual thrill out of it. Their antics were dangerous. 'Sod that for a game of soldiers,' he said. 'There's simpler and more enjoyable ways to get a sexual thrill,' so he quit the macho circus.

When they weren't working, he and a bunch of like-minded cronies played poker for days on end in the Peninsular Hotel overlooking the Star Ferry terminal in Kowloon. Gus was an inveterate gambler and cards were his Achilles heel. While Jake had been a passenger with us he had been invited to join our poker dice school where we played for bar chits, He was ferociously effective in 'Liar Dice' and we would squabble to see who would sit on his left hand. It was the hot seat and Jake could cook anybody – he was the most convincing liar.

Once ashore he had quickly returned the compliment and invited us to the Pen to play poker. I detest card games and am hopeless at them. The only one in which I display any competence is 'Snap' At about three years of age I discovered that a really frightening bellow of '**SNAP!**' accompanied by a thunderous crash of hands on the pile of cards, tended to inhibit the reactions of the more timid players who wished to avoid permanent disablement. As maturity added timbre to my voice and weight to my hand, I never found the technique wanting.

Sadly, they never played Snap at the Pen, but it was quite entertaining to watch the dedicated players. They weren't 'professional' in the sense that they took it seriously. They played for fun and to while away the time; the crosstalk and banter were sometimes hilarious and well worth an occasional idle hour as a spectator.

CHAPTER NINETEEN

Some people seem to attract problems. 'Bubbles', our Kiwi second engineer, was such a man. His life on board was a catalogue of minor disasters which individually didn't amount to much, but the unbelievable frequency of these little events created an aura of hopelessness about him and provided us with non-stop diversions. There seemed to be daily additions to the Bubbles saga.

He had acquired his nickname by what must have been an awful event for him but which was guaranteed to make any onlooker collapse in helpless laughter. Before the running repairs in Singapore and the refurbishment in Hamburg, our main plant and auxiliary machinery were in a pretty poor state; down below something blew up, broke down or refused to function several times a day. Our engineers were a good bunch and they were exhausted by the endless demands made on them. They never knew what it was to stand their four-hour watch then have eight hours off. And, of course, the more senior the engineer, the harder and longer he worked.

Bubbles had surfaced after about eighteen hours of non-stop labour in a killing temperature. He collapsed on the hatch in his sweat-soaked overalls and just lay there breathing in God's good, clean air, untainted by boiler fumes and body odours. In the tropics we had lime juice daily for 'elevenses' as anti-scurvy prophylaxis. It came in big, brown one gallon bottles in highly concentrated form; diluted to the nth degree and served with ice and sugar, it made a very refreshing drink – apart from its preventative properties. Because of their endless Herculean labours in tremendously high temperatures, our engineers were in danger of dehydration. The practice had grown for their stewards to make up batches of the lime juice which were kept in their cabins in the original big brown bottles, so it was instantly available whenever they needed it – day or night.

On that particular day Bubbles had asked his steward to get him a supply of Stergene – a liquid detergent used by the engineers to soak their overalls. The steward had done as requested but unfortunately had used one of the lime juice bottles as the container and put it just inside Bubbles's door. The second eventually staggered along to his cabin, sat on the weather step and picked up the Stergene bottle thinking he had about a gallon of diluted lime juice to hand. He was so exhausted and disconnected that when he tipped it to his lips, he had gulped about half a pint before the awful truth hit him.

Foaming at the mouth, retching and making violent abdominal noises he dragged himself to the quack's cabin terrified that he had irretrievably poisoned himself. Disturbed from sleep at the dead of night the quack was not best pleased; giggling unsympathetically he swamped Bubbles with ice water, which made him foam beautifully, stuck his fingers down his throat, then told him to eat dry bread and not move too far from a toilet. It sounds funny, but it wasn't very amusing really. The man was totally exhausted and needed nothing more that a hot shower and about ten hours sleep. He survived, but he never lived it down.

Bubbles was a slim, dark man with a lugubrious, hangdog expression which intensified unbearably when he realised that once again Fate had emptied a bucket of slops over his head. And Fate seemed to lie in wait for him with an endless supply of brimming buckets. We were lying in Singapore Roads discharging into lighters moored alongside. Bubbles – dressed for the beach – was wearing a brand-new pair of moccasins, hand-made in calf leather in Hong Kong. Suddenly from below there came the extended squeal of metal on metal, followed by a series of diminishing thumps and then silence in some part of the throbbing inferno that the engineers recognised at once was critical.

Conscientious to the last, Bubbles didn't pause to change but dashed below with his men. Some hours later, having won the latest battle with the tired machinery, they came up on deck. The second, in a fit of exuberance at finding himself in the fresh air again, performed a high kick and one of his brand-new moccasins, hand-made in calf leather in Hong Kong, flew off his foot and to his horror just cleared the rail and plopped over the side. He stared in disbelief and self-loathing for a second, swore long and creatively, then with a defiant shout at Fate, he tore off the remaining brand-new moccasin, hand-made in calf leather in Hong Kong, and hurled it at the horizon with all the strength he could muster.

Defiance was a mistake. The shoe was still travelling towards Pulo Bukum at an altitude of thirty or so feet and some seventy or eighty knots, when the first shoe came flipping back over the side. It had fallen onto a lighter moored beneath us and a kindly coolie, recognising its quality, had tossed it back on board.

I was with Bubbles in Nagoya when he received his unkindest cut of all. Nagoya had a porcelain factory where it was possible to order tea and dinner services to your own design or have your choice of device use in decoration. We had spent a couple of very interesting (and bibulous) hours at the factory and were walking back to the town on a beautiful, balmy, spring-like evening. The pavement on which we were walking was formed of large, oblong paving slabs which, unknown to us, covered a sewer. One of the slabs had been removed and we failed to notice it. Bubbles had stopped to retie a shoelace and I had been ambling along by myself for some minutes before it occurred to me that he was taking a long time to catch up. I looked back and to my consternation he was nowhere to be seen.

I retraced my steps and shortly came to a hole in the footpath on the edge of which were firmly glued Bubbles' white-knuckled hands. His head was just below pavement level and he was chest deep in a swirling grey slurry. It smelled of horrible things, long dead. His language was frightening and his situation only marginally less so. The material had the consistency of porridge and was flowing at a smart rate – had he lost his grip he presumably would have met a sticky and a very smelly end. He was terrified to move.

A few Japanese had appeared from nowhere and stood silently with expressionless faces, observing this diverting tableau and offering no assistance at all. I averted my face from the noxious hole and struggled to extract Bubbles without being splashed or getting my hands or clothes contaminated by the noisome soup in which he was marinating. When eventually I had him sitting safely on the side of the pit there was a patter of polite applause and the little crowd, nodding and bowing to us, disappeared whence they came.

We were some distance from the ship and the odd taxi we hailed pulled up just long enough for the driver to get a whiff of Bubbles's distinctive veneer before accelerating smartly away. Presently we came to a little bar that we frequented and the mama-san, sitting outside her establishment on a cane chair enjoying the spring-like evening, called and waved as she recognised us in the distance. As we approached, her smile became progressively more fixed and finally faded altogether.

'Hoi,hoi,hoi,' she squeaked, flapping her handkerchief in her face, 'what t'ing? what t'ing? Go 'way.'

'Hey, Mama-san, moosumaya for was-was. Can do?'

At first she seemed inclined to call the police but, being a kindly soul and in consideration of the considerable investment we had made in her bar over the previous two or three evenings, she eventually called a 'was-was' girl who led Bubbles away to be bathed. Her straight back and neck and her rigid expression were most eloquent, but a slim wad of US dollars enabled Mama-san to ignore her silent protest.

They refused to touch Bubbles's clothes and burned them in a strange, almost formal little ceremony with much theatrical shuddering and waving hands in front of faces while he was having the filth sluiced away. Mama-san lent him a thin cotton kimono – pearly grey with large blue Japanese characters scrawled over it – to wear back to the ship. By the time we got back the balmy, spring-like quality had fled with the setting sun and we climbed aboard in chilly darkness that had poor old Bubbles shivering uncontrollably.

He spent most of the next four of five days under a series of scalding showers in a futile attempt to expunge the incident from his mind long after any bacteria must have been flushed from his skinny shanks. The thought stayed with him for a long time. Months later, he could be sitting and chatting, enjoying a pint, when the memory of being suspended chest deep in Oriental sewage would swamp his consciousness without warning. He would shudder and with a rude Antipodean exclamation of disgust, he would disappear into his cabin to re-appear some time later with his sallow skin scalded crimson and his hair plastered to his skull.

Bubbles was a sleek and competent dancer; even such exotic measures as the samba, rumba and tango held no fears for him. On the dance floor he was smooth and willowy and the ladies loved it. He had a considerable reputation as a ladies' man and he exploited his appeal shamelessly. In Genoa he came close to braining the third mate with a baulk of timber as a direct result of one of his amorous escapades. Relaxing luxuriantly after a successful chase, he was alarmed to hear a door bang and a squeal of fright from the lady by his side. 'My husband,' she said – or something like it in whatever language it was that she spoke – and pushed him off the bed towards the window. Bubbles was fairly quick on the uptake and he realised that the situation was hazardous to his continued good health.

The house was one of a terrace which lay between two roads at different levels on the hillside above the harbour. You entered the ground floor from the lower of the two roads and went upstairs to find that the second storey was at ground level on the upper road. Bubbles didn't know this and thought the lady was being careless of his life and limbs in trying to push him out of the window to save the tatters of her reputation. But her terror communicated itself to him and as he heard thunderous feet on the stairs he gathered his scattered accoutrements, flung open the window and hurled himself into space.

He was jarred almost senseless by the shock of meeting terra firma some eight feet before he expected it. It took some time to collect his scattered wits but when the window was thrown open again and his screaming late-conquest could be seen grappling with a homicidal man who appeared to fill the whole window frame with his bulk, it concentrated his mind most wonderfully. He staggered to his feet and fled.

The scene was witnessed by the third mate who was ambling quietly back along the deserted street. He drew level with the house just as Bubbles exploded out of the window and landed in a crumpled heap at his feet. 'God's teeth,' he thought, 'that bloke might think it's me,' so he put on a spurt to clear the danger area. Bubbles, pre-occupied with more immediate problems, hadn't seen the third mate and hearing the clatter of running feet behind him, thought that the aggrieved husband had descended into the street and was chasing him. Conviction was lent to the illusion by the fact that the man had, indeed, jumped from the window but was contenting himself with raging noisily and screaming at the backs of the two departing men.

The second engineer, head down, was running as fast as he could and as the pounding footsteps sounded right on his heels he had every reason to suppose that he was being hotly pursued. He arrived at the dock gates to find that the guard hut was empty with no policeman to let him in. In desperation he rattled at the wicker personnel gate and bawled for admittance without success.

'Christ,' he thought. 'I've done it this time.'

As the running footsteps bore down on him he picked up a bit of dunnage timber and turned to defend himself as his relentless pursuer staggered into the splash of light from the guard hut and was revealed as the exhausted third mate.

His tribulations were endless and no circumstance seemed innocuous enough not to hide a sting in the tail for our luckless Seconder. We went to a little port in Northern Japan to pick up a couple of hundred tons of oak coffin boards. This was my first and only visit and I can't even remember its name. It was remote and primitive; there were no proper roads, no obvious shops and not even a bar that we could identify. The little houses were clustered on tiny plateaux amid the gullies and crevices in the clay hills and it was difficult to negotiate the slippery slopes between them. It was very cold and snow lay in dirty drifts wherever it could cling.

We went ashore only because it was such an alien place, nobody seemed able to speak a word of English. Our knowledge of Japanese was limited to 'arrigato', 'sayonara' and 'go menasai', so auspices were not good for a frantic evening. We didn't even know where to start so we spoke to the jack stevedore, whose only English appeared to be 'goodbye', and made drinking signs with our hands.

'Ah, so,' he hissed breathily at us, bowing deeply and nodding repeatedly. He stood and pondered the problem for a few moments, then a wide grin split the wrinkled brown face, disclosing a mouth full of steel teeth. He beckoned us to follow him, 'Goodbye, goodbye.'

He led us between the tiny houses where dim lights glimmered fitfully through opaque windows. Stumbling and slipping we followed him into the growing blackness among the slippery, ice-bound gullies until at last the houses began to thin out and the air was redolent with the combined smells of fish and sawdust, so we reckoned we were close to the fish dock and the sawmill that produced the coffin boards. At last he stopped before a low structure, slid back a door and motioned us to enter, 'Goodbye, goodbye'. We were standing in a small room with wooden walls and a bare concrete floor.

The only light came through the wall in front of us – a glazed screen lit dimly from the other side.

There followed a shouted conversation between our guide and two or three other people, none of whom made an appearance. The Japanese always conduct conversations as if they are permanently angry with everyone; they bellow at each other lustily. The guttural exchange came to an end and the screen slid back to disclose a scene I first saw in my 'mixed infants' school geography book, 'Peoples of the World', and have never seen since.

The raised floor of the room was at about knee level for us standing in the foyer and seemed to be constructed of woven reeds or pandanas mats. The walls were made from panels of the same material, with structural wooden members forming verticals and horizontals. The whole was lit by fluttering, paper-shaded lanterns. There was no furniture in the room but in the centre of the floor lay a huge, round, blue quilt embroidered with chrysanthemums of various colours – it was beautiful and would have cost a fortune in Europe. The quilt was humped in the centre and some eight or nine people, of all ages and both sexes were distributed round it like the spokes of a wheel, their lower bodies covered by the quilt and their feet to the humped centre.

Our guide indicated that we were to remove our shoes and we climbed up into the low ceilinged room, which was comfortably warm. A man, whom I presumed was our host, got to his knees and bowed us in – hissing politely at us and making signs that we should join the people under the quilt. Bubbles and I sat down side by side and slid our feet under the cover and the others found positions between the men and women there. On my left was a young woman, breast feeding a tiny baby and beside her lay an ancient grandmother, wizened and still. She could have been mistaken for a corpse until she opened bright, shiny brown eyes which blazed in the sere, yellow-brown face. Her sparse grey hair was pulled back so tightly that it strained from her forehead and the thought of it made me wince inwardly. She turned her head painfully and examined us soundlessly with no change of expression. Her eyes were the bright, optimistic eyes of a happy child.

There was a brief exchange among the gathering as we settled down and we sat, smiling and nodding at each other, as the young girl left the room. She returned with two trays on folding legs, both laden with small dishes containing dried or smoked squid and jars of sake with a multitude of the tiny, thimble-like cups from which to drink it.

We spent a curious evening in that hospitable circle. We knew not a word of each other's language, yet we managed to communicate without undue strain and discovered that it is possible to mime basic jokes, such as 'Isn't it bloody cold?' and 'It does you no good when its as cold as this. does it?'

After a while the assembly fell silent and we looked at each other, wondering what to do next. We had exhausted the mimeable and it looked as if we ought to make a polite exit before the situation became strained.

Suddenly the heavily bearded man who had welcomed us, launched into a harsh, guttural speech. It was delivered with such vehemence that the veins on his throat became distended. At first I thought he was haranguing us about the atom bomb or something similar but that would have been wholly out of context. He wouldn't have been so impolite. The four of us exchanged glances. We were miles from anyone who could help us and we had absolutely no idea how to retrace our steps to the ship. They could have chopped us up and fed us to the pigs and nobody would have been any the wiser. It was an unhappy thought.

I looked at the Japanese lying under the quilt and it occurred to me that they had an air of expectancy, like children waiting for the punch line of their favourite, oft repeated story. Almost simultaneously I seemed to detect a cadence in the man's violent speech and it dawned on me, it was a recitation – he was entertaining us. Blessed relief! Confirmation came almost at once. His speech became spasmodic as if he were having difficulty, then he seemed to be itemising something, emphasising certain elements by pointing savagely at one or other of his audience. They were becoming keyed up – the climax, evidently, was imminent. The rhythm became obvious, even to us, and it cued the audience; suddenly they all joined in and chanted the final words in unison. As the last syllable died away they turned to us and we applauded politely.

I opened the batting for England with 'The Lion and Albert', complete with pseudo Lancashire accent and we swapped recitations and monologues, songs and roundelays all evening. They demanded a repeat of 'Green Grow The Rushes-O' and applauded mightily our harmonised version of 'Sweet Nellie Dean'. The Japanese have quite an ear for Western music. We frequently listened to classical music concerts on Japanese broadcasts, so presumably Western phrasing and rhythms were not totally alien to our audience.

The sweetness of our singing must have affected Bubbles for presently he disgraced himself by dozing off. He had had an exhausting few days prior to our arrival in Japan and was so tired that if he stopped moving for any length of time he was liable to fall asleep where he stood. The warmth of the little room and the endless application of thimbles full of warm sake worked their magic; before long he lay flat on his back, snoring fit to wake the dead.

Our hosts were not in the least put out. They were hard working people, accustomed to cruel labour in a harsh environment and welcomed the soporific qualities of warmth after work, combined with the balm of prolific sake. They were gratified that he felt so relaxed in their company. But his reverberating snores embarrassed the third.

'Turn the noisy bugger over, or prod him. He's driving me crazy.'

I seized Bubbles by the shoulders and eased him gently onto his side; his deep sleep of exhaustion didn't falter for a second, but I had sowed the seeds of his latest debacle.

For perhaps another twenty minutes he lay breathing gently beside me. Then his eyes opened abruptly and it was obvious that he had no idea where he was or what he was doing there. His eyes were glazed as they stared over me at the nursing mother on my left and I wondered what had awakened him. Suddenly, without warning, he slid from under the quilt with a strangled oath, galvanised into action like a scalded snake.

The third engineer chuckled. 'You'd think he was on fire, wouldn't you?'

It was quite perceptive of him. Bubbles **was** on fire. Because I had changed his position and being considerably taller than our hosts, he had somehow managed to insert his toe into one of the breather holes of the brazier that smouldered gently under the quilt. None of the Japanese feet came within inches of it and had he remained on his back and presented the flat of his foot to the heater, all would have been well. The toe of one sock was smoking; he whipped it off and squeezed it between his fingers. Our hosts were perplexed. They were too polite to laugh and looked solemnly one to another, trying to gauge what reaction would be appropriate.

We were not so inhibited. This latest chapter in the Bubbles saga was the funniest of all... it was lucky that we were already sitting or lying down. Our hosts took their cue from us. For several minutes we rolled about the springy floor together, rubbing our eyes and slapping each other on the back... our bearded, solemn host; the young mother; the creaking granny; teenagers; the mother of the family; our tough lumberman/fisherman/stevedore friend and we four foreign seamen. I think Japanese and Englishmen learned a lot about each other that night.

Then came the time to go and we reluctantly prepared to brave the rigours of the freezing darkness and the icy clay hills. It was obvious that we hadn't come to a pub but had been welcomed into the home of the jack stevedore. It was, consequently, inappropriate to offer payment, but we

217

managed to convey to them that we would like to present a gift of money for the baby and it was accepted with grace. We were presented with the little porcelain sake set and we said an effusive goodbye with much pantomiming of burned feet from them and a great deal of chuckling, bowing and patting of hands and shoulders from both sides. We left the human and physical warmth of that odd little haven with real regret.

The jack stevedore came with us and for the next forty minutes we battled over the icy ridges in total blackness, pierced only by the inadequate, cold green flame of the tiny pressure lamp carried by our host. He still had the return journey to make and would be up early in the morning to make his way back to the wharf and lead his men aboard in the frigid dawn. He was a very tough man and like many tough men, was a concerned and considerate one.

While we were preparing to sail the next day, he came to shake our hands and bid us farewell. He got it right this time, 'Goodbye, goodbye'. We presented him with a bottle of brandy for which Chinese and Japanese have an inordinate fondness. His reaction was an odd blend of delight and embarrassment which transcended any language barrier.

CHAPTER TWENTY

The combined British fishing and merchant fleets, in the days before the government connived in the destruction of one and the Unions of the other, provided the most hazardous working conditions in heavy industry. I assume the condition was replicated in fleets of other nations. It's not hard to see why.

Ships operate in an uncontrollable, hostile environment. Men have to work long hours for months on end often teetering around enormous holes in the deck (the hatches) with huge loads swinging over head. They are required to work in risky situations aloft on mobile platforms suspended from ropes where the seaman's old saw – 'one hand for the ship and one for yourself' – isn't always easy to apply. Even a jaunt to the beach for relaxation can present hazards. Leaping into and out of heaving boats onto an unstable gangway platform or onto the foot of a vertical rope ladder isn't always easy – especially if you are rigged for an evening ashore or have indulged rather too liberally.

Down below, the engineers work in their vast, reverberating cavern with high-pressure, super-heated steam and metal surfaces radiating more heat than a cooker hotplate. I have always thought that wartime ships' engineers deserved a medal just for going to sea. The stress and tension of working in an engine room several feet below sea level, with only a thin steel skin between you and prowling U-Boats competing to get you in their sights, is daunting. I have never seen the statistics, but the chances of emerging alive and uninjured from the engine room of a torpedoed ship must have been minimal.

The engine room is partitioned horizontally by grids forming the deck, so tools dropped from above can add to the dangers of oil-slicked floors and narrow walkways winding between operating machinery, which have to be negotiated while the entire structure, heaving and rolling underfoot, is progressing at anything up to twenty-five knots.

In the galley, an innocent pan of grilling bacon or a pot of simmering stew can become a lethal object if it is not handled with due care when there is even a moderate sea running. No matter what the weather, the galley – with a bare minimum of hands – has to turn out three meals a day for dozens or even hundreds of people. Even peeling potatoes is an exercise in agility and perseverance when your seat is rolling twelve or fifteen degrees and dropping vertically every now and then, while your pots and pans are crowding you close one minute and skating away from you the next.

Fishermen are even more at risk. They are the last men in the Western world to make their living as true hunters. The nature of the trade and the techniques employed to drag fish from the sea requires them sometimes to work eighteen or more hours at a stretch when the shoals are running. They are frequently chest deep in freezing water in sub-zero temperatures, standing on a heaving, sometimes icy, deck with the low barrier between them and the sea above their heads one minute and the next at an effective ankle height as the trawler rolls and sways while hauling nets. The vessel is in the toils of the sea, she can take no evasive action while hauling or shooting the trawl.

Cold, tired men are not at their best and numbed fingers can be snagged in a running wire and sheared as if by guillotine, without the victim being immediately aware of it. It is hazardous and requires exemplary seamanship to shoot a trawl in a heavy sea but if you have found your quarry and the fish are running it has to be done. It is not unknown for incautious, unlucky, or clumsy men to go overboard with the trawl and in their heavy weather gear they have little chance of survival.

It is one of the ironies of a fisherman's life that the best and most productive fishing grounds lie in the most inaccessible and hostile waters. In winter ice builds almost as rapidly as it can be hacked away with axes and frigid running gear becomes brittle. In addition to the struggle to find, catch, gut, stow and land their fish, trawlermen in the winter fight a relentless battle to maintain their gear in workable condition so it is instantly available when they find their quarry.

Most people reckon mining to be a hazardous occupation. So it is, but miners are home every night, sleeping in comfort, and report for their next shift rested and relaxed. Their shifts are defined and their working hours limited. Conditions in modern mines don't approximate most people's conception of coal mining. It is mostly the psychological aspects of grovelling in the bowels of the earth that beggar the imagination. Mining accidents are nightmarish and the fate of miners trapped by rock falls, burned in a gas blast or suffocating horribly in powdered coal, is terrible to contemplate. But such monstrous accidents, thankfully, are rare; the mine's greatest hazard is of an industrial nature which threatens any industrial worker in any factory in any country. An electrician loses an arm in a conveyor belt; two men are struck by a collapsing baulk of timber; a crew is trapped and crushed by a runaway truck.

But there is drama in a mining disaster. Television cameras are quickly there to record the aftermath. Grieving relations cluster silently in the mist beneath huge winding engines which stand stark and ugly against the slag heaps. The restrained urgency of ambulances, police cars and fire engines – blue lights flashing, radios buzzing with crisp, coded messages – waiting for the rescue teams to bring up the victims, increases the tension of the scene. The rescuers look tough and competent; their faces, smeared with coal dust and sweat, are harsh and rigid with shock and unremitting effort. Their industrial armour – the leather knee pads and massive boots, the breathing apparatus, the eye shields and stern helmets – gives them an almost brutal aura of discipline and authority and the event makes good television. How many such scenes have we seen in life and in fiction? The fact that the rescuers are brave and dedicated men who willingly and repeatedly risk their own lives in grim and menacing conditions, swells the heart of the onlooker and adds to the dramatic effect.

In contrast a trawler foundering and taking seventeen men with her, scarcely makes headlines anywhere other than her home port. By the time the loss is confirmed it is no longer newsworthy. There are no witnesses to the accident, no on-the-spot coverage of rescue attempts, no fizzing radios, no flashing lights, no solemn procession of laden stretchers. In short, no drama.

A tanker in ballast explodes in the Indian Ocean seven-thousand-miles from home and atomises her thirty man crew. It's terrible, but it might just prompt a thoughtful piece in the City pages of one of the Sunday 'heavies', whose financial correspondent is concerned about the effect of insurance rates on shipping tariffs. There is no visual impact, so no public concern and the bereaved are left to grieve in isolation.

Seamen don't think about these things and certainly don't complain. There is probably not a man afloat who would willingly swap places with a miner, but a great many accidents do happen at sea and an incredible number of ships each year become a total loss. If the uninitiated were to study 'Lloyd's List' – the international daily newspaper for maritime transport and trade – they would be astonished at the number of world-wide marine casualties[15] that occur.

The British Merchant Navy is extremely safety conscious. With hundreds of years of tradition and operational

---

[15] For example: In the decade 1972 to 1982, ships were lost at the incredible rate of one a day by collision, catching fire or exploding, foundering, running aground or simply vanishing without trace. Losses peaked at 473 in 1978 and in 1982, 302 ships were lost!

experience behind the shipping industry, ships are well found and maintained and owners and unions co-operate closely in their attempts to reduce the hazards of the trade. In foreign flag vessels, and fleets of less advanced nations with maritime pretensions but with no tradition of excellence or experience to back them up, there is by no means as much concern shown for the lives and limbs of the men operating the ships.

Stevedoring too, was then a risky trade – no hard hats or safety boots. The father of a friend was killed in a West Country dock while he was in a gang unloading a freezer ship from New Zealand. A cargo net was lowered into the freezer hatch and the frozen lamb carcasses were thrown into it and hoisted to the wharf. One of the carcasses slipped from the net while the hoist was being lowered and struck and killed the victim.

In Keppel Harbour (Singapore) we had three major accidents in one stop over. It seemed almost normal; gear seemed always to be carrying away and things falling or coming unstuck at inopportune moments. Two of the accidents occurred within the space of four hours. We were discharging into lighters alongside and a hoist of corrugated iron sheets – an awkward load to handle – had been incorrectly banded or perhaps had been sloppily attached to the hook. As it was being lowered into the lighter, the strapping broke or slipped, the bundle broke open and the sheets fell like a pack of cards and shredded one of the coolies working below.

Almost before that mess was cleared up and work recommenced, another hoist out of the same hatch, snagged on a deck ladder and spun out of control. Before the winchman could land the load on deck to damp down the swing, it swept the stevedore jack – who instructs the winchman with hand signals from his perch on the side of the ship – into the sea. Fortunately he missed the lighter, but struck and broke his arm on it in passing. He was fished out otherwise unhurt. The next afternoon as we were preparing for sea, the lamptrimmer was severely injured by a falling derrick.

The derrick is a ship-borne 'crane'. It consists of a boom, the lower end of which is attached to a samson post (so called because it is the structural member which bears the weight of the boom – probably about five tons – plus the weight of the load being hoisted) by a hinge. A cable runs from the top of the boom to a block at the top of the samson post, thence down the post to a second block at its foot, then it is fed to a winch drum. The winch is operated to tighten the cable causing the boom, hinged at the lower end against the samson post, to rise from the horizontal and assume whatever angle is required to position the head of it over the hatch. The hoisting cable is then cast off from the winch drum (because the winch will be needed to power the whip-line which hoists the loads from the hatch) and secured to holding bits. This supports the boom while allowing it to swing laterally. When cargo working is finished the procedure is reversed to lower the boom back to its horizontal position to be secured in its cradle for sea.

The tricky moment in rigging or de-rigging the derrick is when the end of the cable which hoists and lowers the boom is cast off from the winch and transferred to the holding bits, and contrariwise. During the transfer the winch, of course, no longer restrains the boom, the weight of which must be supported for a few minutes until the cable is snugged round the bits and secured to take the load.

This is achieved by means of a chain-stopper, a special chain which is wound round the cable and allowed to run into the block at the foot of the samson post. The weight of the derrick drags the chain-stopper into the block, causing it to jam the cable securely enough to hold the derrick while the cable is transferred from the winch to the bits or vice versa.

On this occasion the lamptrimmer had positioned the chain-stopper and cast off the cable end from the bits with the intention of feeding it to the winch drum in order to lower the boom for sea. At that stage only the chain-stopper was holding the weight of the boom and it was either too small, badly worn, or had been incorrectly positioned. Lamps had cast off the cable from the bits and was standing among the coils of wire which were tangled like a mad woman's knitting. The chain-stopper slipped and the derrick fell, dragging the free cable, smoking and screaming through the block. Lamps was standing in a bight of cable and didn't have a chance. As the wire rope ran through the block, the loop in which he was standing trapped his leg against the iron bits, hitting him just above the ankle then skidding up his leg – paring the flesh from the bone as efficiently as a filleter's knife – before snapping the leg off just above the knee, leaving it standing erect with the white bone protruding obscenely from the bloody boot.

Times have certainly changed. Now, the severed limb would be carefully packed in ice and accompany the victim to hospital where there would have been a reasonable chance of re-uniting them. Back then, an AB gingerly picked up the severed limb by the end of a bootlace, carried it to the wall and dropped it over the side. The lamptrimmer was a Lascar and an excellent seaman; it was a puzzle why he had disregarded elementary precautions in rope handling – never stand by a cable under stress and never, ever stand in a bight. It was probably just a momentary lapse, an aberration, but it cost him his leg and probably his only means of support.

Lascar crews always seemed a little pathetic to me. They looked poor and lived in a minor key, moving like ghosts, making hardly any noise. Most sailors are a rumbustious lot – Chinese and Africans are the noisiest, with the Chinese taking the biscuit. Their quarters are throbbing day and night with music, punctuated by the clash of mahjong tiles and hectic argument. It always amazed me that any of them could sleep with such a permanent racket going on.

Steering a ship is a curiously satisfying experience. On the odd occasion that I was allowed to take the wheel (usually in mid-ocean where there was nothing to hit!). I found it thrilling to reflect that at my fingertips and under my control was 5,000 tons of technology, many hundreds of thousands of pounds worth of cargo and eighty-odd lives all being thrust through the water at 12 or so knots. I don't suppose the professionals – the quartermasters (above) – felt the 'romance'.

Maritime terminology is awash with anachronisms. Modern leviathans such as 'Queen Victoria' and 'Monarch of the Sea' still operate against 'sailing schedules' and 'set sail' at the start of a voyage. The titles of many ratings are redolent of Joseph Conrad's era at sea...Even a modern ship of steel and plastic cannot sail without a carpenter (actually a shipwright). His importance is indicated by his fantasy role as one of the triumvirate of officials (surgeon, carpenter and barber) attending the court of King Neptune and Queen Amphitrite in conducting crossing-the-line ceremonies (an ancient tradition first recorded in a ship's log of 1529). On our crew list we carried a lamptrimmer and a sailmaker (above) and our chief steward signed on as 'butler'.

I could never imagine where Lascars went when they were ashore. Most places in the East and Africa have Indian communities, so I suppose that is where they headed. Heaven knows what they did in America and Australia. They had very little money and what they had was mortgaged. They were sadly exploited.

We understood that it was the practice of shipping or recruiting agents to engage the serang (the senior petty officer in engine room or on deck) and he would provide the rest of the crew. Work was hard to come by for Lascar seamen and with no Social Security to fall back on they were glad to pay a premium to the serang for the opportunity to work and eat and send a small allotment to support their families. By the time all the vultures had creamed off their share there was precious little left. Even from that small pittance they would have to pay a percentage to the serang for the length of the commission as a sort of an employment fee and as a 'sweetener' to safeguard their next assignment.

When a member of the crew fell sick enough to be sent ashore, it was required to make an inventory of all his belongings. They were secured and deposited in safe-keeping for his subsequent collection or, if the worst happened, for transmission to his next of kin. I have done a few. With European and Chinese crews their personal belongings sometimes amounted to a considerable value – clothes, watches, jewelry, cameras, radios, musical instruments, cash in various currencies, gifts for home and odd bits and bobs that had attracted them.

The Chinese always carried the most money and sometimes had staggering amounts. We lost one man overboard – whether by accident, suicide or persuasion it was never determined. In his kit I found four passports in different names and nationalities as well as his seaman's book in yet another name. There was nearly a thousand pounds sterling, some four hundred US dollars and other smaller amounts of several currencies. His wage was less than ten pounds a month, so the find suggested all sorts of possibilities. Lascars usually had a few basic necessities and no luxuries at all, apart from a pouch or so of tobacco or a similar substance. It was often a sorry little bundle that accompanied a Lascar seaman ashore.

The social pattern of life ashore was replicated in the pecking order of the crew on board. The lowest form of life was the 'swamper' – usually a grizzled old man – whose job it was to carry out all the most unpleasant tasks and clean up after everyone else. He could never aspire to anything else and ended his career as he had begun it – a swamper. They were sad creatures.

We had an emergency late one night when our swamper became very ill, writhing in agony and burning up with a brutally high fever. He was unpleasant to touch, hot and slimy with sweat. His emaciated and abused physique held no reserves to fight the infection and he quickly collapsed and died. Some days later the post mortem disclosed that he must have been ill for weeks, if not months, and his miserable death had been avoidable.

He had a long standing venereal disease and his urethra had become obstructed with scar tissue or lesions resulting from the infection. As the bladder pressure built up he tried desperately to clear his passage with a sliver of wood. He must have been in an agony of mind and body. A piece of wood had lodged deep within him, making his situation even worse. In ignorance or fear (which are opposite sides of a coin and have much the same effect on the unsophisticated mind) he resigned himself and suffered in silence. Nobody took much notice of him anyway. It was not until he haemorrhaged and the complications of toxemia set in, allowing the infection to rage through his ravaged body, that his troubles became plain enough for everyone to see. They fetched assistance, but by then it was too late.

I'm not sure whether venereal disease qualifies as an occupational hazard, except perhaps for professional ladies, but a grizzly joke then current persuaded us that celibacy was to be preferred. The chief exports of Indonesia, so it was said, were bales of rubber, baulks of timber, ingots of tin, bags of coffee and cases of pox.

CHAPTER TWENTY-ONE

Not all crew injuries were the result of industrial mishaps. There were accidents ashore, or going ashore or returning. Some accidents were the result of sheer exuberance and thoughtlessness and could only have happened to young men. Maturity dispels crassness – usually.

We were anchored off Tjeribon, in Java, in a stiff breeze, working into lighters alongside. *Bellatrix* was ablaze with lights and the offshore breeze was bringing some horrific flying creatures swarming about us. Some, huge and shell hard, were clearly audible as they zoomed and zinged into the lights and portholes or hurtled into your face to stick and scrabble in your hair and beard when you went on deck. They were horrible. Hard on their heels came squadrons of giant bats.

It was rare to see bats at sea although on jaunts ashore all sorts of extraordinary beasts, some as big as rabbits, floated by overhead at times. I think the Far East beats South America and Africa for observable 'nasties', probably because we called in more primitive places in the East. In Africa and South America we usually called only at major ports.

Somebody expressed a wish to examine one of these bats and for several days we did our best to catch one. Initially we tried without success to trap a specimen. Then in desperation we tried to bring one down. Each evening when they appeared and zoomed around our heads we would put up a veritable barrage of coal lumps and nuts and bolts. To no avail. The creatures seemed magical. We would shoot a curtain of missiles aloft and the bats would swoop and teeter their way through it, never once faltering in their normal pattern it seemed to us. Presumably, as well as thumbing their noses at us, they were simultaneously pursuing and devouring the insects that had attracted them in the first place.

They were very accomplished fliers and became an almost obsessive challenge to us. We redoubled our efforts and every night shot a phenomenal amount of fossil fuel and metal waste aloft in an attempt to bring one to earth. When the lightermen alongside complained vociferously that their men were being felled in droves by falling coal and lumps of iron and could no longer see the joke, we had – perforce – to resort to more subtle methods.

The chief engineer was a dedicated fisherman and had an enormous landing net. We devised a scheme which we were convinced would outwit the bats. We rigged a couple of cargo clusters (multi-bulbed, mobile light fittings on cables) just below the top of a samson post. The plan was that the lights would attract the insects and the insects would be hunted by the bats. Because the lights were below the top of the samson post, the mushroom head of it would be in relative darkness and anyone standing there would be almost invisible, especially as the bats would be concentrating on their quarry clustered below the lights. Ergo, anyone standing on top of the post would be in a perfect position to scoop up in the Chief's net any bat he fancied, as it would be focusing on its intended meal as well as being blinded by the lights.

That, at any rate, was the plan. But either the bats had a fifth column or the plan was leaked to them. They were untrappable. Several of us noisily ridiculed the efforts of the net wielder atop the post. The man was clearly inept. From the deck it looked so simple and foolproof that we couldn't think, otherwise, why the endeavour was failing. By the end of the evening some five or six of us had risked life and limb with no success. The nearest we came to a quantifiable result was when a bat on finals adjusted his glide path rather hurriedly at the last moment, seemed to stall and broke off his approach rather abruptly with a confused flapping of enormous wings. If we read the manoevre aright then the bat was either inattentive or slightly demented and shouldn't have been flying at all. The operation could hardly have been described as clandestine and evidently bats don't rely solely, if at all, on sight, so the subterfuge of hiding in the shadow atop the post was a forlorn hope anyway.

The exercise was brought to an abrupt conclusion when the net wielder on the post over-reached himself in his enthusiasm to achieve success where so many had failed. He slipped, let go the net and clung desperately to the smooth surface of the mushroom head, slowly giving way to the inexorable pull of gravity. The bats were not one wit abashed. They continued to flit round his flailing legs which appeared progressively in the splash of light from the clusters. As he lost his grip on the top of the post he grabbed in desperation at the cargo clusters; they gave and the cables pulled out, sparking and fizzing dramatically in the sudden darkness as the lights were extinguished.

He was in luck. We had hoisted the lights aloft by a substantial rope and as he hurtled down, his fall only slightly arrested by the shock absorbing effect of the collapsing light fittings, he grabbed it and despite severe rope burns, succeeded in reducing his headlong descent to a survivable velocity. He fell the last four or five feet and landed on deck with a horrible double crunch. After a moment of shocked silence we ran to help him. He stood up groggily and shook his head. 'Sod that,' he said, I'm not doing that again.'

The burst of laughter that greeted this ambiguity did nothing to smooth his ruffled feathers and he limped off to bathe his hands and have a stiff drink, cursing us for a shower of unfeeling bastards.

He survived his moment of crass stupidity. It could have been a disaster. My moment of crass stupidity occurred in the Philippines and I was lucky not to have been permanently affected. The detritus of war scattered all over the islands in the South Pacific altered the lives of a good many people who were too young to have been involved actively in the war.

Many have made fortunes by reclaiming machines and equipment, recovering and selling scrap metal or collecting souvenirs. Others, sadly, have lost lives and limbs as the result of stumbling over or playing with abandoned military artifacts.

In the Solomons and in several other places it was not uncommon to see human bones sticking out of wind blown sands, or to find an odd boot or piece of equipment still encasing a skeletal portion of its late owner. Certain areas were known to be dangerous and the locals avoided them. Pigs were often killed by rooting up an old landmine or grenade. Occasionally one would come across a damaged weapon or piece of personal equipment left, presumably, where it had been dropped. We found one machine gun emplacement with the weapon, though destroyed, still recognisable with ammunition boxes – not all of them empty – scattered around. It was a very poignant and thought provoking experience.

I don't know if my 'war wound' was a legacy of the Imperial Japanese Navy or of Uncle Sam. I can't remember now exactly where it happened, but it was a good place for spear fishing. *Bellatrix* had a rudimentary forge and we had heated chunks of flat iron, beaten them out and cut some savage fishing barbs. Attached to the end of a rocket stick, which was secured to the wrist by a rocket line, it was an effective harpoon. The sport was good for a while, but the fish grew wary in an astonishingly short time. Using a boat to fish from or standing on the jetty, we would seed the water with food and try to harpoon the fish as they came to feed.

This place had a crude jetty – evidently only intended as a temporary facility on which to land men and materials in a contested area. It was constructed of pontoons which had been towed into place and sunk. There had been no subsequent attempt to modify or strengthen them for general use. The pontoons were in poor condition, apart from jagged holes torn by shot and shell, the whole structure had deteriorated badly and was paper thin in parts, flaking with rust. I suppose we were foolish not to have avoided them, but it seemed safe enough if you watched your step. Unfortunately I didn't. Desperate to get a shot at a large fish which was just out of range, I leaped enthusiastically from one pontoon to another and my right leg went through the corroded metal clear up to my crotch. The rusty iron fangs of the crumbling plate tore a sizeable chunk out of my shin and gouged deep lacerations in my thigh from knee to hip. An American doctor who treated me ashore said I was within millimetres of becoming an instant soprano.

The pain was almost enough to make me grind my teeth down to the gums, but once it had been cleaned up it didn't appear to be too serious an injury. I was to learn a lesson. It became infected; my leg turned as purple as a ripe aubergine and swelled up like an elephant's until my toes were scarcely visible from above. It felt as if it was filled with throbbing, boiling oil. The old man did little for my peace of mind by telling me it was my own stupid fault (which I knew already) and that if I had to have the leg amputated I could claim nothing from the owners as I had done it ashore in my own time and was not covered by their insurance. I seemed everlastingly to be going ashore into hospital for odd days to have it drained and examined or otherwise attended to. It would become quiescent for a time then the infection would flare up again; each time the cycle seemed more virulent and painful and took longer to subside. When it was active I was effectively confined to the ship when we were anywhere but in a major port where I could limp in safety down the gangway.

Cebu was a very primitive port with no facilities – cranes or godowns. I presume there must have been a lockable facility somewhere to secure valuable cargo, but I don't remember one. The wharf was simply an extension of the public highway which led to occasional opportunistic pilfering, but the cargo was no longer the ship's responsibility once landed.

A local trading schooner/fishing boar in the Celebes. The design was supposedly introduced by the Portuguese in the 18th Century and has remained unchanged over the years.

In some of the more primitive places we visited it could be hazardous just getting from the wharf onto the base platform of the gangway on some states of the tide. Although it was normal to stretch a cargo net beneath the gangway platform to catch anybody who misjudged his step or the distance, some men did sometimes contrive to circumvent even that safeguard. One seaman successfully negotiated the leap from wharf to platform and staggered up the gangway to the deck some fifteen or twenty feet above. At the top of the gangway he leaned over to give advice or express an urgent opinion to those following and toppled through the guard ropes. Heaven knows why he wasn't splattered on the wharf, but with the luck of the totally inebriated, he fell between the wharf and the ship into the net.

He was surprised to find himself lying on his back looking up at his shipmates who, the position now reversed, were leaning on the guard ropes and shouting advice to him. He tried to clamber out of the net but in his drunken state found it impossible. He became hopelessly entangled, fell back and went to sleep. The drunken gang came boiling down the gangway again, pushing and shoving, and together manhandled their snoring friend out of the net, shook him awake and bundled him up the gangway.

At the top he leaned over to point out where he had gone wrong the last time and repeated the performance, this time hitting the edge of the net and being catapulted into the water. By now, fortunately for him, the disturbance had roused a few of his more temperate colleagues who came on deck to remonstrate with the ruffians, saw what had happened and were able to fish him out of the water. He was put to bed bruised but otherwise unhurt, protesting loudly that the gangway had been improperly rigged and the third mate ought to be horse-whipped.

This of course, was a vile slander and not to be taken seriously. In fact Gus could have been forgiven for making a botch of almost anything at the time. He had sustained a grievous wound that at one time threatened the loss of his right hand. It was the result of a bite from one of *Bellatrix's* menagerie of pets. Perhaps 'pet' is a misnomer...

In Cebu City in the Southern Philippines there was a grisly bar known as 'Slapsie Maxie's'. There wasn't much to commend it except that it was right on the waterfront by the old Colonial Spanish fort of San Pedro. The ship was only a few yards away within shouting distance. It was very pleasant and relaxing, during breaks from working cargo in the dust and unremitting heat, to sit under the trees sipping icy cubalibras while listening to guitar music and gazing over the sparkling water beyond the ships towards Leyte and the tip of Bohol in the distance. We spent a lot of time there because we could easily be hailed from the ship and be back on board in seconds, should the need arise.

Internally, the bar was grotty to say the least and in the centre was a curious concrete well. It was some time before we discovered that a young crocodile lived there. He led a miserable existence and had to endure the indignity of being bombarded with crown corks, waste food, bottles and glasses and whatever came to hand, or being liberally doused with ice cold beer or coke in an effort to make him react. As a spectacle he was a dismal failure; he just lay like a log. He was shamefully treated and we commented on it once or twice but nobody really seemed to care. It was a bit difficult, in all honesty, to get worked up about an unattractive and morose looking beast.

It wasn't until we discovered that he was also crippled that his circumstances made our corporate conscience itch. We discussed endlessly all sorts of exotic plans to rescue him from his travail, but nobody thought of the simple expedient of offering to buy him from his owner. One day the electrician – a quiet Belfast man – took matters into his own hands. In the middle of an afternoon drinking session when the bar was crammed with customers, he suddenly stood up, stepped into the noisome pit where the creature lived in semi-darkness among a litter of cigarette packs, tab ends, food scraps and varied rubbish, grabbed him under the arms and took him back to the ship.

His audacity was electrifying and totally successful. Nobody but us witnessed the larceny. What was even more remarkable, in view of our subsequent experience of Gimpy's nasty nature, was that Charlie – the electrician – wasn't ripped to bloody shreds. On the way back to the ship the beast was as quiet as a handbag. The theft was not discovered till late that night when the proprietor went into a fit and called the police. They assumed the larceny was recent and as we hadn't budged from the place since about four o'clock, we were judged to be innocent. A bunch of rowdy Norwegians who had, in fact, been the principal tormentors of the creature over the previous few days, were assumed to be the culprits, They were badly roughed up by the gendarmerie, banned from the bar and virtually frog-marched back to their ship; which shows that Justice, though blind, is not daft.

Gimpy was not successful as a shipmate and so far as I know, nobody developed even a rudimentary relationship with him. He was incurably bloody minded – a legacy, perhaps, of the indignities that had been visited on him for most of his short life. We tried to make allowances for him; he was seriously disadvantaged by any estimate. He had been orphaned early, his left hind leg was a stump as a result of a collision with an outboard motor we surmised, and his eyes were badly misaligned. But if you turned the coin over, he also had a lot going for him. He had no competitors and lived like a pools winner in comparison with the appalling squalor of his early life from which we had selflessly rescued him.

Nothing in the way he comported himself suggested any awareness that there were at least grounds for a degree of gratitude – even if he couldn't be bothered actually to display any. Nor did he manifest any evidence of a willingness to compromise. So far as he was concerned we were all just large pieces of peripatetic meat created for the sole purpose of being bitten, if he could possibly manage it. His anti-social behaviour in what was an incredibly enhanced environment for him, made it all the more extraordinary that Leckie had managed to filch him from his hovel in Slapsie Maxie's, carry him back to *Bellatrix* and install him in a bathroom without suffering bloodily for his presumption.

We could only surmise that Gimpy had been shocked into temporary submission by Charlie's pre-emptive strike, or alternatively that he was, perhaps, just bright enough to perceive dimly that bad as things were they couldn't get any worse and might even get a jolly sight better, so he didn't want to rock the boat. Like all saurians he had a sly and calculating look to him.

He had a hacking smoker's cough that worried us at first. We asked the quack to examine him. He stared at us long and hard, one after another, then walked away without saying anything. He was probably right. Later we discovered that all crocs have smoker's coughs. It is their normal way of expressing the single thought extant in their minds – 'I want to bite something.'

Gimpy became a little easier to live with when his supervening ambition and his modus operandi became common knowledge. He would lie still as a rock as if he were dead, until a bit of you came in range, then he would make an astonishingly quick lunge and a mighty snap. Although he was only small his teeth were like needles and inflicted a nasty wound. It was futile to approach him from astern; he had eyes in his tail and he could switch ends with alarming speed. Most of his successful strikes were the result of a rear end approach by the naïve or over-confident. If he was feeling charitable or lazy, instead of his snake-fast strike, he would hiss like a pressure cooker, jaws agape and glare at you with his goat-like eyes. He was pretty horrible really, I can't think now why we bothered.

He caught Gus off guard one day. It was just before we were due to enter port and Gus was moving him from his compound to his pen where he lived when we weren't at sea, I don't know what on earth Gus was thinking of. The only safe way to handle Gimpy was to approach him from about a foot above the back of his neck and make a swift, vertical grab. It was his blind spot and he didn't seem able to look up. Gus was chatting and without thinking reached out leisurely as if he meant to pat Gimpy on the snout. As the croc snapped at him, Gus came simultaneously to his senses and tried to snatch his hand away but succeeded only in converting a 'puncture ' bite into a nasty 'tear' wound with multiple deep lacerations that rapidly became grossly infected. A croc's mouth is a veritable reservoir of bacteria. It cost him months of pain and anxiety before it cleared up.

In Hong Kong we both wound up in Queen Mary's in Pok Fu Lam for treatment and there had the good fortune to meet again one of the sisters who had come out with me in a previous ship a couple of years earlier as a passenger. It was some time before we recognised each other; I had grown whiskers and she looked completely different in her stark uniform. I had been used to seeing her ages earlier dressed only in shorts and a halter or sunbathing in a bikini.

Being utterly without conceit, Gus was oblivious to the effect he had on her. She would light up as if at the touch of a switch when she was around him. It was most amusing. It never occurred to him to wonder what kind of work schedule it could be that had her rushing round the wards all day only to re-appear at eight or nine at night to give us our injections and tuck him up for the night. I was able to observe at close quarters the onset of the fate that ultimately overtook him. It took her two years to nail him down, not from lack of affection on his part or fear of commitment, but from an upsurge of his old insecurity.

The prospect of a one-to-one relationship in a domestic situation terrified him. He simply had no experience of normal domestic life. He was worried about things that someone brought up in a family could never ever perceive as a potential problem... 'what happens in a house with the lavatory in the bathroom, if someone is in the bath and you need to use the toilet?' ... and wrote to me at length on his fears. But he hadn't a chance. A couple of years later I was Best Man at their wedding in Edinburgh and eleven months to the day after that, I was Godfather to Polly and Bess, their twin girls.

CHAPTER TWENTY-TWO

Sometimes a run ashore took on an athletic tinge. Occasionally the local mission padre or sometimes the agent, would arrange a football or cricket match against other ships or a scratch team of residents or expatriates – depending where in the world we were. A football match which produced an unexpected and unforgettable conclusion was played in the islands.

Many of the islands in the South Pacific had been hotly contested in the final days of the war and a great deal of scrap metal in the form of disabled guns, tanks, lorries and ships had been left behind. Over the previous few years it had been steadily collected at strategic points and was being carted back to Japan to feed the embryonic steel industry. We were employed in transporting thousands of tons of it for several months, loading it from various sites scattered round the islands where it had been abandoned at the end of the wars.

It could be a pretty gruesome job at times. It wasn't unusual to find bits of Imperial Japanese remains dangling from the loads being lowered into the hatches. On one occasion I spotted a mangled helmet with a painted badge on it. I picked it up to examine the emblem and dropped it pretty smartish – most of the top half of the unfortunate soldier's skull was still trapped inside. Amos was supervising loading in that hatch; he roared with laughter at my squeamishness, 'Doesn't take you long to look at a helmet, does it?'

At this particular site, the pile of scrap metal had shrivelled progressively and the area on which it had been stacked was a large, flat, very muddy tract of land with oily puddles scattered over it. One evening we were challenged by another ship to an impromptu football match and we turned out on the recently exposed field. We had almost reached the end of the match when a very fast and slippery winger on the opposite team – an Indian or Pakistani – trapped the ball and came racing down the wing. Most of our men were on their last legs by now and nobody seemed to have the reserves of pace and stamina to intercept the speeding winger; as the goalie it was all up to me. He came on like an express train and I steadied myself to receive his delivery when he stepped into a small puddle and completely disappeared, leaving the ball spinning on the oily surface.

He re-surfaced in a flash, eyes rolling wildly in the black face. He was simultaneously spitting out muddy water and strange, wild Hindustani curses. I fancy that most of them – or the naughty bits at least – were directed at us and not at the unsuspecting crater as all of us, including his team mates and a gaggle of local spectators, were unsympathetically clutching our sides and howling with laughter. He glared at us in disgust and trailed disconsolately back to his ship – a picture of utter dejection. We had to abandon the game at that point as we just couldn't regain enough control over ourselves to continue. The extraordinary thing was that the hole was just about on the twenty-five yard line and well in from the side of the pitch – an area I should have thought had been traversed by every player on the field – except the goalies – at some time during the match. Somehow they had all managed to skirt the booby trap.

Amos had been particularly amused at the episode, especially as the winger was his opposite number and had run rings round him. The following Sunday Fate evened the score. We were at anchor waiting for a berth and had a free afternoon. We put the motor gig in the water, loaded up with refreshments and made our way to a tiny island for an afternoon of sunbathing and swimming. While still some distance from the beach we grounded hard. Gus, at the tiller, put the engine astern and it pounded away with no effect at all. He shouted to the bowman to take a sounding with the boat hook. The bowman prodded all round the bow and showed about two feet of water, so Amos threw off his sandals, 'Come on, let's lighten ship and push her off.'

Matching his actions to his words he leaped over the side like Errol Flynn and disappeared from view.

We never discovered whether we had grounded on a high point or whether Amos had jumped into a hole. We pulled him back on board, spluttering and cursing, then we all crowded into the stern and rocked her free while the engine howled in reverse to drag her off her sticking point.

If shallow water has unseen hazards, a beach adjacent to deep water presents considerable danger to swimmers in tropical zones. We were always nervous about sharks but the locals seemed to disregard the menace without being decimated. Near Jose Panganiban (a village re-named to honour a local wartime hero) in the Philippines is a wide, beautiful bay floored with soft, shining sand. It was a perfect spot for swimming, although as it shelved quickly to very deep water it was necessary to keep a sharp lookout for sharks.

Late one afternoon while we were swimming, two young boys came down to the water with a brace of carabao.[16] It was the end of their day's work and the boys drove them into the water to scrub them down and refresh them. Work done, they joined us in frolicking, using the carabao as diving platforms. We had never been so close to the beasts before and the huge sickle horns looked very menacing. What was even more unsettling, was the fact that we were contravening one of the prime rules against attracting shark attack – never stay in the water with animals.

Eventually commonsense prevailed. We left the water and gathered round the boys and their enormous charges to inspect these strange animals. There is nothing like them

---

[16] Carabao – the water buffalo and universal beast of burden in the Philippines and the Far East, although it goes by different names in other countries.

indigenous to Europe. They seemed placid and docile and presumably were tired after their day in the paddy fields, so when Gus and I were invited to ride them we accepted the invitation, not realising it was a challenge. There was no tack; all that was required was to climb aboard the razor sharp spine, ignoring if possible, the effect on our naked thighs of the barbed wire hairs of the hide. We sat upright and urged the beasts into action. All went well for a few minutes after the animals reluctantly heaved themselves into motion. The indolent, slightly rolling gait was very easy to accommodate. We were just settling in when the boys unexpectedly produced goads and plunged the fire-sharpened sticks into the tender area between the animals' hind legs.

My mount took off with a horrible lurching, staggering gait that made the four corners of the beast sag periodically as it operated its legs in a rhythm impossible to recognise and accommodate.

Our progress seemed to be based on a stumbling sequence of half-recovered falls. This unsteadiness was exacerbated by a characteristic I was only just discovering – the carabao's skin is as loose as a healthy dog's. I found myself sliding laterally off the sharp, bony spine as the skin skidded round the animal's ribs. There was nothing to grip in an attempt to haul oneself back onto the summit and it required a great deal of shuffling to stay on board. This was essential, as Gus's animal was bearing down on us at a smartish clip. The thunderous pounding of its plate-sized hooves sounded loud in my ears and I doubted that it would be as agile as a horse. If I came off and was over-ridden I was certain to be turned into paté by the sharp, iron-hard hooves.

The situation was rendered even more perilous by the curious swing of the animal's huge head as he pounded along. I had shuffled forward so as to get my weight as far as possible over his shoulders. This made for a horrible, juddering ride, but at least my seat was marginally more secure as the skidding skin seemed laterally more stable on the shoulders than it was further aft over the animal's flanks. The disadvantage was that the tips of the enormous oscillating sickle horns scythed past my pelvic region – left, right, left, right – and it required only a minimal forward slippage of my seat, or an inadvertent toss of the beast's head to ensure that I would finish the ride as a eunuch.

Gus's beast drew alongside and precipitated the ignominious and painful conclusion to the experience. He had either not discovered that the loose skin was more firmly fixed over the shoulders or, having to concentrate on maintaining his seat on the plunging animal, he had not been able simultaneously to work his way up to the safer perch. As they drew abreast on my right hand, Gus was gently but steadily teetering to his left. It was only a matter of time before gravity combined with the awful staggering gait of the carabao to complete his downfall.

We galloped along, side-by-side, for a few yards more while Gus's list imperceptibly increased. Then he began to fall towards me, slowly and majestically like a felled tree. Unfortunately I was only an arm's length away; at his point of no return he grabbed wildly at me and for a little while longer we clung together, bridging the gap between the racing animals like circus performers. Then came the inevitable. Our mounts moved inexorably apart and we were dumped on the hard, stony road. We were dressed only in swimming gear and it was very painful, but I was luckier than Gus. His beast kicked him hard on the knee as it strode over him and it gave him trouble for months.

Although our carabao race was no race at all – or at least, not intended as such – we did have a race once in which Gus showed the most astonishing agility. It was in Hong Kong and four of us were returning late one night when Amos, who was in an argumentative frame of mind, resurrected an argument that had been flaring spasmodically all evening. Lacking inches himself, I think that when in one of his ratty moods, he slightly resented Gus's excessive height and he was not above goading him on occasion. Amos contended that running speed was a function of muscle tone and a tuned-up nervous system related solely to the power/weight ratio of the runner. Gus argued that, all other things being equal, a man with long legs must have a distinct advantage over one with short legs.

The upshot was that Amos challenged him to a foot race. Gus accepted with the proviso that they did it immediately. Amos refused and the argument wound drearily on and embroiled all of us until finally even the rickshaw coolies were involved. On payment of an enormous bribe, we all changed places with our coolies and at a signal from Amos the race was on. To our astonishment Gus was off and running like a hare. Being so tall he had the rickshaw tilted up at an acute angle and the only view we had of him throughout the entire race was the back of his vehicle with the terrified face of his passenger peering over the folded 'pram hood' at us struggling astern.

The only concrete result of the race was that I never again argued with a coolie over the fare. It was de rigueur to haggle with them and knock off even a few cents in the interests of manifesting occidental superiority; but I discovered what a killing job it was. These skinny, half-starved men could keep up a cracking pace, loping along for mile after mile, even in hot humid, weather and then expect a pittance tossed to them almost with disdain.

Nothing was resolved by the race. Amos protested that Gus had jumped the gun and that anyway his coolie was lighter than anybody else's, which was patent nonsense. All rickshaw pullers come from the same mould. They are about five feet six and about eight stones in weight. They had gaunt, skeletal faces and wide, wedge shaped chests showing every rib and their thighs were shaped like a chicken's, bulging with muscle. Then we learned that Gus had been unable to use his phenomenal stride during the race. The carriages, of course, had been designed for the Chinese pullers. Even a normal European stride was impossible without banging heels and ankles against the contrivance being towed astern, as we had quickly discovered. Gus's astonishing run had been made with an odd little high-stepping gait – like the Pink Panther's furtive trot from dustbin to lamp-post – and Amos, quite reasonably I thought, used this to support his theory. The argument raged on and on, through the dockyard and up the gangway. It persisted while we made and drank coffee in the smoke room. Amos had a good flow when he was fully primed and he swamped Gus's comparatively modest and tongue-tied attempt to counter him, until at last Gus gave in and sat silent and glowering.

But he had the last word. Literally. While Amos was still in full spate, gloating over his apparent victory, Gus suddenly stood up and loomed over him. He towered over Amos radiating his own special brand of silent, trembling menace. Amos's jeering tirade petered out and he sat gazing silently and a little apprehensively at Gus, obviously wondering if he had gone too far and had inadvertently lit the blue touch paper. For a few seconds longer, Gus pinned Amos to his seat with a ferocious glare.

'Bollocks!' he said at last. And went to bed.

CHAPTER TWENTY-THREE

New York was never the same for us after we had met the girls. They lived in the top flat of a tall, brownstone building in Upper Manhattan which became the centre of operations for us while we were berthed in Brooklyn or Yonkers. They were always finding dates for others on board and when money was a bit short – as it often was due to the strong dollar and our income being sterling based – they held fairly hectic parties involving the whole of their apartment building to take our minds off our poverty.

Andrea was completely scatty and boisterous – a complete contrast to the rather solemn seeming Tottie. If Andrea was like an open book which could be read at a glance, Tottie was like one of those complex pictures which require close study before they give up their secrets and always seem to have a surprise in store for the persistent observer.

Their personalities were carried over into everything they did. If Andrea made a cup of coffee for six people, she appeared to rattle around nosily for ages preparing it while the flat filled with steam and the sink with pots and pans. Tottie, on the other hand, seemed able to prepare a full meal for four people in the shoe-box galley while simultaneously discussing plans with her guests, then serve the meal piping hot and enticingly displayed without a wisp of steam or cooking smells pervading the flat. When she sat down to eat, the kitchen would be in pristine condition with not a dirty spoon in sight.

Tottie was highly organised. She did most of the chores, I discovered, while Andrea was planning grandiose schemes to convert the flat into a Mexican hacienda or a miniature Doge's Palace. She would occasionally have a blitz when the prompting of her conscience became importunate. Tottie would come home to find that the flat had been turned upside down and Andrea – having washed every dish, dusted every book and exposed every corner – was now exhausted and had collapsed with the place in total disarray. It would be left to Tottie to re-establish order.

I once asked her how she could stand to live with such an erratic dynamo. She gave her slow, thoughtful smile and typically came up with a comprehensive, well thought out answer.

'She's probably the nicest person I know... she hasn't a smidgen of mean-ness or spite in her. That's very important in a flat mate. I've lived with girls before, and I know. I trust her and besides, she makes me laugh.'

Andrea seemed to be more suited to Gus with his fleeting enthusiasms, than to the rather staid Amos. But she made Gus nervous and was sometimes quite wicked with him. She always insisted on kissing him warmly and noisily in public when they met, as much to infuriate Amos as to enjoy Gus's writhing embarrassment. Every time we returned she seemed to have a new interest. If it wasn't fencing, it was rally driving, or weaving, deep-sea fishing or photography, or painting miniatures or collecting thimbles. It was a hopeless task to buy gifts for her as it was impossible to keep up with her changes of direction. If Amos brought back something suitable for her last known interest, by the time he had given it to her she had moved on.

Tottie just concentrated quietly on getting better and better at the things she did. She had an old Italian concertina on which she was dazzlingly nimble and with which she would accompany herself; she had a pleasing, light but not very powerful voice. Musically it was an odd combination but the result was enchanting. 'I Dreamt I Dwelt in Marble Halls' was my favourite. It always moved her to tears but she would never explain why. When we met she was just getting to grips with the mandolin – a horrifyingly difficult instrument to master. She was very impressive. Her great interest was natural history and specifically birds; her knowledge was encyclopedic and her one regret was that she couldn't paint or draw. That surprised me. She was such a controlled and meticulous person that I thought such a skill would have been well within her capability. The trouble was that unless she felt she could do it to perfection, she wouldn't wish to do it at all.

At that time the Central Park zoo was home to a formidable gorilla named 'Bushman'. He was a splendid specimen. The great apes fascinate me and I can sit and commune with them endlessly. To my delight I discovered that Tottie was a fellow wonderer. We would sit for hours, literally, picnicking and watching this magnificent beast watching us from the other side of his little canal. Sometimes it seemed that he could just lean over and pick one of us up. He would effortlessly twist truck tyres into weird shapes then throw sticks and dung at us with a curious back-hand lobbing action. He did it just to observe our reaction, I think – it didn't appear to be in anger or with any malice. Amos thought we were batty.

New York was our home from home and I could never get back soon enough or stay long enough, although for most of the chaps it wasn't a popular port. It was very expensive and took a disproportionate amount of our disposable cash. Being in New York with insufficient funds is a dismal experience. There was an incredible amount to see and experience but unless you had a local guide you needed money and a lot of it. What you buy precipitately or in ignorance always proves to be expensive. The girls knew their way round so we were able to pick their brains and entertain ourselves relatively cheaply.

SAMMY'S BOWERY FOLLIES — 267 BOWERY — NEW YORK CITY

THE ONLY BOWERY CABARET

Sammy's Bowery Follies — a 'Victorian' music/beer hall. Unaccountably a hangover of the era or a clever replica? They claimed it was a genuine survivor; it felt and smelled undeniably authentic. The 'Red Hot Momma' who so roundly abused us and demanded money for an encore is second left, front row.

We went into the Bowery to visit 'Sammy's Bowery Follies'. I'm not sure if it was a genuine survival of an old music/beer hall or a very clever replica. It had an undeniably authentic aura. I think, perhaps, it had unaccountably outlived its contemporaries and thereby acquired a value due to its rarity and antiquity. The acts were all old timers; some were incredibly skilled and their performance appeared to be effortless. It was sadly spoiled for us by a hard-nosed lady who did a 'Red Hot Momma' act in the style of Sophie Tucker. She was a trouper and had her audience in the palm of her hand. We clapped long and loud in appreciation and she performed a couple of encores. When she finally left the stage she came down to us in her enormous hat with the swooping plumes and her high bosomed, pinch waisted, bustled dress and in a quite abusive manner demanded money from us for the extra songs she had sung. It left a very nasty taste.

The Bowery itself was an eye-opener. One literally stepped over the derelicts and winos lying in the gutter and sprawled over the pavements. The pan-handlers would cadge a few cents then disappear into the nearest bar, drink their twenty five cents worth, then come out and beg for more. I wondered aloud why they did not accumulate a reasonable sum then have a spree. Tottie dispelled my ignorance. 'If they don't spend what they have immediately,' she said. 'They would be 'rolled' by their compatriots' – for a few cents!

Occasionally we would splash out when we were flush and hit what passed for the high life. Jack Dempsey, the boxer, had a bar on Broadway near 50th Street, and he would amble round to greet his patrons. It didn't seem much at the time except as a novelty, to say 'I have shaken Jack Dempsey's hand', but it's a piece of history now. He is dead and his famous fight against Jess Willard that made him world champion is already well over ninety years in the shades.

The Hotel Lexington had a Hawaiian Room where you could drink exotic (and expensive) drinks through straws from pineapples and coconuts. There was Hawaiian music and dance and they worked hard to create the authentic ambience. It was proclaimed to have 'A romantic atmosphere for dining and dancing, an authentic setting complete to a tropical rainstorm'. Maybe, but in my experience Hawaii is warm. The only time we went to the Lexington, the air conditioning was so frigid and the prices so hot, that we couldn't stand either and left.

New York is an exciting place to explore with a kindred spirit. It is well served with museums, theatres and concert halls and must have more restaurants of more varieties than any comparable area in the world. I have toe-curling memories of a bistro called 'The Fourth Estate' – a pasta house to which I took Tottie on one of our first expeditions. It was small and cramped, the tables covered with chintz tablecloths had barely walking space between them. I was wearing my first pair of trousers with zipped flies. As we were going to our seats a laden waiter confronted me in the narrow walkway and we turned back to back and stepped sideways to pass each other. I caught my zip on the corner of a table where four people were dining and it ripped the zip open all the way down. I was faced with the choice of continuing to my place with gaping flies or zipping them up there and then in the middle of the restaurant. Sadly that was the option I chose. When I walked away I found that I had caught the corner of the table cloth in my fly and took it and the plates of the four diners with me. Tottie's reaction convinced me that she was a girl who could handle any situation. Due entirely to her diplomacy and social graces, although she could hardly speak for laughing, we wound up joining forces with the four diners, had an hilarious evening and had made a contact that provided us with several memorable occasions over the next couple of years.

It is impossible to be bored in New York. It had a definite effect on everybody I knew – they either hated it or loved it. Nobody seemed just to tolerate it.Early on we went to a series of open air concerts at Columbia University. If you go by subway it is necessary to go through Harlem. Going through in the early evening wasn't too bad, but the return journey late at night was a little fraught, I thought. I wasn't really comfortable until we were back on our home ground.

We were at the concert the night Marian Anderson got a bee down the front of her dress during the performance. Next day the local paper proclaimed 'Bee buzz-bombs star's bosom'. American newspapers and New York's in particular, bear no resemblance to what we call newspapers. I can't believe anyone has ever read one completely. They are huge and the Sunday papers take as much reading as a Harold Robbins novel. The headlines are decidedly freestyle. The Marian Anderson one was typical. Another I remember headed a story about an increase in the Duke of Edinburgh's annual income. 'Liz ups Duke's payroll' we were informed.

Normally we stayed in New York for three or four weeks each trip, split between two and occasionally three stops. After discharging in New York we would normally go up to Boston and Canada, then return before leaving Southbound for the Central Americas, Panama, the West Coast and the Far East. Sometimes, if we were to be in Philadelphia or Baltimore for a reasonable spell, Tottie would make the journey down for a long weekend in order that we could spend more time together. On one occasion she arrived to find that we had been diverted at sea and would not call in Philly that trip.

While accepting the fruitless journey philosophically, she couldn't resist sending me a tongue-in-cheek telegram.

'It will avail you nothing Englishman. There is no escape. Heh heh heh.'

She handed the form to a wizened little man with a head like a walnut, she told me, and stood waiting for him to check the message and charge her.

'Lady, is this in code?' he asked.

'No, why?'

'Lady, if this is code it makes a difference in charging.'

'But its perfectly plain language!'

'Yeah? What does heh heh heh mean?'

Tottie looked round to discover that she was the focus of a little group of people who were waiting for service and finding her conversation with the telegraph clerk of inordinate interest. She began to regret her whimsy.

'It's supposed to represent a laugh,' she told him, trying hard to keep a straight face.

'Don't sound like no laugh to me', he said and to her astonishment tried it out aloud. There was a titter behind her and the crowd pressed closer, not wanting to miss anything.

'It's meant to be a witchy sort of cackle,' she explained sotto voce, trying to deprive the crowd and not really believing she was living this experience.

'Why,' the little man persisted.

'It's intended as a joke.'

'Lady, you're English ain't yuh?'

'Yes. What difference does that make?'

'How come you call this guy 'Englishman' when you're a Limey too? It don't make no sense. And no sense means I got to charge it like it was code.'

Tottie gave up.

She seemed sometimes to attract the bizarre – a charge she accepted, citing our relationship as corroborative evidence. She accused me of the same thing. We came to the semi-serious conclusion that individually we were reasonably normal, but in combination created weird vibrations that produced odd effects.

We had an alarming experience in one of the side streets off Broadway where the stage door of one of the major theatres was situated. For a few seconds it was intensely frightening. We were on the way to see the late Jimmy Hanley in Rattigan's 'The Deep Blue Sea'; it was raining and we were late so had taken a taxi. As we approached Broadway a dense crowd of women blocked the road ahead. The taxi slowed down to negotiate the mob and was instantly surrounded by a horde of seemingly demented women, not all of them young, who surged round us, rocking the cab and squealing, peering through the windows, pushing and rapping on the glass. One of them discovered that the door was unlocked and the next thing we knew it had been wrenched open and a gaggle of crazed women were inside tugging at us and screaming deafeningly. The storm passed quickly, we weren't who they expected and hoped we were. They were waiting to greet Johnny Ray – the 'sobbing' crooner.

I didn't realise till then what a hazardous business he was in. I'd heard of crooners being mobbed and having their clothing torn off as souvenirs, but I'd always assumed it was a publicity gimmick orchestrated by their agent. For the brief few minutes we'd been on the sharp end of a rampaging mob of hysterical fans I'd been really alarmed. They seemed so mindless and yet had an obvious, uncontrollable and almost inexorable power. When they discovered that we were only 'ordinary' people, their disappointment and hostility were palpable. An agitator could easily have sent them over the top. It was an object lesson in 'people power' to me.

CHAPTER TWENTY-FOUR

We'd left the States bound for the Far East and a strong rumour was circulating that we wouldn't be having many more trips on this run; the charter was coming to an end. It depressed me – New York and what it represented was the most important thing in my life. The thought of never going there again was too awful to contemplate and I was considering whether to join one of the lines that ran to and from New York regularly.

A few days into the run I was glancing idly through an old Daily Telegraph when I spotted an advert for a job that seemed tailor made for Tottie. I wondered what she would think of a job in Hong Kong, but it was only idle speculation, the deadline for applications was only a few days away. It preyed on my mind. It seemed such a dismally wasted opportunity. The paper had come aboard in Vancouver and I cursed fate that I hadn't seen it a few days earlier when I could have sent it to her.

I was always engaged in writing a continuous letter to Tottie. I spent a few minutes each night adding to it and would post it at whatever stage it had reached, in the next port of call, then continue straight on. By that time she must have accumulated the equivalent of a Dickens novel in letters from me. I was telling her of my discovery when it flashed into my mind – 'Radio it!'

There and then I made a precis of the advert, appended a brief note and shot along to the radio shack. It cost me an arm and a leg, but within minutes my message was in the system and when I sat down to continue my letter, the missive was probably already en route via Western Union from the West Coast radio station to New York.

By one of those rare combinations of chance and circumstance, everything worked smoothly. Tottie was at home, sick, that day so precious hours were saved. She reacted immediately and being highly organised it required only a few minutes to up date her C.V. We worked out later that probably within eighteen hours of my reading the advert in mid-Pacific, her letter of application was en route to The Crown Services in Millbank, London. Every link in an enormously complex chain of coincidence had flexed smoothly and by the time I got back to New York a couple of months later, she was bursting to tell me the news. She had landed the Hong Kong job. It seemed unbelievable, but so convoluted were the dealings resulting in her successful application that even sceptics would have been obliged to accept that it and the consequent events, were ordained elsewhere and were meant to happen. The most extraordinary coincidence of all was the fact that her putative Hong Kong boss was in New York on a private visit, having stopped-over en route to Hong Kong from the UK and had conducted some interviews in New York.

Andrea was delighted for Tottie but depressed on her own account. They had lived together since Tottie had arrived in America nearly four years earlier and they were a perfect combination. Andrea knew it would be impossible to replicate it. The whole of that stay in New York was spent in planning and talking, arranging and speculating. Unknown to us the girls had planned a farewell stunt which had unforseen consequences leading to a rather embarrassing impasse which clouded the relationship of Andrea and Amos. They planned a final holiday together in California. Tottie had always wanted to go and this would be her last opportunity. The holiday was so timed that they would be there when *Bellatrix* arrived Northbound to 'Frisco on the homeward leg of the voyage to the Far East. They intended to surprise us on our arrival in Long Beach. It was a lovely plan.

While they were visiting the Agent to check our itinerary, they saw that we were proceeding from Long Beach to 'Frisco, Astoria and Seattle before leaving for Manila. In a mad moment, without thinking it through, they cancelled their holiday arrangements and booked themselves in *Bellatrix* to Seattle. In Long Beach we were surprised to find that we had passengers to Seattle and when the agent escorted them aboard, the roof lifted. The old man thought that Amos and I had connived at the event, carpeted us most thoroughly and refused to accept the girls as passengers.

This irritated the agent, a bellicose gent, and he almost came to blows with father in an argument about turning away custom which adversely affected his figures and therefore his profits. The old man was deeply offended and once again hauled Amos and me before him to give an explanation. Amos by now was so furious, embarrassed and patently innocent, that he succeeded in convincing the old man that we were as surprised as he was. By now the row had become general knowledge throughout the ship and it came to the ears of the girls, who were well known on board. They had visited *Bellatrix* dozens of times and a good many of those on board – including the old man – had been guests in their flat or had been found dates at one time or another.

They were extremely distressed at the furore generated by their innocent seeming little scheme and sought an audience with father. Once they had him face to face and explained what had happened, he stopped reacting to an imagined situation and sanity was restored. They told him it was a spur of the moment decision and that we did not even know they were in California – the **intention** had been to surprise us. Tottie related it all to her new life in Hong Kong and a final fling with Andrea. Before long he was eating out of their hands, he even gave her the address of friends in Kowloon who might be able to help her find accommodation. When they offered to cancel their bookings rather than create a difficult situation on board, he would have none of it.

Incredibly, he even arranged a family discount on their fares and when we left Long Beach he had all four of us in individually and delivered a fatherly dissertation on our responsibilities. He lent me fifty dollars from his own pocket, which was a Godsend. We were always broke on the West Coast homeward after being so long on the Yankee coast. We relied on the long Pacific crossing and our bartering round the islands to build up cash in the ship ready for our next coast-wise jaunt.

San Francisco was a different city that trip. It was the first time in my life that I had explored a new place with somebody. Previously I had escorted people round places I knew or I was in their home territory and they were guiding me. A hire car cost $5 a day and eight cents a mile at that time and we had three days of glorious weather completely free from the Golden Gate fog. It was fun playing tourist. We did the lot. We goggled at Mount Tamalpais and the Muir Woods. The ascent to the top of Tamalpais is by a hair-raising series of S-bends, but the view from the summit car park at sunset is staggeringly beautiful and well worth the terror of descending the serpentine trail made malevolent by the onset of darkness. At the base of the mountain is an incredible grove of gargantuan trees (the Muir Woods), claimed to be the oldest and largest trees in the world. It's not difficult to believe. They are an awesome sight. Some are reputed to be over two thousand years old.

We were berthed on the Embarcadero, a short step from the world-famed Fisherman's Wharf. I have always found it disappointing. Apart from the Golden Gate, Fisherman's Wharf and the cable cars are the two facets of 'Frisco that the world knows best. In consequence they are over exposed and find it difficult to live up to their image.

The Golden Gate itself is a bit disappointing too. Not in its setting or its structure, the rampant elegance of its towers or the magnificent sweep of its carriageway and the graceful parabola of its supporting cables, but in the rather tatty, orangey-coloured paint in which it is finished. It's not as you'd expect and isn't golden at all. We found other, less well publicised, aspects of San Francisco more charming. China Town gave Tottie a taste of what she could expect in Hong Kong and the restaurant at the top of the Mark Hopkins hotel on Nob Hill, although we had to queue to get in, presents spectacular views of the city and the entire bay area. The vista is particularly attractive at dusk as the surrounding counties begin to light up.

On the last evening we blew all we had left on a meal in a German café on Telegraph Hill. I know nothing about German or Bohemian food but the place felt authentic. It seemed to underline the cosmopolitan charm of 'Frisco. I've always thought that 'Frisco and New Orleans are the most 'European' cities I know in the States.

We left San Francisco glowing and broke. We were sad that Amos and Andrea seemed so stilted with each other; I thought he was being needlessly stiff-necked and I told him so. Somehow it took the shine off my enjoyment. So far as everybody else was concerned everything had come right in the end, but Amos's dignity was very delicate and had been badly bruised by his having been placed in an embarrassing situation. He resented it bitterly. By the time we got to Seattle they seemed to have recovered a bit, but when the time came for the girls to depart Amos found it impossible to accompany us ashore, although everyone was co-operating like mad to give us spare time. I had used up months of favours. It was left to Gus and me to escort the girls to the trans-continental bus that would take them home.

They left us on a bright, sunny day. It was autumn and the air, though warm, was thin and sparkling. When you drew a deep breath it seemed to squirt clear through your body until your extremities tingled. It produced a feeling of well-being quite out of keeping with the looming imminence of a dreaded goodbye. We had coffee in a pleasant, pine-lined restaurant then ambled through the sunny streets to the bus station where Andrea and Gus wandered off. We weren't inclined to talk much. As time pressed on Tottie became more and more pensive, throwing me occasional quizzical glances. It worried me a bit.

'Is anything wrong?' I asked.

'No, of course not...' she paused, '...are you glad we came?'

'Honestly. I can't tell you how glad. It's been marvellous, absolutely marvellous.'

'I don't think Amos would agree. I think we've spoiled something.'

'Well, you know Amos! Unless everything is planned and discussed endlessly weeks in advance it's unworkable.'

She gave me a shrewd look. 'Is it because he has a girl in 'Frisco?'

'How did you know that?'

'Grampus told me. Did I upset anything for you? It's something we hadn't considered.'

I took her by the shoulders and turned her to face me, wanting to be sure that she could see my expression and understand me exactly. 'I haven't got a girl in 'Frisco. You didn't upset anything for me and I couldn't be more glad that you did what you did. I'm sorry things went sour for the others, but Andrea knew he was a bit of a killer. He's never pretended otherwise. I told you so when we first met!'

She giggled at the memory, then over three years old. 'I remember it well. I thought you were jealous.'

'So I was madly jealous. I thought you were smitten and that Amos had snared another panting maiden, leaving me as an also ran. It happens all the time. Ahem, correction. **Used to happen.**'

We strolled calmly, arm in arm, back and forth in companionable silence, Tottie still in a brown study. She evidently reached a conclusion for presently she stopped abruptly, dragging me to a halt beside her. She looked directly at me.

'Look, I'm in the middle of an immense upheaval in my life just now and it's all due to you in a curious way. I've never thought about this before and probably haven't the right to ask, but is there anyone else? You can tell me to mind my own business if you like.'

'No,' I said. 'There's no one else in the way you mean. We don't have a great deal of opportunity you know.'

An odd, fleeting expression swept over her face and we turned and recommenced our walk. She snuggled my arm to her and sighed.

'Have you known lots and lots of girls?'

'No. Not lots. Sufficient, I'd say.'

'What a funny word! Sufficient?'

'Sufficient to know there's something different about you, about us.'

She gave me a long, searching look. 'Do you know the best thing about these last few days?'

'I can think of lots of best things.'

'Idiot! Seriously... it's saying goodnight to you knowing I'd be seeing you at breakfast.'

I felt as if someone had dropped an ice cube down my back. We reached the end of the strand and turned to stroll back. Gus and Andrea were walking towards us.

'There's some delay,' Andrea said. 'Half an hour or so. Gus and I are going for a coffee.'

We stood in silence and watched them walk away. Tottie turned to me. 'It's strange to think that the next time we meet we'll be in Hong Kong.'

'Mm. I wonder what I'll do in future in New York? I'll have to go back to the Astor and see what else turns up.'

She pinched my arm. 'Pig... Do you spend much time in Hong Kong? Shall we see each other lots?'

'Well, its our home port insofar as we have a home port. We usually dry-dock in Taikoo. Probably three weeks or so is the longest we'd expect to stay in one chunk.'

She suddenly hugged my arm. 'Isn't it exciting? Hong Kong, who'd have thought it?'

'Free white ladies over twenty-one are at a premium in Hong Kong, you know. You'll be snapped up before you leave the airport.'

She turned to face me and took my hands in hers, looking earnestly up at me. 'I don't think so. You've wrought a curious change in me. I'm happy all the time; when you have to leave it saddens me, but I'm not miserable. I never seem to stop being happy.'

The loudspeaker above our heads blared. The New York coach was boarding. Tottie was blinking and smiling shakily. I felt sick. 'Are you happy now?' I asked.

'No,' she said. 'I feel bloody miserable.'

We laughed aloud at her inconsistency. It seemed, somehow, to dull the sharp pain of parting. We stood close, hands in hands – securely and warmly at ease with each other, grinning like foxes. But it was a brief contentment. Andrea ran up, threw her arms around me and gave me a smacker, dead centre. 'Aren't they awful? They said half an hour; you won't forget where I live will you?'

She turned and bussed Gus for good measure then bounded up the steps into the coach, her skirt swirling about her slim, brown legs. Tottie arched her brows and rolled her eyes heavenwards in a silent comment on Andrea's exuberance and smiled at me.

'I can't kiss you in front of all these people. You don't mind do you?'

She took my hand and pressed a long kiss in my palm. Her eyes were closed and moisture glistened on her lashes. She looked up at me as she folded my fingers into my palm, one by one, trapping her kiss. 'Keep it safe my love. It won't be long before I reclaim it.'

Her eyes were glowing and had an expression in them that I had never seen before; it made my heart stumble. 'Much less than usual,' I said. 'About seven or eight weeks I should think.'

I helped her up the steps into the coach and she made her way to where Andrea was sitting, smiling and blowing kisses through the window at Gus. The door hissed shut and the huge diesel came alive with a shuddering growl.

Tottie sat high above us gazing down with that same odd expression. I pressed my lips to my palm where hers had left their imprint and held them there, looking up at her. She got the message. She leaned forward suddenly as if she had come to a decision and with her forehead pressed against the window, she mouthed a few words at me, forming them slowly and carefully. I can't lip read very well, but I understood what she said. She had never told me that before. It explained her expression.

We stood and watched the huge silver coach slide from its bay with a deafening blast of its siren, rumble to the end of the station and turn the corner out of sight. It was extraordinary. I had never known such desolation. She seemed to have taken with her all that was worthwhile, leaving only bleakness and emptiness. I was glad it was Gus who was with me and not somebody else. He knew when not to chatter.

CHAPTER TWENTY-FIVE

My gloom at parting from Tottie was lightened that evening by an encounter with Jumbo, our eccentric cook, whose meals varied whimsically between five star quality and swill. He was a small but solid man with only one eye and a huge ginger beard.

Having cleared Cape Flattery we had turned on track for Manila on the long haul across the Pacific. We were steaming Westerly, directly into the eye of a flaring sunset which was blinding in its intensity and had set the entire Western horizon aflame. Amos, having relieved the mate for dinner, was on watch and I was standing in the wheelhouse with him, filling him in on the details of the girls' departure. Jumbo brought some hot sausage rolls up to the bridge and exclaimed at the beauty of the sunset. He was a photography buff and specialised in cloud formations, sunrises and sunsets.

'Ah'd loike ter git that bogger,' he told Amos.

'Well, go ahead, it's free.'

He went below for his camera and returned to stand by us in the wheel-house, twiddling his dials and peering through his view finder.

'S'no good. Thass too bloody dazzlin'.' he said.

'No problem,' said Amos in a moment of whimsy, 'move outside.'

To our astonishment Jumbo took him at his word and went on the wing of the bridge. He placed his good eye to the view finder to discover of course, that as the target was the same, the fifteen feet change in viewpoint hadn't improved matters at all! He looked across at us to see Amos in near hysterics, absolutely hugging himself with delight and he gave him a venomous look of such evil intent, that Amos became nervous of Jumbo's food for several days.

Jumbo was an unusual character and in hind sight many things he did had an hilarious aspect. He had saved up for ages to buy a natural looking false eye. Whenever he had accumulated sufficient funds, however, some family emergency or disaster had always supervened and he was back to his starting point. Came the day when he had surmounted all the obstacles and the money was in his hand. His dream was achievable. The big day dawned and off he went to have his National Health marble replaced by a private enterprise false eye.

When he returned he was walking on air. His dream had taken so long to be realised, that technology had overtaken him. The money he had accumulated so painstakingly could have bought him two or three plastic eyes – light weight, made to measure and a perfect match to the surviving orb. When the magic eye was installed, everyone determined not to notice anything new and he was equally determined that someone should. He would go to inordinate and sometimes acrobatic lengths to meet directly your most casual glance, leaping out of the periphery of vision into full confrontation where he would boggle his eyes at you like a mad toad.

The silent battle was waged for days; at last the chief steward weakened and asked the vital question. The floodgates opened. We were regaled endlessly with the specification of his new eye, the traumas involved in accumulating the necessary funds for it, its cost, its longevity and the fact that it was so light that it would, he was sure, move to some degree in unison with the true eye, thus heightening the illusion of a full set.

Gus had a pretty short fuse at times and one freezing day he had just come off watch and was having a mug of Bovril and a quick warm-up in the galley, when Jumbo buttonholed him and the marathon began. Exasperated beyond endurance by Jumbo's endless, boring recitation of the merits of the new eye, Gus cut him short in mid spate. He looked blankly at him and asked innocently and with palpable sincerity, 'Can you see through it?'

Jumbo looked at him as if he had suddenly grown horns.

'Course I can't see through it!'

'Well, what bloody use is it then?'

Poor Jumbo was completely deflated. He turned to his stove and as Gus left the galley he heard him rattling his pans and muttering to himself in tones of deep disgust, 'See through it? See through it? Course I can't ----ing see through it. Stupid born bastard.'

* * * * *

A seaman's life is one long series of farewells and it doesn't do to dwell too much on partings – you just get on with the job in hand. I would be seeing Tottie in Hong Kong much earlier than had she stayed in New York and that gave me some comfort. In Manila a plump and happy letter awaited me. It was cheerful and chatty and bubbled with excitement at what the next few weeks and months would bring. I had just settled to read it when Gus appeared at my door. He saw the letter in my hand and withdrew. 'Tottie?' he asked.

I nodded.

'See you later then,' he said, and left.

The next morning I was checking some bills of lading when he came in and stood awkwardly in front of me. He looked tense and unhappy. 'What's up, Gus?' I asked.

He drew a deep breath and looked straight at me. 'Afraid I have some bad news for you old son.'

My mind flew to my teeming family in England. 'From home?'

He shook his massive head slowly, never taking his eyes from mine. 'New York.'

It was then that I spotted the telegram form in his hand and my throat constricted so savagely that I could scarcely speak. 'Very bad?'

'Worse possible.'

It's a marvel to me that anyone understands anything about anyone else in this world. It's impossible to know what goes on inside the head of even those closest to you. When Gus reported our encounter to Amos later, in response to his enquiry, he told him that I had closed my eyes and sighed. I would have described it differently. I had closed my eyes because I felt as if they were about to burst out of my head with the sudden pressure that seemed to build up inside. My sigh was a gasp for breath. My chest was so tight that I could hardly breathe and felt sick and dizzy.

Gus placed the telegram on my compendium and left. After a while I smoothed it out; it was crumpled and damp from his hands. It was from Andrea. 'Such terrible news. Darling Tottie died accident 12th. Letter Singapore. So sorry my love'.

Peewee had received the cable the previous day and not wanting to hit me with it out of the blue, had taken it to Amos and asked what to do. Amos discussed it with the mate and Gus and it was decided that Gus would break the news personally. When he had come to tell me, I had just started to read Tottie's letter and he couldn't face it. 'We'll let the poor bastard have another peaceful night.' he went back and told Amos.

In Singapore there were two letters, one from Andrea and another from Tottie. I couldn't bring myself to read it. In a fit of pointless rage, I tore it up and threw it in the bin. Andrea's letter was brief and to the point, but couldn't disguise her grief and shock. Tottie, in the inimitable Tottie style, had decided to take lessons in Cantonese so she would have a head start in Hong Kong. On the way back from a class she had accepted a lift from fellow students. When they were crossing a major intersection, the driver had suddenly spotted a car coming hard up the highway against the lights. He had no chance. He had tried to accelerate out of trouble, but had merely succeeded in aligning the rear compartment of his car with the bonnet of the speeding and inattentive or drunken driver. Both of his backseat passengers were killed instantly.

I sat and wrote a brief note to Andrea then changed my mind about reading Tottie's last letter, picked the pieces out of the bin and began painstakingly to fit them together. I hadn't got very far before it became obvious that it was a duplicate of her Manila letter. Knowing how erratic were our schedules, my efficient little lady had wished me to have her thoughts, one way or another, at the earliest opportunity.

When we hit the American coast a couple of months later, I rang Andrea from San Francisco but it most unsatisfactory. I had taken her by surprise and she wept bitterly, making no sense at all. In New York a rather anxious Amos begged me to come ashore with him, whether for his benefit or mine, I can't now fathom. I couldn't face it. I never went ashore in New York again. Andrea and I spoke on the phone for a few minutes after Amos had arrived, then I left them to their own devices.

Amos came back aboard just after midnight and rapped on my door. I was reading. He came in bearing an old BOAC flight bag. 'Andrea found a few of Tottie's books after she had cleared up,' he said, 'and thought you'd like to have them.'

He dumped the bag on my settee and left. After a while I investigated the contents. One was a copy of 'Palgrave's Golden Treasury' and as I held it, it fell open to a bookmark. The marker was a photograph of *Bellatrix* on which one of our photography buffs had incorporated a few sprigs of holly and a brief message to turn it into a Christmas card. I had sent it to Tottie the previous Christmas. I glanced down the page marked by the photograph and felt my scalp constrict and my back hairs twitch. It was one of the most eerie experiences of my life.

I went immediately to the phone and called Andrea. It rang a long time before she answered. She was weeping. I apologised for the late call, thanked her for the books then steeled myself for the big question. 'Andrea, do you think it's possible that Tottie had any premonition?'

She was silent for so long that I wondered if she had heard me. I was about to repeat the question when she answered.

'Impossible,' she said at last. 'She was full of excitement and plans. Nothing was further from her thoughts.'

'Where did you find the poetry book?'

'By the bed. She often browsed through it last thing at night if she was too tired to read.'

'Did you mark any pages?'

'No. I just picked it up and stuck it in the bag with the other two.'

'You didn't put anything in the book?'

'No. I told you. I simply put it in the bag as I found it. Why?'

'Well, she seems to have marked a particularly relevant poem, that's all, and it rather spooked me.'

I heard her sharp intake of breath and waited for her to speak, but she was weeping again. I thanked her for her thoughtfulness in sending the books, apologised once more for disturbing her, then hung up.

Back on board I sat with Tottie's beloved late night reading and turned to the poem she had marked, knowing she had marked it because it had moved her. She was very close and her presence enveloped me, warm and comforting. I was reluctant to break the spell by closing the book, aware that the action would be more final, in a curious way, than even the dreadful event that had torn her from me. She could only recede from me now; we would never again be so close. She had stopped, but I had to go on. This realisation induced a mild panic. Attempting to prolong the sense of communion, I read again and again, over and over and over, those words of Thomas More's – Tottie's last gift to me – achingly sad yet joyous, of love remembered struggling against the realisation of unbearable loss.

> 'At the mid hour of night, when stars are weeping, I fly
> To the lone vale we loved, when life shone warm in thine eye;
> And I think oft, if spirits can steal from the regions of air
> To revisit past scenes of delight, thou wilt come to me there
> And tell me our love is remembered, even in the sky!
> Then I sing the wild song it once was such rapture to hear,
> When our voices, commingling, breathed like one on the ear;
> And as echo far off through the vale my sad orison rolls,
> I think, O my love! 'tis thy voice, from the Kingdom of Souls
> Faintly answering still the notes that once were so dear.'

CHAPTER TWENTY-SIX

Running regularly to Japan where cameras and photographic equipment were cheap and of excellent quality, everyone in *Bellatrix* was bitten sooner or later by the camera bug. We must have bought up every gigantic condenser lens in Japan. The engine-room must have been nearly denuded of brass and copper strip and stainless steel tubing to perform as runners and rails for ever bigger and better enlargers.

Gus was a man of fleeting and intemperate enthusiasms; it was a forgone conclusion that he could not long resist the attractions of the hobby. But the old man surprised us, he became obsessed and bought indiscriminately every gadget he was shown. He had his bathroom converted into a darkroom by the carpenter and electrician. I never inspected it but it was reputed to be the equal of professional facilities ashore. He drove everyone crazy by sneaking around and taking what he termed 'character' shots – which to us meant ruthless close-ups of ears, nostrils and dental amalgam disclosed in unguarded moments. But, to be fair, he also turned out some pretty high quality work including pictures of the birth pangs of a marine volcano off Luzon. We monitored it over several trips and it grew at an astonishing rate —from a wisp of smoke and steam emerging from a still sea to an impressive cone of ash and rock within a matter of months.

We were lying in Surabaya in Indonesia with steam up awaiting the pilot when the agent called.

He had arranged a last minute consignment of exotic animals as deck cargo – destined for a Californian zoo. Three boxes came on board. Two contained lizards and in the third was a python.

They were secured in a quiet corner and an awning was rigged over them to keep them shaded. All we were required to do was to hose them down on hot days. They had recently been fed and would be semi-comatose until arrival at the zoo.

When we had dropped the pilot and squared away for sea, the old man summoned the carpenter. He was a wizened but ingenious Chinese craftsman whose conversational English was rudimentary, but who could cuss fluently in every major European language. The skipper pointed at the snake box. 'Makee open', he commanded.

Then twiddling his exposure meters and range finders and twirling his lenses, he sank down on one knee and waited. With an almost insolent display of reluctance and a hair raising string of mumbled, polyglot obscenities, Ho Chiu prised open the snake box. He plied his crowbar diligently for a couple of minutes then fell back with as terrified howl when, predictably, a triangular head followed by a muscular two feet or so of thick python, shot out of the box and knocked him on his hunkers.

It is obvious in hindsight, that even a semi-comatose snake imprisoned in a stifling box which has been rattled around on the back of a lorry, hoisted aloft by derrick, then bumped and banged about on a steel deck, is likely to become rather less that semi-comatose and feel considerably put upon. The two feet of angry serpent thrashed about and everyone leaped out of range.

'Grab a sack...' the old man shouted '...and get it over his ---ing head.'

The snake had other plans. With his head and, one might say, his shoulders out of the box, he formed an elongated, muscular wedge. The box lid, now insecurely held by the started nails, was progressively prised loose and his enormous length flowed out onto the deck. There his disposition deteriorated even more. The deck was rough and hot as a hob; his motion took on a frantic aspect and we witnessed the curious spectacle of an angry python 'walking on tiptoe'.

Nobody on board could be considered even a passably competent snake handler. Nor did anybody bother to try. Everyone was clearing the area as quickly as possible and the need to keep a weather eye on the angry snake produced some spectacular collisions. Only the old man seemed to be thinking clearly, and he was clearly thinking of his lost cargo bonus and the considerable rocket he would get if valuable cargo was damaged or lost through his stupidity.

The snake by now had left the rough deck and was coiled round the safety rails that overlooked number five hatch. The starboard well-deck ladder was well within his reach and he had a go at anyone trying to use it. Few tried. Chippy had acquired a hessian sack and was flapping it half-heartedly in the snake's face instead of approaching him resolutely, as the situation required, and slipping it over his head. You could hardly blame him, despite the old man's colourfully expressed encouragement. The snake seemed exceptionally irritated and disinclined to co-operate.

The contest went on for some minutes. Chippy flailing with his sack like a demented toreador and the frightened snake striking savagely at it. The inevitable happeded. The beast snagged his fangs in the coarse hessian and on recoil pulled Chippy off his feet. Ho Chiu let go the sack as if it were on fire and with a terrified squeal scuttled like a crab to safety. The python, surprised to find it had won the unsought contest, didn't know what to do with the trophy. To the confused beast it must have seemed as if he were in the toils of the sack and not the other way round. Having no hands with which to divest himself of the sack, he became frantic in his attempts to escape it.

In his efforts to free himself, he loosed his grip and fell in a sort of sliding roll from his position on the rails, straight into the canvas plunging pool which had been rigged on the hatch below. It was being filled and had about three feet of water in it. It must have come as a pleasant surprise to him after the hot, rough deck. He punted round for a few minutes considering this development and the old man used the brief respite to arm his troops with sacks and distribute them round the pool. The snake was at a loss now as he had no strong point and nothing to grip.

He investigated several possible exits and induced near convulsions in one inattentive seaman. After exchanging ribald comments over his shoulder with one of the onlookers, he turned back to the job in hand to find himself literally in a nose-to-nose confrontation with a reptilian head about the size of a loaf of bread which was peering at him over the side of the pool. His reaction was impressive, if a touch extreme. He reflexively hurled himself bodily backward off the pool staging and landed with a crunch in the scuppers some feet away. For the rest of the operation he sat with his head in his hands, shuddering extravagantly and taking no further interest in the proceedings.

Then we struck lucky. A particularly resolute or fortunate seaman was standing with his sack at the ready just as the beast stuck his head up within a few inches of him. It was difficult to say which of them was the more surprised, but the snake was severely disadvantaged. Rudely awakened from what he had thought was to be a three week siesta after a heavy lunch, he had spent thirty minutes expending an enormous amount of nervous energy; it was hardly surprising that his reactions were blunted. The seaman struck first. We were fortunate too, in that this seaman was armed with a lifeboat sail bag – a canvas sausage skin about six feet long in which lifeboat sails were stored. He got it over the animal's head in a swift lunge and pulled the drawstring tight. After a couple of frantic heaves the snake relaxed, then to our relief, being unable to retreat, he moved gently forward into the bag for two or three feet. He was lost.

With the beast's business end immobilised, our salty crew regained its fire. A dozen pairs of willing hands hoisted the relaxed length from the pool while retaining a firm grip on the sail bag. Now came the ticklish business of how to get him back in his box. But first, father decreed wisely, we must examine him for any injuries. He was tied with wide bandages to a timber spar, then the canvas bag was cut away from his forward end so we could see his magnificent length in safety.

He lay helpless. His black tongue flickered in and out and his handsome, sinuous body made little rippling movements between the broad bands securing him to the spar. Sadly, he had been injured. About three feet back from his head where his body thickened quite distinctly, were two long, deep slashes which gaped obscenely. He had evidently forced his way out of the box between two nails which had gashed him badly. The quack applied liberal quantities of sulfa powder and used up all his sutures, reinforced with Elastoplast to hold the cuts together and we stuffed him back in his box.

But it was useless. Some days later a vile smell emanated from his box and, with extreme caution, we pried open the lid. He raised his head weakly and without threat, then draped it over the side of the box. The wounds had gone gangrenous; he was obviously in extremis. We observed him for a few hours then put him out of his misery with a fire axe. It was a very sad and rather silly end for a magnificent creature. Before we consigned him to the deep – despite the protest of the bosun who was allowed to skin him but who also wanted to salvage what meat he could – we stretched him out on deck and measured him. He was fifteen feet seven inches and weighed one hundred and twenty-five pounds.

Gus reminded me of Toad of Toad Hall. His enthusiasms were embraced recklessly with avowed intent of total commitment – until something went wrong. Then he would become furious with the project, abandon it and within hours could quite happily denounce it as a passing fancy which hadn't really excited his interest at all. So it was with photography. I was with him when he took what I really believe could have been the 'photograph of the year'. It was on the same day that he lost his camera and with it, all interest in the art form.

We were lying at anchor in Tobago in the Philippines, waiting for a berth, when Gus conceived the idea of climbing the imposing volcano that dominates the island. I wasn't whole heartedly in favour but went along because nobody else would and because Gus's enthusiasms often generated something to laugh at. We packed a haversack and with Gus festooned with all his camera gear we set off on the expedition. It was Gus's project so I had left the logistics to him – foolishly as it turned out. He had neglected to look at the chart or consult a local map.

After a substantial lift in a policeman's jeep, we had been trudging in the steamy heat for about three hours and the beautiful, completely symmetrical cone was as far away as ever. Frustration was setting in and we were becoming testy with each other. For about the tenth time, it seemed, I asked him 'How far is it now Gus?'

'Not too far I should think.'

'How far is that?'

'Stop bloody nagging.'

'Seems a perfectly reasonable question to me. You've no idea, have you?'

'Course I have.'

'Well then, how far?'

'Look, either come or not. I don't give a damn. But if you're coming then quit bloody whining.'

I stopped and lowered my pack. 'That's it Gus. I'm not going another inch until I know how far it is.'

To my surprise he seemed relieved, sat down beside me and opened a couple of beers. He squinted up into the sun at the distant volcano shimmering like a mirage in the heat haze and grinned at me.

'Bloody marvellous isn't it? You'd think it was right on top of us, wouldn't you?'

'Didn't you lay off the distance before we set out?'

'Nope, seemed just down the road.'

'I bet it's twenty-five miles if it's an inch.'

'You're probably right.'

I looked at him with loathing. 'You idiot! You haven't got the brains of a clapped out rocking horse. And you were giving **me** a hard time. It'll take us days without transport.'

'Don't think we should bother. It's much too far and we've got to get back tonight.'

I stared at him furiously, but he ignored me and continued unabashed.

'Look, old son, there's not much point in trekking all that way. Then we'd have to climb it; it's obviously a major expedition. Let's poke around here. There's plenty of good shots round one of these barrios.[17]

We sat and talked while we ate a brief meal then drifted over to a nearby barrio where Gus photographed some youngsters with a team of carabao. On the way back we passed through a bamboo grove and there in a clearing was one of the most horrific sights I have ever witnessed. A huge, hairy spider was crouched over a sparrow-sized bird, tearing at it like a dog. Gus halted abruptly and unslung his camera. 'What a shot! Don't frighten it.'

I laughed nervously. 'You must be joking. I wouldn't go within a mile of it.'

The spider stopped its assault on the dead bird and became ominously still, making me a little uneasy. Gus shifted slightly to improve his angle and the beast sidled round to keep him in view. My scalp constricted sharply.

'Gus,' I hissed, 'the damn thing's watching you. It's not the least bit scared. Don't go near it.'

He was crouched about five feet from it, peering through his view finder. I have never forgotten the feeling of raw horror it induced. It was evidently a thinking, confident animal and was clearly aware of us and taking precautions or making preparations, or both.

---

[17] Barrio – village.

… 'a wee beastie you could squash between your fingers!'

Climbing the beautiful, symmetrical cone of Tobago's spectacular volcano was to become an unrealisable dream.

Gus looked up at me, 'Can you give it a poke? I want it nearer the bird.'

'Give it a poke? with what?'

The creature had moved imperceptibly some inches away from its victim and was looking at Gus in a speculative manner. Gus pointed to a longish bamboo pole on the ground. 'There, that should do the trick and keep you out of harms way.'

I reluctantly picked up the pole and prodded the beast. I didn't see it move. One minute it was on the ground and the next it was perched on the pole inches from my hand. I don't know if that represented the limit of its initial attack or whether it was simply wondering what to do next. Did it run, jump or fly? I don't know, but it had cleared about four feet in a flash. I multiplied its leap by a factor of five and I swear I was twenty or so feet away looking back on the scene while the pole, with its passenger, was still in the air where I had left it.

Gus had collapsed and was quaking with helpless laughter. He was on one knee, elbow on his thigh and his head in his hand. Tears of mirth were rolling down his cheeks.

I was shaking with fear and fury. 'What's so bloody funny?'

'I never thought to see you move so fast', he gasped. 'And all for a wee beastie you could squash between your fingers!'

'Right!' I said, 'squash away me handsome,' and pointed between us.

The spider was advancing steadily on Gus with absolute confidence, waving its front two thick, hairy legs in the air. He stood up with satisfying alacrity and looked around him. 'How do I get round it?'

'Squash it between your fingers,' I suggested helpfully.

'Blast your eyes.'

He retreated until he was on the edge of the clearing.

'I wouldn't go among the trees,' I advised, 'where there's one there must be others.'

Gus stopped abruptly and looked decidedly unhappy. I relented, picked up the discarded pole and with a hefty swipe clocked the little beast a good one. Gus had been right. It was supremely squashable. What had appeared to be as hard as a crab was extremely vulnerable; the animal disappeared in a little gout of body fluids. An aggregate twelve feet seven inches and thirty-two stones of humanity marched from the clearing, leaving behind an ugly, eight inch smear of bloody tissue from which protruded eight hairy legs. I felt shaky and a little ashamed.

We got a lift back to Tobago on a sugar cane lorry and entered the outskirts of the little town as the sun was declining. We turned the corner to cross the square when the peace of the evening was shattered by the sudden, horrendous clatter of a machine gun interlaced with the searing blasts of grenades accompanied by hoarse screams and shouting. We exchanged panic-stricken glances.

'Christ,' said Gus. 'Huks.'[18]

We dropped like kestrels. As we rolled for the safety of the monsoon ditch I felt a heavy blow on my foot and heard Gus cry out in pain. I lay for a second, face down in the filthy detritus in the bottom of the ditch thinking 'What on earth have we got ourselves into now?' Then I remembered Gus's howl of pain and called to him. There was no reply. 'Dear God,' I prayed, 'please let him be all right.'

I wriggled over onto my back and looked at him. He was lying between my feet, face down.

'Gus, where are you hit?'

I stirred him with my foot; to my relief he moved and groaned loudly. 'Shut up imbecile,' I whispered urgently. 'Are you OK?'

He raised his head and my stomach heaved. His face was a mask of blood smeared with filth from the bottom of the

---

[18] Hukabulaps – Marxist insurgents, an endemic menace among certain of the islands at that time.

trench. He looked dazed. As he focussed on me his expression changed to one of fury. 'You clumsy bastard, you nigh on stove my ----ing head in.'

I felt sick with relief and recalled the heavy blow on my foot. 'You're lucky I didn't kick you where it could have done some damage. Shut up and listen.'

Silence reigned above, broken by occasional blasts of gunfire and confused shouts.

'They sound like Yanks,' Gus said. 'What the hell's going on?'

'Take a quick peek,' I suggested.

He moved to comply then sank back. 'Not bloody likely, you stick **your** head up. You owe me one.'

A further exchange of fire rattled out above us. I had my second breath now and with it a measure of objectivity. There was an odd quality to the gunfire that I couldn't quite identify. I was steeling myself to take a quick look over the top when a shadow fell across us.

My heart did a flip and I looked up, expecting to see an olive-green clad Huk with a red head rag menacing us with his weapon. Instead, two ragged little girls and a tiny boy clad only in a diminutive vest which scarcely reached down to his pot belly, stood above us gazing down in wonderment. It gave me an entirely new perspective on the origins of life. I was terrified for them although they seemed unconcerned. 'Hey, muchachas,' I called, 'viene aqui. Muy malo hombres, pistoleros.'

I raised my hand and pointed my finger like a pistol – 'Bang, bang'.

The solemn tot raised his hand in reply and shot me back 'Pahang, pahang'.

I beckoned sharply. 'Viene, viene rapido; asesinar.'

My vehemence alarmed them and they backed away a little. The oldest girl shook her head vigorously and pointed into the trench. 'Ahas,' she said.

I seemed to recognise the word, but wasn't sure. 'Ahas?' I queried.

She nodded violently and repeatedly and the other children joined in until it seemed they must give themselves headaches. Something was scratching at the back of my mind. 'Hey Gus, what dialect do they speak here?'

'Tagalog, I suppose.'

'She said 'ahas'; I think that's Tagalog for snake.'

My mind was working only intermittently. I lay in the trench having come to terms with Gus's apparent demise and now I had another puzzle. Then I began to put it all together. Evening – damp trench half filled with rubbish – beetles – grubs – rodents – SNAKES! The little girl repeated 'Ahas, ahas,' making sinuous movements with her arms, pointing down at us. That clinched it. I was lying on my back actually looking between my feet at Gus when he made the connection. One moment he was there and the next he was standing upright on the edge of the trench two or three feet above. He had gone from the supine to the perpendicular in one explosive movement. I followed a fraction of a second later, the threat of the guns submerged in a more primitive fear.

A small crowd of people was making its way towards us when we appeared. For us the effect was comical. It must have been heart-stopping for them. One second they were looking at three tiny children talking animatedly to something in a hole; the next, two enormous (to them) hairy creatures, one covered in blood and both filthy in the extreme, exploded into view as if by magic, like pantomime demons. All that was missing was a resounding 'boin-ng-ng' and a cloud of green smoke.

The entire crowd swayed backwards and everyone pressed the backs of their hands to their eyes, fingers clawed rigidly while gasping 'Aeieee' in unison, like Hollywood film extras witnessing the destruction of the temple by Victor Mature. Only the little boy was not affected. He reached over his head and tugged the hem of Gus's shorts. As Gus bent down to look at him, the child raised his gun finger, aimed and fired 'Pahang, pahang.'

Gus placed his enormous forefinger like a cannon against the tiny snub nose and repaid the compliment.

As with many seemingly impenetrable mysteries, the explanation of what we had construed as a guerilla action, was simple. The combatants **had** been Yanks, fighting their interminable film war against the Nipponese hordes. For a reason that we could never discover, the cinema in Tobago relayed the soundtrack of films through loudspeakers so the citizenry could enjoy the proceedings without going into the place, I assume it was intended as advertising; its something I've never seen anywhere else.

Everybody was very polite about our apparent aberration but as things warmed up and the explanation of our unorthodox behaviour became general knowledge, so manners slipped. Everyone crowed with laughter, slapped our backs and dug us in the ribs. We could have floated *Bellatrix* in the St. Miguel beer and Canay rum that was pressed on us and a sort of carnival developed. Music throbs just under the surface throughout the Philippines and it takes only a scratch to release it. Clouds of young girls, brilliant as butterflies, drifted around us giggling and pointing at Gus's tree trunk legs whose girth was considerably more than that of any one of their waists. Everyone tried to talk at once and stick their fingers in our beards. It was a very congenial party. We were eventually escorted back to the boat dock and with many shouted good wishes of 'Mabuhi' we took a sampan out to the ship.

An interesting highlight of the Philippine character was displayed a day or so later after we had come alongside the wharf. The morning after our adventure we realised that Gus had dropped his camera either in the scramble to the ditch or had left it in the ditch itself. Either way, that was it, he thought, he'd never see it again. That evening a little group of people gathered shyly by the foot of the gangway, hissing for our attention and waving the curious upside-down beckoning signal peculiar to the Philippines. When we went down to investigate we found that they had come to return Gus's camera. He eventually swapped it with the second engineer for a pair of binoculars.

We returned to Tobago two or three times subsequently. We never did get to climb the volcano, but our visits were always the signal for a repeat performance of the original party. They were cheerful, hospitable people and, I think, regarded us as amiable lunatics. We certainly liked them.

CHAPTER TWENTY-SEVEN

Seamen, and I suspect most seasoned travellers, quickly learn that foreign officialdom has no sense of humour. It is foolish and may be downright dangerous sometimes, to assume that uniformed foreigners in authority can be treated in the same slightly patronising way that most Britons regard their police. It is possible to joke with the British Bobby. But a gentle rapier thrust of wit directed at foreign upholders of the law, is likely to be parried with the flat of a sabre or a lead-cored truncheon in many countries.

Bellatrix had a hard core of incorrigible jokers. Practical jokes, not many of them funny, were almost daily fare. The joke that led to an expensive delay in Japan, had its genesis in Timor at the tail end of the Indonesian archipelago. This chain of islands, resembling the skeleton of a gigantic fish, stretches nearly three thousand miles from the middle of Malaya to New Guinea, separated from Northern Australia by the sparkling waters of the Arafura Sea.

Gus was supervising stowage when one of the coolies fell from a sheer cargo face some twenty or so feet into the empty lower hold. Gus and I quickly descended to him to see if we could help while waiting for the quack. He lay groaning and barely alive, transfixed by pieces of dunnage, limbs twisted and blood pulsing from every aperture in his body. We loaded him onto a stretcher and hoisted him out of the hatch. On examination the doc noticed that the injured man had an impressive collection of buboes in his groin and armpits. He was a new and naïve quack and not as wary as he might have been. He instantly diagnosed bubonic plague, which was prevalent in some of the islands at the time. That was bad enough, but the situation was further complicated when he sent an independent report to the agent in Singapore without letting father vet it. He later protested that medical matters were confidential and concerned only the doctor and patient. It's a brave doctor who attempts to uphold that philosophy on board – the old man is privy to everything!

The coolie was sent ashore, heavily sedated and splinted but otherwise untreated. Within hours he had died of his appalling injuries and, as is the custom in those climes, within hours he was buried. There the matter ended – we thought! Due to a series of oversights, errors or simple bloody mindedness on somebody's part, the quack's original and damaging diagnosis was widely circulated. The incident increased in magnitude as the story spread until the port where we had killed the coolie became a 'plague port' with all the attendant problems for subsequent inward port clearances.

Meanwhile it had been fairly rapidly established that the victim we had landed had suffered not from bubonic plague, but from an exotic and probably terminal form of syphilis. There the matter should have ended, except for Gus, who for weeks after learning of the dead man's affliction, examined his entire body night and morning, searching for signs that the disease had been transmitted to him. We didn't help his peace of mind much either; we would shrink from his approach with shrill cries of alarm and make a detour round him if we encountered him on deck.

It should have ended, but it didn't because of the extreme caution of the Japanese Department of Health. On arrival at our entry port we were instructed to anchor off. After some delay the authorities came aboard to tell us that we could not be cleared inward until samples had been given by everyone aboard – even a couple of passengers who had joined us subsequent to the suspected plague port. The old man protested and showed our various clearances and clean bills of health from the various highly competent authorities for the ports we had visited between the incident and our arrival in Japan. But they were adamant. They would do it their way.

No samples, no clean bill of health, no bill of health, no inward clearance.

They left a large stainless steel container, some tiny bottles for the urine and a supply of round, waxed cardboard cartons – like pillboxes – for the solid samples, together with a supply of wooden tongue depressors. They would return the next morning to take the specimens for analysis. Furious at the delay, father gave the boxes and bottles to the chief steward together with crew and passenger lists. 'Here you are, Ike,' he said, 'get your lads to fill these damned things up and label them ready for the morning. I'm not going to bother everyone with this nonsense. It's a waste of bloody time.'

The container with the samples, all neatly labelled, was duly collected next morning and we waited in confident expectation for the necessary documentation and a berth allocation. At about two o'clock the wharf became a frenzy of activity. White cars with blue lights, sirens howling, threaded their way through hordes of white coated figures and others in blue uniforms and white steel helmets who were rushing about. Eventually two launches put out from the wharf and laden with officials of every uniform combination possible headed for *Bellatrix*.

Father met them in the saloon, which was the largest public room we had and the only one that could accommodate the regiment of officials. They all seemed to be talking at once and were fairly gobbling with anger. He accosted the ship's agent. 'What the hell's wrong with them? What's all the bloody fuss about?'

The agent rolled his eyes, shrugged his shoulders and called the senior doctor who strutted over, followed by a bearer carrying the stainless steel container. The doctor glared at the old man for several seconds before snapping a guttural order at his acolyte. The little man opened the container and withdrew one of the pillboxes which he placed gently in his boss's hand.

The doctor turned to father, holding the box balanced on the upturned palm of his hand, like a Harrod's assistant offering a delicate and expensive piece of jewellery for inspection by a favoured customer.

'Ingorish sayror meka shoke, hai?' he asked huskily and offered the box to the captain. The old man hesitated for a moment as if he had been offered a live snake, then he snatched the box and opened it. We couldn't se the contents but we could see father's face; it was all we needed. He was normally a cold, self-contained man whose face registered nothing at all of what he was thinking. But not this time.

His bushy brows shot up into his hair line and his face went purple. He glared round at us, his eyes watering. He looked on the verge of apoplexy and obviously didn't trust himself to speak. He passed the box to the mate who looked into it without speaking, put it on the table then walked quickly to the porthole to gaze across the shimmering water at the smoky shoreline, his shoulders shaking with suppressed laughter.

Meanwhile the assistant had methodically opened the top layer of pillboxes and set them out neatly on the saloon table. He would have made a tidy window dresser; he laid the lids flat on the table in a straight line and propped the boxes against them, tilted so the contents were in full view. Each had been tastefully garnished with a sprig of parsley!

The 'English sailor's joke' misfired badly. When the furious officials left they had their specimens and they wouldn't allow us alongside or permit anyone to go ashore until they had been analysed. It took nearly two days.

We were fairly sure who was the perpetrator although we could never prove it. We had a Cape coloured second cook/baker who had a ferocious sense of humour. He was the only person I have ever known who had no concept of cause and effect. If he felt like throwing a bucket of galley slops over a Russian armed guard in Vladivostock 'for a joke', he would do it and be genuinely astonished at the consequent uproar.

On one occasion we were anchored in the stretch of water between Panay and Negros in the Philippines waiting to enter Iloilo We had been there for days, swinging round the hook, seeming to have no priority at all. Everyone was becoming bored and fed up. One afternoon the old man had given permission for a swimming party provided we put look-outs in the crosstrees with whistles to warn of any approaching sharks. The water was as clear as gin and not a minnow could have approached within half a mile without being seen from that height. Scrambling nets were rigged along the ship's side and as an extra precaution – to provide us with a bolt hole – we put the motor-gig in the water with the engine idling, then plunged in with a will. I am an arrant coward when it comes to exposure to marine animals, so I kept close to the ship's side where I could leap out of the water like a penguin if the alarm should sound.

Some hardy souls swam well clear of the ship and were porpoising and gambolling, enjoying the clear, warm waters. Suddenly the look-out in the foremast spotted a sinuous shadow hugging the bottom and cruising purposefully towards us. He blew long and hard on his whistle and everyone rushed to get out of the water. Pongo and his more foolhardy mates were some way off; the cox'n in the gig gunned his engine and roared towards them expecting them to rendezvous with him and be plucked out of the water. Instead, most of them made a mad dash to close the ship and climb to safety up the scrambling nets where several of us were already hanging, shouting encouragement to the men in the water who were swimming for their lives.

Even in that life-threatening situation, Pongo's homicidal sense of humour manifested itself. He could swim like a fish but on the way towards us he sank out of sight with an anguished scream and our hearts went into our mouths. Then one of his companions screamed in terror, threw up his arms and vanished. We were deeply shocked; somehow a shark had penetrated our sight screen and tragedy had struck. Then

Pongo re-surfaced, followed by the second man who was swearing horribly. They all made it in safety back to the deck where Pongo's compatriot, a much smaller man, turned and felled the cook with a single, stupendous blow, powered by the manic rage and terror still surging through him. 'You half-chat bastard,' he howled, 'I'll ----ing kill you!'

While Pongo, heavily concussed and bleeding profusely, was carried below to his quarters, the scullion showed us his thigh which carried a clear imprint of Pongo's magnificent white teeth.

CHAPTER TWENTY-EIGHT

Amos was greedy for new experiences. We persuaded a Badjo guard to take us hunting one night. Badjos were convicts who came aboard under armed guard, usually in Macassar, and travelled round the tiny, copra-producing islands with the ship as a mobile work force. A typical plantation was only a few acres in extent and produced a few tons of copra annually. They had no labour force other than the two or three families who tended the coconut plantation and eked out a minimal existence by subsistence farming and fishing.

With the Badjos and their jailers we shipped two or three surf boats and a tiny tug. A gang of Badjos under guard would land on an island in the surf boats, shovel the dried copra into sacks, stitch them up and load them into the surf boats. The boats were towed back to the ship, the sacks hoisted aboard by the ship's derricks, slit open with crude knives, the contents dumped into the hold and the sacks returned for a refill. By this means we collected thousands of tons of copra from tiny island plantations all round Indonesia, few of which produced more than a few hundred tons.

At night the Badjos were herded into cages on the foredeck and the majority of the armed guards stood down. They carried rifles with an enormous bore you could stick your finger down.

One island we visited was famous for its wild pig and deer, so we talked the head guard into taking a party of us ashore one night to hunt them. Amos had been hunting since a boy; the killing didn't appeal to me but I went along for the experience. It was a hot, black night with the moon appearing only intermittently. Within minutes we were running with perspiration, every rubbing surface on our bodies became a point of scalding discomfort; the spiteful whine of mosquitoes was all about us.

We climbed steeply at first up a rocky, uneven, invisible path and, at last, after what had seemed to be hours of unremitting effort, we reached a plateau and rested awhile, My legs ached, my chest internally seemed consumed by fire, my face was badly bitten and we had only just started the wretched adventure. After only a few minutes to catch our breath we started off again and a couple of hours later came to a village.

There wasn't much to see, A few huts were illuminated by pressure lamps that gleamed fitfully through cracks in the structures and one or two smoky fires burned in the open. As we arrived, our escorting Badjo guards shouted and one by one, dim figures shuffled into view. When they realised we were visitors they made us very welcome. We sat on boxes by one of the fires and smoked hot, bitter cigars of local tobacco to keep the mosquitoes away.

'Hey boong,' a guard said to me , 'mau minim?' and made a drinking sign with his hand.

'Saya. Saya terrimakassi.' I was gasping and would have mugged a pensioner for a draught of ice cold water. A few minutes later an old lady shuffled forward and passed out beakers. It was warm, a slight disappointment but any drink was welcome. I took a long pull and nearly choked. The drink for which I had trekked so far and needed so desperately was warm, weak cocoa made with water only – no milk or sugar – and had a liberal coating of dry cocoa powder floating on the surface. It was the most revolting drink I have ever had.

Amos took a sip, blinked and swallowed hard, then he gazed into his mug. They were very poor people and milk and sugar were luxuries for which they had little use. It was a puzzle how they had come by the cocoa. It was expensive and not a drink I would have associated with rural Indonesians. They knew Europeans drank it and they were offering us their best hospitality. I glanced across at Amos. He grinned wryly, raised his beaker… 'Prosit…' and downed the contents in two or three gulps. I was very impressed but lacking Amos's moral fibre I wasn't able to grasp the nettle, so sipped mine slowly. Fortune smiled on me and put two fingers up to Amos. The old lady rushed forward, all solicitude, snatched Amos's mug from him and refilled it.

His face was a picture but his perfect manners didn't desert him. He raised his beaker to his hostess, squinted at me over the fire and repeated his performance, this time thanking the old lady profusely, and politely but firmly refusing another drop of the nectar. His charade went down well and gave me a clue to how I could avoid a refill.

We rested for half an hour while our escorts questioned the Kepala Kampong,[19] then we took off again. We split into two parties each with an escort – Amos and his partner in one and the third engineer and me in the other. Another half an hour of stumbling over rocky paths and tripping over tree roots brought us to a plateau that was knee high in grass. We stopped, lay down in the moon shadow beneath some trees and prepared for the arrival of our prey, for this was their grazing area. The newly risen moon had transformed the black night; its cool, milky glow suffused the scene and the grass moved gently in a light breeze; it gave me the odd impression of being underwater.

I had the only gun and we waited for a very long time. I was becoming disenchanted with hunting. Suddenly I received a sharp poke in the ribs which refocused my attention. Our escort was wagging his finger towards the clearing and I realised that I had dozed off. When my vision cleared there, belly deep in the milky green grass, stood a doe as clear as day – head high, ears twitching. I didn't sight the gun. I knew I couldn't kill it, or even attempt to.

The third grabbed the gun from me in disgust just as World War Three appeared to be breaking out on our right. I

---

[19] Kepala Kampong – headman or senior village elder.

was looking straight at the deer. It just disappeared. I didn't see it move. One second it was there and the next it was gone. I was glad. While we were waiting for the fusillades on our right to ease off, the third abused me roundly as a lily-liver, but it didn't change my mind – I was glad our quarry had escaped. After a while the shooting from Amos's party ceased, my partner fell silent and I fell asleep again.

I was shaken awake and came to, stiff and aching. My bites were on fire, my left eye was swollen shut by a strategic bite, right in the corner, and my legs were trembling with fatigue. It was time to return and we hadn't fired a shot. By the time we had retraced our steps and stumbled into the kampong, Amos's party had been there for some time. They had secured a trophy and were standing round it, drinking mugs of water.

I went to look at their victim and there on a piece of bloodstained sacking, lay a shaggy little animal about the size of a corgi but with longer legs; its shoulder was crusted with blood and the throat gaped from ear to ear.

'Bloody funny deer,' I said.

'Wild pig are exceptionally difficult shots,' Amos replied in his snootiest, most hoity-toity manner. 'They are fast and low slung.'

'Were you aiming at it? That grass was pretty deep. Taller than that sorry little beast, I should have thought.'

'He didn't even see it,' Amos's partner said. 'We fell over it after he'd fired at the deer. We thought he'd frightened the poor little bugger to death at first, then we found it'd been hit in the leg, so we put it out of its misery.'

'What was all the shooting about? Sounded like a battle.'

Amos looked chastened. 'Don't exaggerate. I let fly at the deer and missed it; that put up the pigs so I had a crack at them.'

'And winged one…?'

'I'm not used to shooting by moonlight and besides, I had a narrow squeak. There was one big bastard who nearly did for me'.

'Good Lord Amos,' I said. 'I'm sorry, I'd no idea… did he have a gun?' Amos glared at me, 'Well, what happened to him…?' I continued.

'He, er… changed his mind.'

Amos's partner chuckled. 'You mean he changed his mind about climbing your tree.'

That was the final straw. The thought of Amos being treed by an indignant porker was just too much to bear. It almost made my stings and bites worthwhile.

Amos was not amused. 'It's not so funny. They can rip you to pieces.'

'Yes, damned dangerous things,' said the Third thoughtfully, turning over Amos's tiny victim with his toe.

Dawn was breaking and the village was beginning to stir. Amos gave the piglet to the Kepala Kampong, we thanked them for their hospitality and made our way wearily back to the beach some hundred feet below us and five or six miles away. By the time we got back on board we were in a pitiful state. We had all been badly bitten, despite liberal coatings of various creams, lotions and unguents. My eye gave me trouble for weeks and the Third's bites all went septic – no joke when they were constantly being scoured by sweaty, oil contaminated overalls in the brutally high temperature of the engine room.

'It was an experience,' Amos said guardedly when asked about it on board, But even he had to agree that it was hardly worth the pain and effort.

CHAPTER TWENTY-NINE

Badjo trips were not popular. Apart from the fact that it is unpleasant to see men herded like animals, it is very unsettling to have fifty or so convicts living within yards of you for weeks on end – a ship is home to the men working her. Many, if not most, of the wretches were degenerate or had been brutalised. They lived their lives on a standard that we could hardly recognise, let alone share. Yet, in effect, that was what we were required to do.

The men were formed into labour gangs, some in the surf boats, some on shore and the rest on board. Each group was heavily guarded. When the nets containing the sacks of copra were swayed up from the surf boats, the string securing the neck of the sack was cut and the contents emptied into the hold. The empty bags were then collected into tens and sent back on shore for re-filling. There was a constant battle between us and the Badjos who tried to steal the sacks. They were worth only a few cents each, but to a convict living at subsistence level in a primitive prison, a few pence would buy a disproportionate amount of comfort or privilege.

The whole business dragged on interminably and we never got used to the noise and the smell. The Badjos lived on the foredeck behind their fences and the effluvium of their life was shared liberally by everyone on board. We slept behind locked doors and tightly secured portholes. It was hot and uncomfortable and depressing. We hated it. Each morning they were counted by having an ink dab on their foreheads and each evening they were issued with their food in bulk. It seemed to consist mainly of bags of rice and casks of fish heads. They cooked it themselves and it smelled very unappetising.

We had arrived back in Sulawezi where the Badjos were to disembark. It had been a particularly hot and horrible trip and it had seemed endless. Now the end was in sight. In a matter of hours we would be back at sea. Thousands of gallons of sparkling sea water would have sluiced away the evidence of weeks of residence by the miserable wretches who had shared our lives. We would be able to hook back our doors and open our ports to let the sharp sea air blow away the accumulated vapours of over-heated living. Life would once again revert to the smooth, restful tenor of a ship shouldering her leisurely way through endless summer seas.

Bellatrix was alongside the wharf and being deep laden on a falling tide, the maindeck was about at wharf level, so the bulwarks formed a low wall between them. The lorries to transport the Badjos were drawn up on the wharf, the loading grills of the wire cages latched back to give the men access. Armed guards were distributed about the wharf and on the ship as the Badjos were searched and then filed down the almost horizontal gangway; Amos was at the head of the gangway, tallying off the men on a little clickstop counter we used for tallying sheep.

I had finished feeding and playing with Lorrie and had locked her back in her cage when I heard a whistle from the bridge. I walked to the forward end of the midships boatdeck where her cage was built against the engineroom casing, to see Gus standing on the port wing of the bridge, signalling me to get the drinks in. He had just finished testing the gear prior to sailing. Acknowledging his signal I turned to go below when out of the corner of my eye, I saw one of the Badjos step out of line and punch Amos in the stomach. It seemed impossible. It was done so deliberately and coolly, with a total lack of drama or signalled intent, that I couldn't believe what I had seen. My daze was broken by the culprit racing to the bulwark, vaulting it and disappearing in the crowd of convicts on the wharf as Amos doubled up.

'Cheeky devil,' I thought and ran to the side of the ship to see if I could spot the man responsible but he was lost among the seething mass of men on the wharf. They were all shaven headed, wearing filthy head rags, torn singlets and dusty blue or khaki shorts. All were barefoot. I watched the crowd for a few moments, smiling to myself and wincing when I thought what Amos would have to say about it. He would be beside himself with fury and would bend our ears about it for weeks to come.

Turning back to jeer at him, I was astonished to see him half collapsed against the hatch coaming. My heart almost stopped when I saw the blood. He had staggered backwards and was only just keeping his feet. I don't recall what happened next in strict sequence, but we put it all together in due course. I cleared the rail to the hatch below and got to him just as he lost his footing. He fell against me and someone on the other side of him helped me to lift him gently onto the hatch. He made no sound at all.

Leaning over him to shield his face from the sun, I put my hand under his head. He seemed not to notice. His eyes were clear but confused and they had a pronounced tremor; they wandered all over my face, yet he seemed not to know me. He raised a violently trembling hand and passed it clumsily over his eyes as if he were trying to brush away an invisible cobweb or a recalcitrant hair. I grasped and held it and as I watched in shock and disbelief, I sensed a growing stillness beginning at his core and spreading slowly outwards, as if his life force were seeping simultaneously through all his pores.

The large, luminous grey eyes framed by the dark, girlishly-long lashes, seemed to shrink and recede into his head. The deep tan faded before our eyes and within a very few minutes Amos no longer inhabited the pile of bloody rags, sprawled on the oil-stained canvas. It seemed an anti-climax almost – so much less dramatic even, than the unprovoked attack which had caused it. I remember the flies, how they worried me because I knew Amos would have hated them. I recall standing up foolishly, not knowing what to do next. Gus had raced down off the bridge, alerted by my suicidal leap, but it was all over. Several people were standing about, speechless, just staring at each other. I don't remember much else.

I spent the Christmas after Amos's death with his family. It wasn't a success, our loss was too fresh and raw. Three of his four beautiful sisters still lived at home. They all looked like Hedy Lamarr.

CHAPTER THIRTY

Amos's death seemed to trigger a series of mishaps and disasters that ultimately spelled the end for *Bellatrix*. His replacement lasted just over five weeks after joining us in Singapore.

Accidents are usually the result of carelessness or poor housekeeping and this one was no exception. I had gone down the hold to survey some damaged or broached cargo and the new second mate was with me checking stowage. The job finished, he mounted the vertical iron ladder in the forward end of the hold, with me following a few rungs below.

A hatch can be covered in various ways. In *Bellatrix* it was done by a series of heavy transverse beams which spanned the hatch opening from side to side, six feet apart. The space between the beams was bridged by heavy, iron-bound, six feet by two feet, two-inch-thick hatch boards laid fore and aft. The whole was covered by a heavy canvas tilt, held in position by a number of flat iron bars dropped inside retaining fingers under the outside rim of the hatch, which were then snugged down by hard-driven wooden wedges. The principle was rather like covering a jar of home-made jam with cellophane or plastic film, secured under the rim of the jar with an elastic band.

On this occasion, three of the hatch boards had been removed over the ladder for access (leaving a six feet square hole) and placed on the deck beside the hatch coaming, thus sowing the seeds of almost certain disaster. Standing orders made it mandatory that hatchboards should be placed in the scuppers – the point furthest away from the hatch, to provide a clear deck round the hatch opening for safe working. But everyone was in a hurry!

We had been loading dried peas or lentils and various bags had, as usual, been holed by hooks or had fallen from the hoists and burst on deck There was a comprehensive scattering of dried peas all over the deck. The hatch boards could hardly have been more unstable had they been placed on ball bearings. When the second mate reached the top of the hatch, he stepped over the coaming onto the three stacked hatch boards and as his weight came on them at an angle, the boards skated on the peas, moving away from him and he fell backwards down the hatch.

I heard his yell and looked up just as he hurtled past me, his flailing feet catching me in the face and neck and tearing me loose. I followed him down backwards. But I was luckier, being much heavier and not having fallen half so far. He hit, and fortunately for me, destabilised some bales of tobacco then bounced into another drop to fall on some crates of machinery. My arrival a split second later was cushioned by the collapsing bales of tobacco which gave beneath me, absorbing my impact to some extent but burying the second mate. I lay on the bales covering him, all the air driven out of me, unable to move a muscle and struggling to inflate my lungs. I was quite sure I was suffocating – the dust cloud was dense.

It was a very strange experience; things seemed to happen in slow motion. As I fell I was looking upwards and clearly saw heads appear round the access hole, while the hole itself seemed to float away from me in a curiously leisurely manner.

The second mate sustained severe injuries. After some time in a local hospital to stabilise his condition, he was transferred to hospital in Singapore before being flown home to complete his recovery. He was back at sea again a year or so later. He was very lucky.

For a while there was talk of Gus being bumped up to fill the vacancy but he declined. Ultimately a new seconder arrived and within months had involved us in a disastrous collision, although he was not responsible and was subsequently cleared of all responsibility for the disaster.

It was a complicated accident. The second mate had signalled his intention to carry out a manoevre with the requisite blasts on the siren. The first blast had not sounded but had released a cloud of steam and hot water, so he had pulled the siren's lanyard again. The other navigator had apparently initiated his response based on the puffs of steam he saw, then realised they did not accord with the sound signal but it was too late to recover and the result was the collision.

We were lucky; we had only two casualties, neither serious. A galley hand threw out his hand to steady himself when he was thrown off balance as she struck. Unfortunately he was standing by the stove and burned his arm on the hotplate. The other was somebody just getting out of a bath who was thrown across the bathroom and sustained cuts to the head and a bruised shoulder. *Bellatrix* was not so lucky. She was old and corroded in parts visible and invisible. The impact distorted or displaced her engine mounts which caused the propeller shaft to become misaligned. When she was surveyed in Hong Kong the tragic result was a write off. She was simply too old and worn out for major repairs; costs would inevitably escalate as one problem led to another during the course of renovations. So they took the insurance and sent her to the breakers.

It seemed unbelievable to us. Her bows were scarcely damaged and there was hardly any visible evidence of her grievous injuries. Obviously the speed and angle of the shunt must have been critical. Some months earlier in dense fog off the California coast we had clouted the Long Beach breakwater with a far greater impact and the damage had been mostly cosmetic. It was very sad. Over the years she had carried thousands of tons of steel scrap from the battlefields of the South Pacific and the South China Sea to Japan. Now she was to be towed to the same knacker's yard in Japan to be broken up. We would much rather she had sustained immediately fatal damage and gone down with dignity.

The magnificent 10 mile long harbour of Hong Kong; one of the
five most spectacular in the world. This photo was taken from the
summit of Mount Parker which looms over Taikoo dockyard
where Bellatrix was cannibalized. The Eastern entrance to the
harbour – the narrows at Lye Mun – are to the right just out of
frame.

It seems incredible that such a massive structure as a crank –shaft could be damaged. But apparently we managed it!

There are few trees in Hong Kong and no indigenous hardwoods – timber is available at a premium. When 'Bellatrix' was condemned her teak decks were torn up and her teak-headed rails sawn off (above). In the cabins all the (mostly) mahogany furniture – bookcases, bunks, compendiums, desks, lockers and wardrobes – were dismantled and the wood paneling in cabins, staterooms and public rooms was removed. She was stripped of everything valuable – chronometers, binnacles, solid brass fittings, boats and even the clock in the saloon – which I'd had my eye on! When we waved her off on tow to the knacker's yard in Mitsubishi-land she was an empty shell.

Rickshaws awaiting passengers at the Star Ferry terminal in Victoria. A common sight in the fifties but apparently the Chinese Government has banned rickshaw coolies as "undignified labour".

After seeing *Bellatrix* off, Gus and I elected to stay on in Hong Kong. I had always wanted to go to Macao but had never before had the opportunity. Although we knew that it would probably be several weeks before we could be fixed up with another ship, we agreed not to be repatriated but hang on and play tourist as long as the money lasted. Polly (Pauladius – the youngest of the three brothers Sikkim) gave us an address of a pension in Macau and off we went. It was a salutary experience like nothing I had ever known. I felt like a character in a Somerset Maugham novel. It was a strange, rather unreal place. Hong Kong was bustling and purposeful while China was committed and muscular; Macao in contrast, seemed like a film set waiting for the action to start. I could easily imagine that the pretty, colour-washed frontages, so alien to the Far East, were simply facades propped up out of camera.

Gus was an inveterate gambler and it quickly became apparent that his money would soon be dissipated. Gambling to me is an incomprehensible vice and I prevailed on him to hand over his money for safe keeping. He regularly patrolled all the casinos and ultimately fell hopelessly for a sleek, shiny Portugee-Chinese girl who was a croupier in one of the salons. He was really hooked and thereafter I didn't see him much, during her hours of duty he spent all the time in the casino where she worked. She was certainly beautiful but I couldn't help feeling she was a little practiced and was glad I had extracted Gus's money from him.

The pension was cheap and clean and it seemed we could roost there for ever, which pleased Gus. However, a few days after we had settled in, I received a wire from the office. Thinking it was a recall to join a ship, I ignored it. Another one arrived a couple of days later couched in very ungentlemanly terms which was impossible to ignore. Reluctantly I phoned the office to find that they had received a cable from Amos's father addressed to me inviting Gus and me to spend Christmas with the family. He had generously sent a money order to cover our fares. I was delighted. Macao and its attractions was already beginning to pall. I was sure Gus would jump at the opportunity.

To my astonishment, when I broached the subject that evening, sitting on the flower filled balcony overlooking a street straight out of Southern Europe, he declined. He sat opposite me at the rattan table, his slim glass of beer almost lost in the compass of his huge hands.

'Come on Gus, don't be stupid,' I said. 'What is there here?'

'I can't'.

'Of course you can. Think what it will mean to them, apart from anything else.'

Dipping his finger in his beer he contemplatively stroked the rim of his glass, making it ring sweet and clear, He looked at me from under his bushy brows and I was astonished to see that his eyes were bright and watery.

'Right then,' he growled. 'I bloody **won't!**'

There was nothing more to be said. I had felt Amos's death acutely, but previously Gus had given no indication that he felt so deeply about it. He surprised me constantly. On reflection I don't know why I should have been surprised. Early in our relationship I knew Gus to be perceptive and soft hearted, but it was not until Tottie's death that the true depth and quality of his character became evident to me. It was Gus who intercepted the telegram and took it upon himself to break the news personally. Amos's view was that it would be a devastating blow whatever they did.

'There's no way to soften it. Just leave him alone.'

Although Amos was sympathetic and supportive, he had a streak of pragmatism in him that sooner or later would make him impatient with grief.

It was Gus who was always there when needed but never intruded. In the bad times he was always ready to play chess at two in the morning, or sit silent and unembarrassed, sucking on a cold pipe, while I used him as an emotional punch bag to work off my anger and grief.

Depression is dangerous at sea. Ships are desperately easy places to commit suicide and the easy access to alcohol makes the depressive doubly vulnerable. About half past midnight one morning I was leaning on the boat-deck rail, lost in self pity as I gazed at the fluorescence unfolding beneath us, when I was suddenly aware of Gus's shadowy bulk beside me. I turned on him petulantly.

'I don't need a bloody nursemaid. Leave me alone.'

He handed me a mug of cocoa, said ironically, 'Cheers,' then leaned in silence on the rail beside me while we sipped our cocoa. It occurred to me that whenever I was pacing the boat-deck or propped against the rail late at night or in the early morning wrapped in misery, it was never long before a silent Gus appeared with a mug of cocoa. He stayed long enough to assess my mood, then silently withdrew, or sometimes stayed to talk.

It was a comforting thought and I felt ashamed of my sour outburst. 'Look, I'm sorry Gus. You've all put up with a hell of a lot from me haven't you? I'm grateful, truly.'

'You're such a daft bastard,' he mumbled, embarrassed.

'A miserable one,' I conceded. 'But I'm OK now. Honest.'

He turned to face me, leaning his elbow on the rail and studied me for some seconds. 'Yes,' he said at last. 'I think you are. I really think you are. Welcome back.'

He was a complex man, but considerate and a good companion; I always felt comfortable with him. I was very sorry that he would not join me on what I regarded almost as a pilgrimage. But once Gus had made up his mind there was no shifting him. He had decided not to accept the invitation from Amos's father, so that was that. I gave up. We talked for hours and ultimately agreed that I would go and he would stay in Macao; it was cheap and cheerful and he was engaged in pursuit of the delectable Mei Hoon.

I returned to Victoria the next day on the ferry and Polly booked me to Singapore by Cathay Pacific. On arrival at Paya Lebar, then the airport for Singapore, I bumped into one of our old card-playing charter pilots from the Pen in Kowloon. 'Hello,' he said. 'Where are you off to?'

'Aussie, I came down this morning.'

To my disgust I discovered that I had wasted about a month's salary.

'Bad luck,' Jake said. 'I got in last night from Kaitak, you should have come down with me.'

He was flying some machinery down to Balik Papan and had been delayed by incomplete documentation. 'Never mind', he continued, 'you can come down to BP with me.'

It wouldn't have helped. I had visions of being stuck in Borneo or some other equally inconvenient watering hole from where it would have been difficult to continue South. 'Thanks Jake, but old man Sikkim has fixed me up in 'Criterion', the skipper is an old friend of his and he'll get me to Bunbury. From there I'm not sure.'

'Bunbury! Christ, you might as well go to the bloody moon. Look, come and have a jar and I'll see if anyone's going your way.'

But there wasn't. I caught a sampan from Ocean Wharf and went out to the roads. 'Criterion's' master was a surprisingly young, very fat American. He made me welcome and within three hours we were away. It was bad luck that we left so promptly. About three months later I met Jake in the Tiger Balm Gardens in Singapore. As usual he had an extraordinarily pretty girl on his arm.

'Ha!' he exclaimed. 'I wondered when I'd bump into you. You missed out at Christmas, we were diverted to Freemantle the afternoon I saw you. I tried to find you but you'd already left.'

Still, it all worked out pretty well. 'Criterion', after stops in Djkarta, Tjirebon, Surabaya and Banjuwangi, was herself diverted to Freemantle where we arrived on December 18th.

Amos' father had retired from farming some time previous to my visit. He had lost interest, Amos told us, when his only son had decided on a career at sea. He retired to Western

Australia and kept a fair sized cruiser in the Swan River and spent a lot of time sea fishing. Then he became restless, bought a batch in the Darling Range that traps the Indian Ocean breezes on the coastal strip and devoted his time to building and improving a second family home. We spent Christmas there. When the house was completed, he divided his time between fishing and disappearing to the opal fields in New South Wales for weeks on end. He was very restless and unsettled and all the time I was there he was hardly to be seen. He rose at dawn and reappeared at dusk.

A taciturn, solitary man, he would ride alone for hours – a legacy of his active, very physical life as a farmer. Tall and blocky, he bore no resemblance to his son at all, apart from colouring. As a young man he had probably had Amos's baby-fine, light brown hair. This had all but disappeared now and the deeply tanned, lined face under the freckled bald head was the face of a total stranger with no familiar aspect at all.

Amos clearly had inherited his twisted smile and mobile, whimsical face (and a great deal more) from his mother. At sixty she was as slim and active as a ballerina and her face registered every change of mood and nuance of thought. What went on inside her head was mirrored instantly in her face. I liked her enormously. I caught her looking searchingly at me several times, but whenever I met her eye she would break the contact and look away. Occasionally she would start to say something, then evidently change her mind and talk of something else. My arrival seemed to underline their loss and although they did everything to make me welcome, somehow there was a flatness that we couldn't overcome in the time we had. It wasn't a success. I wished I had used the money Amos's father had sent me to fly down although it had seemed to be taking advantage, but he had insisted on paying for my return flight. Perhaps with four weeks instead of ten days we could have lifted the barriers. It may have made a difference too if Gus had been there, but who can say?

It wasn't until we were travelling to the airport on my return to Hong Kong that Amos's mother felt able to bring up the matter which had evidently been troubling her throughout my stay. She was driving and perhaps the concentration required made it easier in some way for her to broach the subject that so concerned her. She turned to me, 'You were with him, weren't you?'

'Yes.'

'Well did… I mean…'

'Do you know what happened?'

'Yes. Mr Sikkim told us everything. He was very kind.'

'Amos didn't suffer, you know. It was all so quick that he couldn't have known a thing. I was with him throughout. I caught him. He didn't know what happened, I promise you.'

We pulled up at the airport and she turned to face me; tears were running unchecked down her cheeks. We stared dumbly at each other for a while, then got out of the car and walked slowly arm-in-arm to the check in. She dabbed her eyes and blew her nose.

'I'm sorry. This must have been a miserable visit for you, not at all as I planned. Can you come back?'

'It's been a sad visit but not miserable, truly. It could hardly have been otherwise, could it? I'd love to come back when we've all had a chance to come to terms with it a bit more. It must have been very hard for you all to have me here. I think perhaps it was a little too early.'

'I'm sorry.'

'There's nothing to be sorry about, honestly.'

I looked down at her tear wracked face and patted her hand. I felt almost as if I were her father. 'Old Amos would soon have snapped us out of it wouldn't he?'

She smiled wanly and took my hand. 'You're a dear boy. I hope you **will** come back.'

It seemed as if I was deserting her and I felt wretched. 'If only we could have reached this stage a week ago,' I thought.

Pulling my head down to her, she cuddled her cheek briefly to mine, then stood back. 'I'm sorry Gus couldn't come, perhaps you will give him our regards. We feel we know you all so well, Alexis[20] used to write reams about your doings. I'll miss that.'

My flight was announced and for a second she looked haunted and seemed about to cry again, but she got a grip. 'It might seem funny, but we shall miss you. I wish things had been different. Write and let us know what happens won't you.'

She looked desperately sad and fragile and somehow hopeless. I wanted to put my arms round her and regret to this day that I didn't follow my instinct. It was what she needed. 'Of course I will. With a house full of beautiful daughters you'll have problems keeping me away.'

A smile came then, a serene and proud smile and I knew from whom her daughters had inherited their staggering good looks.

---

[20] Amos's nickname was derived from a transliteration of his initials. A.O.M-S.

CHAPTER THIRTY-ONE

I touched down in Kaitak in the late afternoon of January Second. Gus was there to meet me. He looked terrible.

'Good God, Gus, you look like a corpse.'

He groaned and rolled his eyes. 'Yankee pilots and Suntory whisky are a lethal mix. Thank God you're back. They're still celebrating New Year and you were a good excuse to break off.'

'Thank you very much. Where're we staying?'

'Don't know. I had a room somewhere but I can't remember where. I've been playing poker at the Pen since New Year's Eve.'

'What happened to the luscious Mei Hoon?'

'Ships that pass in the night, old son; ships that pass in the night.'

'Not even a tiny collision?'

'Not so you'd notice. Where's all my bloody money?'

'In Polly's safe. Why, are you broke?'

He gave me a smug grin and pushed his hand inside his jacket, pulling out a wad of American money. 'There's six hundred smackers here. Frightened me to death.'

'What on earth d'you mean?'

'I took over this bloke's hand when he was called away and at one time I was down 250 dollars. We were playing for markers and I thought the stakes were in Hong Kong dollars. When they paid me off to meet you, I collected my winnings in US dollars. How about that?'

It was quite a coup. The relative values were about seven shillings and sixpence (US) against one and threepence (HK). He was incorrigible. I shook my head in despair.

'Honest Gus, you're not fit to be let out on your own. Do you think you could find your hotel room? I'm shagged out.'

We never did find his hotel room. I doubted that it existed but he was adamant that it did. Fortunately, like all good travellers, he was never separated from his documents and his heavy gear was at the office. All he lost were a few bits and pieces together with two days of his life.

We found a room at a Portugee hotel on the Shaukiwan Road out towards Taikoo dockyard and took a couple of rickshaws from the Star Ferry terminal without too much bother. Usually the coolies blanched and argued among themselves to decide who would take Gus. On the way past HMS Tamar, the Royal Navy shore establishment, we were hailed by two men in crumpled civvies. The larger one in a thick, slurred Scottish accent demanded of Gus 'Wheer the hell did ye get tay?'

He stood swaying and tugging at his back pocket to extract his wallet, nearly falling flat on his face as he slipped off the kerb in the process. I tensed for trouble and glanced at Gus; his face was blank.

'Here, ye jammy big bastat', the Scot said and thrust a handful of notes at Gus. He accepted them in amazement as the two men clung to each other and staggered happily off, chorusing 'Happy New Year.'

'What on earth was that all about?' I queried.

Gus shook his head and counted the money, 'Damned if I know, I've never seen him before.'

I accepted that with reservations. 'You mean you don't **remember** having seen him before. It's not quite the same thing. He obviously remembered you.'

Gus grinned and shrugged. He must have had an incredibly bibulous three or four weeks, I thought.

When we got to the Alcoba, the coolies thankfully dropped the shafts and stood waiting for payment. Gus split the wad of notes the Scot had given him and gave half to each of the men. They couldn't believe their eyes. They'd been expecting, perhaps, five or six dollars.

'How much was there, Gus?' I asked him as the coolies took off like Derby winners before he could change his mind.

'Kung yi fat choy (Happy New Year)...' he bellowed after them, then turned to me... 'Oh, I dunno, hundred and fifty, hundred and sixty[21] dollars I suppose. I didn't want it, didn't really seem like mine. I wonder where it came from?'

'Doesn't matter does it? You've certainly given them a bright start to the New Year. It's probably assured you a place in the Chinese Heaven at least.'

'Not too bloody soon, I hope.'

I slept for ten or twelve hours non-stop. When I awoke Gus was sitting in the armchair drinking coffee. He was fully dressed. I still felt tired. 'What's the time?' I asked him

'Well, I've just had lunch – guess.'

'What happens now?'

He was silent for a long time, staring at me but not seeing me. It made me uncomfortable. I waggled my hand at him. 'Gus! Gus?'

He came to with a start, 'Well your future's decided old son. They want to see you in the office this afternoon. I was there this morning to get some cash.'

'Any idea what's on the cards?'

'Nope. It was Tiktok,[22] you know what he's like. He'll probably keep **you** in the dark until the last minute.'

'Polly **said** six weeks, didn't he? Looks like he was bang on; nothing in the wind for you then?'

He shook his head slowly then looked out of the window. 'Strange old world isn't it?'

---

[21] About ten pounds sterling. Hong Kong dollars were then about sixteen to the pound.

[22] Tiktok, a rather cruel nickname. He wore a set of enormous, plastic false teeth with bright orange gums. They were ill-fitting and when he spoke they made a curious, hollow 'tik-tok' sound.

'Agreed, but what sparks that profound thought?'

He was in a very strange and introspective mood that I'd never seen before. He shook his head again absently. 'Nothing... nothing really.'

We were at the office about half past three. Tiktok, the smallest, baldest and meanest of the three brothers greeted us. I was to go to Kobe to join *Rosa Ephron*. It was a delivery job. She had just finished repairs and was to be delivered in ballast to her new owners in Mogadishu. It would probably mean less that a month's work and I was a bit put out. If I took the *Rosa*, I might miss out on a proper job and a steady berth. It also occurred to me for the first time that Gus and I would be splitting up. It was inevitable of course but needed to be assimilated. To split up for a proper job was one thing but this was a fill-in, and I said so.

Tiktok was on his dignity and put on his hoity-toity manner which was very impressive if you simply listened to the well modulated, fruity English tones and didn't look at him. 'Really, we have been very generous to you and this is an important contract for us. Deliveries are a new venture. You are here and it is convenient to us that you should go to Kobe. We hope it will not be necessary to insist.'

Put like that I had no reasonable counter argument and I needed the money anyway. Although Tiktok was worse than an exposed tooth nerve, the company had been excellent employers. It was just bad luck that Tiktok had been duty man that afternoon. Had it been Polly, he would have shaken my hand vigorously, holding it moistly in both of his, then he would have pulled a wad of notes from his pocket and peeled off a sheaf. 'Expenses to get you to Kobe, my friend; *Rosa* is a good ship, I hope you have a pleasant trip. There will be a money order and an air ticket in Mogadishu; go to the Travellers' Rest hotel and we will be in touch. Bye, bye.'

I would have been carried away on the flood of his enthusiasm and warmth and gone with absolute confidence. Tiktok, however, seemed so shifty and mean that I always felt as if he were trying to get rid of me and do me out of my money into the bargain.

We left the office and ambled down to 'Jingles' in Nathan Road where I ate and Gus sat to keep me company, drinking stupendous amounts of coffee. I was to go by Glenline to Kobe, leaving the next day. It all seemed so sudden that I felt disoriented and depressed. It occurred to me that Gus must have guessed something like this was in the wind and it accounted for his odd introspective mood. That evening was spent quietly mooching round our usual haunts doing nothing in particular. It was not the least strained, it was as if we had forgotten tomorrow.

He came with me on the Jardine Matheson launch which took me out to the ship which was lying at the A1 buoy. I stowed my gear and we strolled up onto the boat deck to observe the flurry of activity that inevitably precedes sailing – it seemed odd not to be personally involved – and to see how these sleek 'civil service' ships and crews conducted themselves. We listened to the gear being tested and in a jangle of engineroom telegraphs and the shrilling of whistles, punctuated by the bass boom of the siren, we walked down to the gangway. The launch, all shiny mahogany, gleaming brass and snowy decks and awnings – was lying at the foot of the ladder. A smartly dressed, wrinkled Chinese seaman was standing on the scrubbed foredeck with his bare feet braced, holding the surging launch to the gangway platform with a boat hook snagged into the chain.

From the engineroom there came the jangle of the bridge telegraph's double ring; the engineer's answering ring sounded clearly to us, then a loud hiss of compressed air blasted the massive twin diesel motors into life. Their low grumbling vibrated the deck and a heat shimmer appeared over the squat funnel as the ship moved dead slow ahead to slacken off the mooring cable so the buoy jumper could unshackle her from the buoy.

Gus stood, hands thrust into his jacket pockets, shoulders hunched, glowering at me. I noticed one or two apprehensive looks from the odd passenger or crewman and it amused me. I had grown accustomed to Gus's aggressive stance and his menacing expression; they no longer registered on me. To a stranger it must have looked as if he was about to launch an attack. The agent came bouncing down the accommodation ladder from the bridge followed by the smart-as-paint fourth mate. 'All ashore,' he said brightly, extending his arms sideways and swinging them as if he were shooing chickens. The gesture irritated Gus; he turned in his deliberate manner and looked hard at the young man, probably just out of his apprenticeship. The poor chap held Gus's eye for a mini-second, then busied himself with a totally unnecessary adjustment of the gangway strops.

Gus turned back to me. 'Take care,' he said. 'You're such a daft bastard.' He didn't offer to shake hands.

'Bye Gus.'

He turned and stumped down the gangway, making it bounce and clang against the ship's side.

Free from the buoy, the ship was gathering way now and a little bow wave fluttered at the stem of the launch. The Chinese sailor leaned back, throwing his weight on the boat hook to hold her head close in. Gus jumped from the gangway platform onto the foredeck, his weight and impetus making the slim launch curtsey and roll sharply, throwing the little seaman into a mild panic as he shuffled to keep his footing and disengage his boat hook from the chain. Gus recovered his balance and leaned on the awning spar. It was a chillingly evocative replay of the first time I had seen him stumbling and slipping on the wet logs in Zamboanga. I felt the goose pimples break out.

I climbed to the boat deck and leaned on the rail between the lifeboats to watch the launch pull smartly away, cutting a creamy curve through the blue water. The cox'n gunned his engine, the stern sat down with a muffled chuckle and her bows lifted as she headed back to Holt's Wharf in Kowloon. Gus stood on the tiny foredeck looking back at us over the length of the boat as we slipped towards the narrows at Lyemun. After a minute or so, he briefly threw up his right arm in a sort of sloppy Nazi salute, then disappeared from view, hidden by the cockpit awning.

END